Expanding Psychoanalysis

Expanding Psychoanalysis explores the work of the acclaimed psychoanalyst, writer, and activist Susie Orbach.

The book studies Orbach's multifaceted career in five sections, examining her multitudinous contributions to the mental health profession, from the creation of feminist psychotherapy to the enhancement of media psychology, to the growth of political and social consultation. The book contains clinical, historical, and personal chapters, examining Orbach from a range of perspectives. Each chapter investigates a key aspect of Orbach's work and its impact on the professional, the social, and the personal level. The book concludes with an epilogue by Orbach herself.

Expanding Psychoanalysis will be essential for all readers interested in the work of Susie Orbach.

Professor Brett Kahr has worked in the mental health field for over forty years. He is Senior Fellow at the Tavistock Institute of Medical Psychology in London and, also, Visiting Professor of Psychoanalysis and Mental Health at Regent's University London. A trained historian, Kahr is both an Honorary Fellow as well as the Honorary Director of Research at the Freud Museum London. He is the author of twenty books and series editor of over eighty-five further titles. He serves as Chair of the Scholars Committee of the British Psychoanalytic Council and, additionally, as a Consultant Psychotherapist at The Balint Consultancy. He works with individuals and couples in Central London.

"Brett Kahr's meticulously edited text gathers cutting-edge clinicians to honour Susie Orbach's pioneering work. They pay tribute to Orbach's impact, which radically weaves political, cultural, gender-power dynamics, and psychoanalysis. This inspired book confirms Orbach's enduring influence in challenging toxic psychosocial messages about the body and countless other critical mental health topics."

Dr. Zack Eleftheriadou is a parent-infant, child and adult psychotherapist and a Fellow of the British Psychological Society, as well as a member of The Bowlby Centre, London.

"This outstanding volume captures the essence of Dr. Susie Orbach's brilliance and her profound impact as a thinker, clinician, writer, feminist, and social activist. The prominent contributors bring multiple perspectives that illuminate Orbach's work as a beacon of knowledge, hope, and empowerment for people all over the world."

Dr. Galit Atlas is a Faculty Member at the New York University Postdoctoral Program for Psychotherapy and Psychoanalysis, and the author of *Emotional Inheritance*.

"Susie Orbach has made many great achievements in the mental health field for over half a century; in consequence, I commend this enriching and glowing tribute of her professional life and work. Brett Kahr has prepared a beautifully edited *Festschrift* in Orbach's honour, and I hope that the chapters contained herein will encourage us all to read and re-read Orbach's many enlightening publications."

Julia Samuel is a psychotherapist and the author of *Grief Works: Stories of Life, Death and Surviving*.

"This book not only celebrates the life and work of the iconic feminist Susie Orbach, it also deepens, extends, and enriches it, and does so critically. The collection of essays will be of interest not only to the psychotherapist, but also to the 'ordinary' citizen."

Dr. Farhad Dalal is a group analyst and a psychotherapist, and the author of *Thought Paralysis: The Virtues of Discrimination*.

"Susie Orbach's remarkable career has brought a brilliant integration of clinical commitment, feminism, and psychoanalytic-political insight to the widest public audience. This book is an essential guide to her radical *and* intimate sense of how 'the personal is political', leavened with personal honesty and great common sense."

Professor Stephen Seligman is Clinical Professor at the University of California, San Francisco, and at the New York University Postdoctoral Program in Psychoanalysis and Psychotherapy, as well as a Training and Supervising Analyst at the San Francisco Center for Psychoanalysis and at the Psychoanalytic Institute of Northern California. He is the author of *Relationships in Development: Infancy, Intersubjectivity, and Attachment*.

"The work of Susie Orbach has changed how we think about the body, how we speak about it and how we inhabit it. Over several decades, she has campaigned tirelessly against social injustice and ideologies of bodily blame, as well as having a huge influence on the promotion of emotional literacy and the powers and possibilities of therapy. This marvellous and highly readable collection of essays shows the scope and importance of her work, as well as containing many chapters which add original research and thinking into the mix. It offers not just an introduction to Orbach's work but a significant review of developments in her field. A pleasure to read."

Darian Leader is an author and a psychoanalyst at the Centre for Freudian Analysis and Research, London.

Expanding Psychoanalysis

The Contributions of Susie Orbach

Edited by Brett Kahr

Routledge
Taylor & Francis Group

LONDON AND NEW YORK

Cover image © Sarah Ainslie

First published 2025
by Routledge
4 Park Square, Milton Park, Abingdon, Oxon OX14 4RN

and by Routledge
605 Third Avenue, New York, NY 10158

Routledge is an imprint of the Taylor & Francis Group, an informa business

British Library Cataloguing-in-Publication Data
A catalogue record for this book is available from the British Library

ISBN: 9781032746159 (hbk)
ISBN: 9781032861951 (pbk)
ISBN: 9781003470090 (ebk)

DOI: 10.4324/9781003470090

Typeset in Times New Roman
by Newgen Publishing UK

To the Next Generation of Mental Health Practitioners

Contents

Contributors

Sarah Benamer is a relational attachment-based psychoanalytic psychotherapist and supervisor who works with individuals and couples. She qualified originally as a psychotherapist at The Bowlby Centre and has trained subsequently as a psychosexual and couples therapist and as a Somatic Experiencing Practitioner. Prior to becoming a psychotherapist, she was a community worker, advocating for those in crisis within the N.H.S. psychiatric system, supporting individuals living with chronic pain, long-term illness, and severe physical disabilities. In addition to therapeutic trainings, she has earned a master's degree in Applied Anthropology – a grounding that informs her "participant observer" approach to clinical practice. Sarah Benamer has a particular interest in the many roles of the body in our emotional and relational worlds. In her clinical and written work, she seeks to integrate psychoanalytic and attachment understandings with an appreciation of individual body narrative. She is deeply committed to anti-discriminatory practice, to the accessibility of therapy, and to the theory that is relevant in the clients' world. Her publications include the books *Telling Stories?: Attachment-Based Approaches to the Treatment of Psychosis* and, also, *Trauma and Attachment: The John Bowlby Memorial Conference Monograph 2006*, as well as articles such as "Killing Me Softly: A Relational Understanding of Attachment to Pain" and " 'Not So Hysterical Now': Psychotherapy, Menopause, and Hysterectomy". Her website address is: www.theintimacyclinic.co.uk.

Luise Eichenbaum, together with Susie Orbach, co-founded The Women's Therapy Centre in London in 1976 and The Women's Therapy Centre Institute (now known as The W.T.C.I.) in New York in 1982. She has co-authored many books with Susie Orbach, including *Understanding Women: A Feminist Psychoanalytic Approach*, as well as *Between Women: Love, Envy and Competition in Women's Friendships*, and, also, *What Do Women Want: Exploding the Myth of Dependency*, in addition to numerous articles on issues related to feminism and psychoanalysis. She serves on the Board of Directors of The W.T.C.I., working to sustain and continually grow a feminist-run psychoanalytic institute. She maintains her private practice in New York City.

Jane Haberlin trained as a psychoanalytic psychotherapist with the Arbours Association and worked at the Arbours Crisis Centre and at the Women's Therapy Centre in London. She is a founder member of The Relational School. A Partner and Consultant Psychotherapist with The Balint Consultancy, she works with couples and individuals, and she offers executive coaching and organisational consultancy as well.

Professor Brett Kahr is Senior Fellow at the Tavistock Institute of Medical Psychology in London and, also, Visiting Professor of Psychoanalysis and Mental Health at Regent's University London. He serves as Chair of the Scholars Committee of the British Psychoanalytic Council and, also, as an Honorary Fellow of the United Kingdom Council for Psychotherapy. A trained historian as well as a clinician of long standing, Professor Kahr is both an Honorary Fellow and, also, the Honorary Director of Research at the Freud Museum London, where he has worked in many capacities since the museum's inception in 1986. Additionally, he is Senior Clinical Research Fellow in Psychotherapy and Mental Health at the Centre for Child Mental Health. Having served for many years as Resident Psychotherapist at the British Broadcasting Corporation, Kahr has also become a Visiting Professor in the Faculty of Media and Communication at Bournemouth University. Formerly the Advisory Editor-in-Chief to Confer Books and to Karnac Books, he has authored twenty books and he has served as series editor for over eighty-five additional volumes, having created such monograph series as "The Library of Couple and Family Psychoanalysis", the "Forensic Psychotherapy Monograph Series", "The History of Psychoanalysis Series", as well as the "Freud Museum London Series". His solo-authored books include *D.W. Winnicott: A Biographical Portrait*, for which he received the Gradiva Award; *Sex and the Psyche* – a *Sunday Times* bestseller – based on his research for the British Sexual Fantasy Research Project; *Bombs in the Consulting Room: Surviving Psychological Shrapnel*; *Freud's Pandemics: Surviving Global War, Spanish Flu, and the Nazis*; *How to Be Intimate with 15,000,000 Strangers: Musings on Media Psychoanalysis*; *Hidden Histories of British Psychoanalysis: From Freud's Death Bed to Laing's Missing Tooth*; and *Forensic Psychoanalysis: From Sub-Clinical Psychopaths to Serial Killers*. His impending books include a collection of essays on *Volcanic Spouses: The Art of Couple Psychoanalysis*, as well as an edited volume of the memoirs written by one of the grandchildren of Sigmund Freud. He works in full-time independent practice for individuals, couples, and families in Central London.

Dr. Roanna Mitchell is a performance-maker and movement artist, and Senior Lecturer at the University of Kent, where she specialises in psychophysical performance practice. She is also co-founder of The Chekhov Collective UK, the leading United Kingdom-based practice research centre exploring contemporary uses of Michael Chekhov's technique in the arts and beyond since 2013. From 2010 until 2018, she worked closely alongside Dr. Susie Orbach as artistic director and project coordinator of the charity AnyBody UK. As a maker, she has created, directed, and movement-directed performance internationally, including collaborations with Richard Schechner in India and the United States of America. Dr. Mitchell has published on actor-wellbeing, body activism, the Chekhov technique in actor-movement and dance, and dialogues between theatre training and therapy. Her recent work focuses on applications of psychophysical performer training techniques in community and mental health settings, especially in relation to supporting survivors of a borderline personality disorder diagnosis. She has been facilitating creative support for this community through the *'Inappropriate' Anger* project since 2020. Her website addresses are: www.roannamitchell.com and www.chekhovcollectiveuk.co.uk.

Andrew Samuels was Professor of Analytical Psychology at the University of Essex. He works in private practice in London and is a Training Analyst of the Society for Analytical Psychology and a consultant to political leaders, parties, activist groups, and think tanks in several countries and, also, to the National Health Service. He is Director of the management consultancy TELOS: Putting Imagination to Work, as well as the co-founder of Psychotherapists and Counsellors for Social Responsibility and, also, the Psychotherapy and Counselling Union. His books have been translated into twenty-one languages and include *Jung and the Post-Jungians*; *A Critical Dictionary of Jungian Analysis*, written with Bani Shorter and Fred Plaut; *The Father*; *Psychopathology*; *The Plural Psyche*; *The Political Psyche*; *Politics on the Couch*; *A New Therapy for Politics?*; and *Persons, Passions, Psychotherapy, Politics*. With Emilija Kiehl and Mark Saban, he co-edited *Analysis and Activism: Social and Political Contributions of Jungian Psychology*. His website address, containing a selection of videos, is: www.andrewsamuels.com.

Dr. Valerie Sinason is a widely published poet, writer, child and adolescent psychoanalytic psychotherapist (retired) and an adult psychoanalyst and now a novelist. She has specialised in trauma and disability for over forty years and lectures nationally and internationally. The founder and now the Patron of the Clinic for Dissociative Studies UK, Dr. Sinason is also President of the Institute for Psychotherapy and Disability. Additionally, she serves on the Board of the International Society for the Study of Trauma and Dissociation from whom she received the organisation's Lifetime Achievement Award in 2017. In 2022, the British Psychoanalytic Council presented her with its award for Innovation Excellence. She has been a Consultant Psychotherapist at the Tavistock Clinic, at St. George's Hospital, University of London and, also, an Honorary Consultant Psychotherapist at the Cape Town Child Guidance Clinic in South Africa, as well as the Acting Chair of the Friends of the Bushmen Heritage Centre, New Bethesda. In addition to her classic book, *Mental Handicap and the Human Condition: New Approaches from the Tavistock*, her more recent books include *The Truth About Trauma and Dissociation: Everything You Didn't Want to Know* *and Were Afraid to Ask*; *Trauma and Memory: The Science and the Silenced*; *Treating Children with Dissociative Disorders: Attachment, Trauma Theory and Practice*, co-edited with Renée Potgieter Marks, and *A Refugee's Story*, co-authored with Professor the Baroness Sheila Hollins. Dr. Sinason's first novel, *The Orpheus Project*, appeared in 2022, published by Sphinx Books.

Kate White is an activist, writer, and speaker, with lived experience as a care partner in the field of Dementia Care. She is a retired attachment-based psychoanalytic psychotherapist and member of The Bowlby Centre, which she co-founded with John Southgate in 1988. Together they developed its unique attachment theory-informed and radical relational approach to psychotherapy. She is currently the Series Editor of *The Bowlby Centre Monographs*, published by Routledge, and served for ten years as co-editor of the journal *Attachment: New Directions in Psychotherapy and Relational Psychoanalysis*. Her most recent publication, *Trauma and Loss: Key Texts from the John Bowlby Archive*, was co-edited with Professor Robbie Duschinsky. They are currently collaborating with Professor Erik Hesse on a forthcoming posthumous publication of a book by Professor Mary Main and, also, organising two issues of the journal *Psychoanalytic Inquiry* to honour Main's immense contribution to attachment theory. With colleagues, Kate White co-edited *Exploring Memory Loss and Ageing from an Attachment Perspective*, which reflects on current and developing thinking about the applications of attachment theory to the world of dementia, memory loss, creativity, and ageing. She combines this understanding with her deep commitment to social justice.

A Note on Confidentiality

Although this *Festschrift* contains only a small number of clinical vignettes of encounters with patients, rather than fully-detailed case histories, the editor and the chapter-writers have anonymised all of the descriptions contained herein, thus preserving the privacy and the confidentiality of the individuals who have sought our psychological assistance.

Introduction
Susie Orbach and the Modernization of Mental Health

Brett Kahr

Many long decades ago, as a young psychology student, I enjoyed a quiet after-noon in the university library, researching a paper on the psychoses and, also, preparing for an end-of-term examination. One of my female friends – a very intel-ligent psychology undergraduate called Ellen – happened to be perched nearby in an adjoining cubicle. At one point, keen to take a much-needed break from this intense studying, I closed my extremely heavy, early-twentieth-century textbook on schizophrenia and I began to chat to this young woman. As Ellen and I attended the very same classes, I expected that she, too, might well be deeply immersed in the same psychopathology text, but, I quickly noticed that she had instead chosen to read a rather more modern tome in paperback, which bore a most unusual supra-title, namely, *Fat is a Feminist Issue*[1] – a book which I certainly had not noticed on our official reading list.

As a rather naïve person, who had not yet begun to investigate the complex-ities of gender, I found myself rather surprised that this fellow student should be devoting her precious study time to this seemingly "unauthorised" book. In fact, I believe I muttered, "Gosh, Ellen ... *Fat is a Feminist Issue*? But you're really slender. Why are reading a book about fat women?" Ellen looked at me with utter disdain, rolled her eyes, and replied, "You men ... honestly! This book has nothing to do with weight. You should read this one day. It challenges our stereotypes about the human body."

In reply, I nodded quietly, and then returned to my enormous schizophrenia text-book, worried that Ellen might not pass our impending examination or might not even graduate. Little did I realise that within a matter of years, the author of this cunningly titled book, *Fat is a Feminist Issue ...: The Anti-Diet Guide to Permanent Weight Loss*[2] (Orbach, 1978), later known solely as *Fat is a Feminist Issue*, would become a much revered figure in the mental health profession from whom I, and many millions of others, would learn so richly.

Back then, few people understood much at all about the psychology of the human body, not least our relationship to size and weight. During the nineteenth century, physicians did, from time to time, treat certain women who starved them-selves of food in a truly perilous manner. Indeed, round about 1873, long before Dr. Sigmund Freud (1896, p. 166) coined the term "psycho-analyse" – the original

DOI: 10.4324/9781003470090-1

French-translated word for "psychoanalysis" – an English physician, Sir William Gull, introduced the notion of *anorexia nervosa*, as a means of encapsulating the psychiatric frailty of female patients who refused to eat and who became extremely emaciated, often on the verge of death (cf. Bell, 1985). My teachers of psychopathology would, occasionally, mention the work of Gull – one of the physicians to Her Majesty Queen Victoria – and, whenever they referred to this psychopathological condition, they would underscore that, fortunately, very few women would ever become clinically anorexic and that, in all likelihood, my fellow students and I would probably not encounter very many such cases in the course of our impending psychological practices.[3]

At that point in time, most of us regarded the notion of body weight in a rather straightforward matter. One either weighed too much and thus tipped over the scale or, in fact, one weighed too little and could thus readily wear a pair of tight jeans. Most people, as it happened, seemed to weigh just the right amount. Little did we know that numerous women had begun to refer to themselves as "compulsive slims" and that many considered themselves obese, even if they looked quite trim to others. Few of us appreciated that certain women would even vomit up their food, while many others would starve themselves. In fact, little did we suspect that one could boast a very ordinary-looking body of seemingly normal weight and yet still harbour massively hateful feelings towards one's own corporeality.

In this extraordinary book, *Fat is a Feminist Issue ...: The Anti-Diet Guide to Permanent Weight Loss*, Susie Orbach, then a mere youngster, no older than thirty years of age at the time, dared to challenge the concrete, traditional notions of the female body and offered a refreshingly new lens through which psychopathologies such as compulsive eating or compulsive starvation could be understood more thoroughly, not as forms of madness *per se* but, rather, as ordinary manifestations of the universal human struggle to inhabit a body. Nearly one hundred years after the emergence of the more traditional medico-psychiatric approach to anorexia nervosa (cf. Lacey, 1982; Bell, 1985; Vandereycken and van Deth, 1989, 1990, 1994), Susie Orbach began to reconceptualise the female body (and, by implication, the male body as well) and helped to destigmatise these very common corporeal challenges.[4]

Orbach (1978, p. 13) explained that she had written this 192-page book, in part, to examine the psychology of those in deep distress, which might include "Feeling awful about yourself as someone who is out of control" or "Feeling awful about your body" (Orbach, 1978, p. 13). And in both a pro-feminist and, also, an antipsychiatric fashion, Orbach explained that physicians have often contributed to a worsening of this problem by having encouraged women to undergo surgeries in order to remove fat cells. Indeed, Orbach (1978, p. 185) concluded her tome in a passionate manner, arguing that, "Compulsive eating is an individual protest against the inequality of the sexes. As such, medical interventions as detailed here are not part of a solution but are part of the problem. The situation requires a major reorientation of medical and scientific education, organization and practice based on the demands of the women's health movement."

How did the incredibly youthful Susie Orbach become such an expert about these much underappreciated psychological bodily challenges?

Throughout the 1970s, the vast of majority of mental health professionals – mostly males[5] – treated their patients psychopharmacologically, especially those who presented with any overt bodily complaints. Others would provide behavioural therapies, owing to the tremendously influential publications of the clinical psychologist Professor Hans Eysenck, who detested the work of the traditional talking therapies (e.g., Eysenck and Wilson, 1973a, 1973b; cf. Eysenck, 1984, 1985). And although esteemed psychotherapy organisations such as the British Psycho-Analytical Society, the Hampstead Child-Therapy Course and Clinic, and the Tavistock Clinic – all based in London – provided psychoanalytically orientated treatment, very few women across the nation could access these services, and very few – especially those who might have suffered from sexual abuse – could be certain that they would be able to consult a safe female practitioner.

Aware of the lack of affordable, publicly available mental health services for British women, Susie Orbach, who had recently completed her graduate studies at university, co-founded The Women's Therapy Centre in London, in 1976, in conjunction with her American colleague Luise Eichenbaum. This new clinical service – an out-patient facility – offered both psychotherapy and counselling to thousands of women in need. Additionally, this clinical resource centre would be staffed entirely by women and, within due course, it became both quite popular and, moreover, extremely essential. Indeed, before long, The Women's Therapy Centre received an overwhelming number of referrals and requests from prospective female clients, so much so that the Institute of Psycho-Analysis in London – the training arm of the British Psycho-Analytical Society – actually approached The Women's Therapy Centre, requesting that Orbach and Eichenbaum might refer some patients, as that esteemed organisation needed referrals for its training candidates (Kahr, 2016)!

In 1981, some five years after having inaugurated The Women's Therapy Centre in London, Orbach and Eichenbaum co-founded an American version, namely, The Women's Therapy Centre Institute, in New York City, New York, which not only provided psychotherapeutic interventions for women in need but, also, created a radical, new three-year training programme in feminist-informed psychoanalytical psychotherapy for mental health workers. Orbach co-directed this institute as well for several years before returning to London to embark upon a full-time clinical psychotherapeutic practice.

In the decades which followed, Orbach built upon her foundational work in the late 1970s and early 1980s and soon became an experienced and esteemed practitioner, teacher, supervisor, organisational consultant, writer, broadcaster, and political activist, engaging with a wide range of psychological topics.

Perhaps Orbach will be best known across the world as a result of her many writings. During the 1990s, Susie Orbach published regular columns in both *The Guardian Weekend* section of *The Guardian* newspaper and, also, in the *New Woman* magazine, all of which attracted a very wide readership and a very loyal audience of admirers who benefited greatly from the ways in which Orbach discussed essential topics through a psychological lens, having addressed not only the dilemmas of our private lives but, also, how personal biographies interconnect with a whole range of economic, political, and social topics. Orbach wrote most compellingly and with engaging titles, including "The Third Party Liabilities" (Orbach, 1994a), "Why Tongues are A-Wagging" (Orbach, 1994b), and "The Hidden Signs of Insecurity" (Orbach, 1995). Moreover, she continued to produce a stream of highly popular books, which have since become classics, including, *Hunger Strike: The Anorectic's Struggle as a Metaphor for Our Age* (Orbach, 1986), *The Impossibility of Sex* (Orbach, 1999), and the prize-winning *Bodies* (Orbach, 2009).

Dr. Susie Orbach contributed not only through printed publications, but, also, as a presenter on both radio and television over many decades. Perhaps, most memorably, Orbach created a fifteen-part series entitled *In Therapy*, which debuted on 15th February, 2016, broadcast on B.B.C. Radio 4, and which resulted in not one, but two, beautifully written and accessible books, *In Therapy: How Conversations with Psychotherapists Really Work* (Orbach, 2016), followed by a sequel, *In Therapy: The Unfolding Story* (Orbach, 2018), each published in conjunction with the Wellcome Collection – a true indication that Orbach's exploration, popularisation and, indeed, expansion of modern psychology had become truly a part of health-care history.

In the space of such a brief communication, one cannot do justice to the half-century of Susie Orbach's contributions. In addition to her work as a psychotherapist and psychoanalyst and as a writer and broadcaster, she has served as a teacher and lecturer at innumerable institutions across the globe from New Zealand to Peru, and has spoken at such culturally iconic settings as the Royal Festival Hall in London, the Royal Society of Medicine, Harvard University, and the University of Oxford, as well as Exploring Parenthood, the International Bank for Reconstruction and Development, and various others, including the United Nations.

As an organisational leader and political activist, Orbach not only co-founded The Women's Therapy Centre in London and The Women's Therapy Centre Institute in Manhattan but, also, helped to create Psychotherapists and Counsellors for Social Responsibility, as well as Antidote – a collective designed to promote emotional literary in schools and businesses. Likewise, she has provided consultancy not only to Dove, assisting with the organisation's new initiative, helping to champion a more sensitive promotion of the diversity of women, but, also, to the World Bank, advising on the psychological aspects of poverty reduction and social development, And, in 2002, she became the Convenor of AnyBody, a working group that launched a global campaign to protect the next generation of young girls from the ravages of body hatred. As a result of these essential sociopolitical consultancies, Orbach ultimately served on several government expert committees.

In recognition of her academic and popular and political contributions, she has become the recipient of numerous honorary doctoral degrees from a range of institutions on both sides of the Atlantic Ocean, including the London Metropolitan University, the University of Roehampton, Stony Brook University (part of the State University of New York), the University of East London, the University of Essex, and the University of Westminster. She also earned an appointment as Visiting Professor at the esteemed London School of Economics and Political Science in the University of London. Likewise, she has served as a visiting fellow, a trustee, an academic visitor, or a board member to many other organisations ranging from The Bowlby Centre in London to the New School for Social Research in New York City, and has also received appointments as a Fellow of the Freud Museum London and of the Royal Society of Literature, as well as a similar post at Hertford College in the University of Oxford. In 2017, Orbach secured the very first Lifetime Achievement Award from the British Psychoanalytic Council as an acknowledgement of her multitudinous achievements.

The vast majority of mental health professionals spend our days sitting quietly in small consulting rooms, welcoming patient after patient. Sometimes, in the evenings, we might attend a seminar or deliver a lecture or write a paper. But few members of the psychotherapy or psychoanalysis communities have contributed to the growth of modern mental health in the way in which Dr. Orbach has done, and, in consequence, she has garnered much appreciation and deep praise from millions of people worldwide.

On 22nd April, 2017, several months after Orbach's seventieth birthday, Jane Ryan, the founder and Director of Confer – one the United Kingdom's most esteemed continuing professional education organisations – hosted a special event on the sixth floor of the iconic Foyles bookshop on Charing Cross Road in Central London, right in the heart of the theatre district, in order to pay tribute to this remarkable woman. This special event, entitled "Psychotherapy is a Cultural Issue: The Influence of Susie Orbach's Work on Theory, Practice and Values", proved so rich and so stimulating that we decided to invite the speakers to expand their talks into chapters, which now constitute the bulk of the content of this *Festschrift*.

In the pages that follow, readers will be able to enjoy a range of tributes to Susie Orbach from a multitude of perspectives. In the first section, "Orbach in Context", long-time collaborator Luise Eichenbaum, who has worked closely with Susie Orbach since the 1970s, offers her special reminiscences of the early days at The Women's Therapy Centre in London and The Women's Therapy Centre Institute in New York City, New York. Thereafter, we have the opportunity to read a transcript of a more recent interview with Dr. Orbach, which I hosted for "Radio Karnac" in 2016, in which we had the opportunity to discuss various matters, including her contributions to the media. In the second part, "Orbach in the Consulting Room", two more colleagues, Jane Haberlin and Sarah Benamer, have prepared thoughtful essays which demonstrate the ways in which Susie's psychological insights have enhanced clinical daily practice. In the third section, "Orbach in Politics and Society", and in the fourth section, "Orbach in the Media", we learn much more about how the Orbachian body of work has penetrated culture more widely. Professor Andrew Samuels has provided readers with an encapsulation of Orbach's influence on political psychology, and Dr. Roanna Mitchell has shared her excellent insights from a 2018 birthday tribute for Orbach, examining the links between Susie's theories about the human body and its impact on the acting profession and society more broadly. My own chapter on the history of media psychoanalysis explores the ways in which Susie Orbach has extended the original contributions of such figures as Dr. Donald Winnicott – the first regular psychoanalytical broadcaster at the British Broadcasting Corporation, back in the 1930s, 1940s, and beyond – helping to challenge the long-standing insistence that psychotherapy and psychoanalysis must remain the so-called "silent" professions! And in the fifth and final part of this *Festschrift*, "Orbach from a Personal Perspective", two more colleagues, Kate White and Dr. Valerie Sinason, have offered warm, personal reminiscences of our celebrant. Although most *Festschriften* rarely include contributions from the celebrant, Dr. Orbach has generously supplied us with her own response to the various chapters contained herein.

Many years ago, I had the privilege of lunching in London with a rather brilliant and, also, rather outspoken American colleague and scholar of long standing who, over the course of his own rich career had the opportunity to meet virtually every psychoanalyst of note worldwide. This gentleman, to whom I shall refer solely as "Dr. X.", lamented that most clinical mental health practitioners, though all warmhearted, compassionate, professional people, do suffer, alas, from a true lack of creativity. At one point, Dr. X. moaned, "Most psychoanalysts are nothing more than plumbers. All they do is delve into their patients' minds and empty the drains." One might well argue that by helping our clients or our analysands to "empty the drains" of their internal messiness could well be considered a truly vital achievement. But I do understand Dr. X.'s concern about the lack of activism and public creativity among many mental health workers.

The actively creative Susie Orbach, by contrast, will not only have helped to drain the ugliness from the minds of many patients over the years, but, moreover, she has also drawn upon her immense energy and aspiration and generosity, and has thus helped to drain the world of much of its messiness through her expansion of psychotherapy and psychoanalysis. In this respect, she serves as a great role model to us all, and it gives us much pleasure to be able to celebrate her many unique achievements.

Notes

1   I wish to express my deep gratitude to Dr. Susie Orbach (2023) for having kindly enlightened me about the origins of the publication of her now iconic book, known as *Fat is a Feminist Issue*, or, sometimes, by the acronym *F.I.F.I.* Apparently, the publishers had hoped to entitle the book *Fat is a Female Issue*, but Orbach (2023) objected, having complained that such a styling "would have taken away its punch"; and, fortunately, she managed to retain her original preference for the main title. Regrettably, the publishers did insist upon the subtitle, namely, *The Anti-Diet Guide to Permanent Weight Loss*, in the hope of increasing sales in the so-called "diet market" at that time.

2   As I have indicated, this now-classic book bore the original full title *Fat is a Feminist Issue ...: The Anti-Diet Guide to Permanent Weight Loss* (Orbach, 1978). Apart from my own historically orientated chapters in this *Festschrift*, I have, at the request of Dr. Susie Orbach, rendered the title more concisely as *Fat is a Feminist Issue* in all of the other chapters and bibliographies.

3   For those who wish to learn more about the early history of the treatment of anorexia, I warmly recommend Susie Orbach's (1986) highly readable and hugely insightful book *Hunger Strike: The Anorectic's Struggle as a Metaphor for Our Age*, in which she has framed her contemporary work against the much more primitive interventions offered by her psychiatric predecessors.

4   Fortunately, after the publication of Susie Orbach's inaugural book, the medico-psychiatric approach to anorexia nervosa – though increasingly influential in certain circles – became challenged more acutely, due to the bravery of Orbach's work.

5   Other female mental health practitioners, such as the influential German-born, American-based psychiatrist and psychoanalyst, Dr. Hilde Bruch (1973, 1978), had also made important contributions to the humanisation of anorexia and related conditions.

References

Bell, Rudolph M. (1985). *Holy Anorexia*. Chicago, Illinois: University of Chicago Press.

Bruch, Hilde (1973). *Eating Disorders: Obesity, Anorexia Nervosa, and the Person Within*. New York: Basic Books.

Bruch, Hilde (1978). *The Golden Cage: The Enigma of Anorexia Nervosa*. Cambridge, Massachusetts: Harvard University Press.

Eysenck, Hans J. (1984). Lecture on "How Wrong Was Freud?". Oxford Psycho-Analytical Forum, Corpus Christi College, University of Oxford, Oxford, Oxfordshire, at the Department of Experimental Psychology, University of Oxford, Oxford, Oxfordshire. 30th April.

Eysenck, Hans J. (1985). *Decline and Fall of the Freudian Empire*. Harmondsworth, Middlesex: Viking / Penguin Books.

Eysenck, Hans J., and Wilson, Glenn D. (1973a). Introduction. In Hans J. Eysenck and Glenn D. Wilson (Eds.). *The Experimental Study of Freudian Theories*, pp. 1–15. London: Methuen and Company.

Eysenck, Hans J., and Wilson, Glenn D. (1973b). Epilogue. In Hans J. Eysenck and Glenn D. Wilson (Eds.). *The Experimental Study of Freudian Theories*, pp. 385–396. London: Methuen and Company.

Freud, Sigmund (1896). L'Hérédité et l'étiologie des névroses. *Revue Neurologique*, *4*, 161–169.

Kahr, Brett (2016). Interview with Susie Orbach. 10th March.

Lacey, J. Hubert (1982). Anorexia Nervosa and a Bearded Female Saint. *British Medical Journal*. 18th December – 25th December, pp. 1816–1817.

Orbach, Susie (1978). *Fat is a Feminist Issue ...: The Anti-Diet Guide to Permanent Weight Loss*. London: Paddington Press.

Orbach, Susie (1986). *Hunger Strike: The Anorectic's Struggle as a Metaphor for Our Age*. London: Faber and Faber.

Orbach, Susie (1994a). The Third Party Liabilities. *The Guardian Weekend*. 8th January, p. 21.

Orbach, Susie (1994b). Why Tongues are A-Wagging. *The Guardian Weekend*. 19th February, p. 44.

Orbach, Susie (1995). The Hidden Signs of Insecurity. *The Guardian Weekend*. 4th February, p. 8.

Orbach, Susie (1999). *The Impossibility of Sex*. London: Allen Lane / Penguin Press, Penguin Books, Penguin Group.

Orbach, Susie (2009). *Bodies*. London: Profile Books.

Orbach, Susie (2016). *In Therapy: How Conversations with Psychotherapists Really Work*. London: Profile Books.

Orbach, Susie (2018). *In Therapy: The Unfolding Story*. London: Profile Books / Wellcome Collection.

Orbach, Susie (2023). Personal Communication to the Author. 25th April.

Vandereycken, Walter, and van Deth, Ron (1989). Who was the First to Describe Anorexia Nervosa: Gull or Lasègue? *Psychological Medicine*, *19*, 837–845.

Vandereycken, Walter, and van Deth, Ron (1990). A Tribute to Lasègue's Description of Anorexia Nervosa (1873), with Completion of its English Translation. *British Journal of Psychiatry*, *157*, 902–908.

Vandereycken, Walter, and van Deth, Ron (1994). *From Fasting Saints to Anorexic Girls: The History of Self-Starvation*. London: Athlone Press.

Part I

Orbach in Context

Chapter 1

A Tribute to Susie Orbach

Luise Eichenbaum

As I contemplated my contribution for this collection, acknowledging the work of my dearest colleague Susie Orbach, I became aware of the unique nature of my relationship to her extensive body of work. In the earliest days of theorising and finding a home in The Relational School, Susie and I were collaborators. Our friendship and political activism, however, pre-dated our co-founding of The Women's Therapy Centre in London, The Women's Therapy Centre Institute in New York,[1] and co-authoring work on feminist psychoanalytic theory. Our shared political commitments are what drew us together and subsequently laid the foundation for our work.

Others in this collection will discuss Susie's contributions to relational psychoanalysis. I join them by discussing our concept of separated attachments not only because I believe it continues to resonate as usefully today as it did nearly forty years ago, but because it exemplifies the inextricable influence of feminism and political theory on our collaborative work and, I believe, on the entirety of Susie's body of work.

Feminism, left politics, historical analysis, and the belief in social change was the menu which first brought us together. Filled with the energy of the late 1960s and early 1970s, Susie and I had the great fortune of coming of age in a youth culture that believed we could change the world. We were set on it. Inspired by the civil rights movement and the anti-war movement that followed, we had a taste of what it meant to be a part of something much larger than our own individual development and aspirations. We have written about those early days elsewhere including the chutzpah of youth that had us depositing our first mailing into the Chalk Farm post box announcing the opening of The Women's Therapy Centre in April of 1976 (Eichenbaum and Orbach, 1988). By then we had each moved from New York City where we first met – for Susie, back to London, and, for me, living outside of my hometown for the first time.

In New York, we had begun, along with our feminist colleagues,[2] a critique of Freud and psychoanalytic theory through a feminist lens. What now appears to be a most obvious question – how does gender influence psychological development, psychic structure, and clinical practice – was then an entirely new one.

DOI: 10.4324/9781003470090-3

As I write this, I am acutely aware and encouraged by how much has transpired in the discourse concerning gender in the last ten years. The last several years have seen the deconstruction of gender by feminists, queer and trans folk, microscopically magnifying and questioning the very category of gender itself. The complexity of gender assignment and the psychological disruption it created for so many had previously been insufficiently understood.

In 1973, developmental theory both inside and outside of psychoanalysis was one size fits all babies in a world that was highly structured around gender inequalities. The unisex version was typically descriptive of male experience and was devoid of any analysis of sexual politics. Through our newly found feminist lens we knew girls and boys were not coming into being on an even playing field. How one came to know oneself, how one was seen by others, how one thought about a future and adulthood, were deeply informed by the body and gender one inhabited.

Our psychoanalytic study of gender had two foci – the experience of the daughter being raised female and the experience of the mother for whom gender identification or disidentification permeated the relationship with her newborn (Eichenbaum and Orbach, 1983a). Prescriptions for masculinity and femininity needed to be teased apart in order to begin the work of theorising a roadmap for girls' and women's psyches which more adequately reflected how the outside (patriarchal social relations) got inside (Eichenbaum and Orbach, 1982), becoming the bricks and mortar of internal life. We found our psychoanalytic home with the Middle Group and, more specifically, the seminal theory of Ronald Fairbairn. The work of Harry Stack Sullivan in the United States and John Bowlby in the United Kingdom had not yet influenced our project and yet both Sullivan's detailed enquiry, and attachment theorists' emphasis on the minutiae of what transpired between mothers and infants, paralleled our own approach to writing a gendered developmental theory and examining its implications in the clinical setting.

At the heart of our work was the complexity of emotional dependency. In retrospect it makes sense that our focus was dependency rather than attachment *per se*. Dependency was more ideological at the time. Independence was highly valued by feminists. Indeed, feminists within the field applauded the concept of separation-individuation, arguing this developmental achievement was the new goalpost for girls. Dependency was seen as something that inevitably weakened women, keeping them childlike, while boys and men, by striving for and achieving apparent independence, could, symbolically, be strong individuals.

Susie and I turned that notion on its head, claiming that patriarchal social relations in which women mother and provide nurture curtailed, for girls, the security born of the ongoing ability to rely on another for emotional and intimate care. Girls had to absorb the tough lesson, transmitted by mothers, that they would become the providers of that support, but could not expect equivalence.[3] This, we suggested, made for the paradox of women appearing, and even feeling, clingy and dependent while being the person upon whom others depended. In the very legitimate quest for emotional security, women often do hold on tightly within their relationships, only adding more fuel to the erroneous supposition that women are the dependent sex (Eichenbaum and Orbach, 1983b).

It made sense that feminist ideology celebrated independence, seeing it as a necessary objective for the advancement of women. Historically, economic dependence limited women's life choices. Feminist ideology celebrated economic independence, increasing self-confidence, breaking barriers and glass ceilings. These were all charges of the time for good reason. But we knew that misogynous culture worked in insidious ways to keep women in their place, and the beauty of psychoanalysis, and why we turned to it, was that it offered a practice by which one could access the unconscious. We did not come to psychoanalysis to practice the art and brainy appeal of this relational profession. Feminism and the desire for change were our motivation. The former were icing on the cake.

Psychoanalysis offered the possibility of deep change, lasting change, internal structural change. Our initial interest was not mental health *per se* but determination to change sexual inequalities. Our project led us to deeper understandings of how those inequalities saturated the interpersonal and domestic realm. Not only was there a need to change institutionalised sexism,[4] but in order to do that effectively we, at the same time, had to penetrate our psyches to change structurally both conscious and unconscious self-states. For us, the women's liberation movement's slogan – the personal is political – got extended to include the fact that political is also deeply personal.

Recognising the infusion of patriarchal social relations into the very cells of our psyches necessitated a revision of developmental theory. Even as late as the 1970s, women were still the primary caregivers to infants and children, and so the primacy of the mother-daughter relationship was evident. The glaring omission of a more precise understanding of the subjectivity of the mother, and of her gendered internal object world, spoke volumes. In clinical seminar after clinical seminar, mother's psychology was referenced when diagnosing the pathology of the child. In psychoanalytic theory, mother was the object for the infant's internalisations, projections, frustrations, ruthless desires, and so on, and with that object status came an appalling lack of understanding of mother's *particular* psychology, as a subject in her own right.

We can find easy agreement across a spectrum of schools, both within and outside of psychoanalysis, that the achievement of a secure, differentiated self is a desirable, developmental achievement. In the consulting room, practitioners continuously draw on their theory of choice and, for most, politics is something that exists outside of clinical practice. That being said, many of those psychotherapy relationships can be life-changing.

A perspective informed by sexual politics, however, takes the very same psychological achievement, a secure and differentiated self, and contextualises it with an infusion of the realities and consequences of a gendered schema.

Achieving a separated attachment is not straightforward for girls. Differentiating and occupying an embodied self is rife with caution warnings, prohibitions, and danger signs. The blurred boundaries of gender identification, social inequalities based on sex, and the fostering of mutual emotional dependency create a synchronicity between mothers and daughters. We suggested that a merged attachment with mother was far more ubiquitous. A merged attachment, unlike a separated attachment, dovetailed with the necessities of patriarchal constriction. Controls and constraints have taken up residence in our minds.

Starting a centre for women and families to have access to psychotherapy informed by social critique was a political act, although we always maintained that our work in the consulting room was not political activism. Psychotherapy, informed by feminism, could contribute to the much-needed resistance to forces, both internal and external, that women encountered from birth through adulthood.

Others in this volume have spoken of Susie's work on the body and its widespread influence. From the first words in *Fat is a Feminist Issue* (Orbach, 1978) to her most recent writings, whether it be about the multi-billion-dollar beauty industrial complex, or how members of the British public are responding to Brexit, or revealing what goes on in the mind and body of analysts as they sit with their patients, a social analysis is always at the heart of her work. She is a prolific writer and educator and seemingly inexhaustible. She says "yes" to invitations to speak and columns to write both inside and outside of the field because she is passionate about the work and that passion has not subsided.

Our dedication in *Between Women: Love, Envy and Competition in Women's Friendships* (Eichenbaum and Orbach, 1987, n.p.) says: "This book is written in recognition of our relationship, our deep love for one another and in the hope that it will speak to other women". Words written almost forty years ago. We could write the very same dedication today. Our collaboration was, for the most part, broken by our living 3,000 miles apart, raising children and losing the daily intellectual contact that came with sharing an office or a desk. We were youngsters when it began, and it was a fertile time. Fertile seems fitting because we had the great fortune of being part of birthing a feminist presence within psychoanalysis. Our collaboration took place during a most generative time for feminism and, for us, there was an opportunity to marry seamlessly our wish to change the world, our love of women, and our intellectual hunger.

I have treasured our collaboration and continue to feel sorrow for its interruption by our choices to live in our respective home countries. A collaborative relationship can exemplify, by its very nature, feminist principles in its intermingling of minds and valuing the thoughts of the other. In this dialectical process of each bringing an idea to the table, tossing it back and forth in an exciting playground for the mind, the collaborators jointly produce a new narrative. But it also requires room to disagree, to reject the other's idea, to tweak it, to weather the refutation or to trust the tweak, to both merge and to let go. In that sense our collaboration represents our efforts towards our own separated attachment, holding the thread which connects us while recognising and commending the autonomy of the other.

In this chapter I have set out to highlight the political lens through which one must read all of Susie's work. Her ability to translate political reality into psychoanalysis is matched by very few. The tribute that this volume offers is, without question, one well-earned.

Notes

1 Together with our colleague Carol Bloom.
2 Carol Bloom, Lela Zaphiropoulos, Laura Kogel, and Cathy Stillson.
3 This is as relevant today. In an article in *The New York Times*, entitled, "The Bad News on 'Good' Girls", Jill Filipovic (2017, n.p.) has written, "While girls are being taught to be emotionally competent, they also learn to be responsive to the needs of others – not a bad thing in theory, except that it can cross over into subservience."
4 This applies equally to racism and the internalisation of structural inequalities.

References

Eichenbaum, Luise, and Orbach, Susie (1982). *Outside In ... Inside Out: Women's Psychology: A Feminist Psychoanalytic Approach*. Harmondsworth, Middlesex: Penguin Books.

Eichenbaum, Luise, and Orbach, Susie (1983a). *Understanding Women: A Feminist Psychoanalytic Approach*. New York: Basic Books.

Eichenbaum, Luise, and Orbach, Susie (1983b). *What Do Women Want?: Exploding the Myth of Dependency*. New York: Coward-McCann.

Eichenbaum, Luise, and Orbach, Susie (1987). *Between Women: Love, Envy, and Competition in Women's Friendships*. New York: Viking Press.

Filipovic, Jill (2017). The Bad News on 'Good' Girls. *New York Times*. 24th November. *The New York Times*. [https://www.nytimes.com/2017/11/24/opinion/sunday/girls-parents-boys-gender.html; accessed on 29th August, 2021].

Orbach, Susie (1978). *Fat is a Feminist Issue*. London: Paddington Press.

Chapter 2

Radio Karnac
An Unpublished Broadcast with Dr. Susie Orbach

Brett Kahr

Introduction

For many years, I enjoyed a very creative and stimulating collaboration with Oliver Rathbone, the owner and Managing Director of the psychoanalytical publishing house Karnac Books, who, during his long-standing tenure, produced quite a number of my books (e.g., Kahr, 2016, 2017, 2018). Round about 2012, Oliver launched a new website called "Karnacology", with the assistance of his colleague Dr. Rod Tweedy – a platform which provided mental health practitioners with an opportunity to post interviews, blogs, reviews, obituaries, and other pieces of communication.

Keen to expand upon the success of Karnacology, Oliver approached me in early 2016 to discuss the creation of a new podcast series, and he very kindly invited me to serve as the presenter of "Radio Karnac". As we discussed potential speakers whom I might interview, and topics that we might discuss, both Oliver and I agreed that Dr. Susie Orbach would be the very best guest to inaugurate this new project and, with great generosity, she kindly agreed to participate. In due course, on 10th March, 2016, after a long day in the consulting room, I had the privilege of facilitating a most memorable conversation with Dr. Orbach about her career and, in particular, her contributions to public outreach.

At that time, the first series of Susie's iconic radio programme, *In Therapy*, had begun to appear on the British Broadcasting Corporation and would soon become transformed into two highly popular and influential books, namely, *In Therapy: How Conversations with Psychotherapists Really Work* (Orbach, 2016), and, also, its sequel, *In Therapy: The Unfolding Story* (Orbach, 2018), in which she would chronicle her unique sessions with trained actors. Orbach did not, of course, possess any details of the private lives of these actors; instead, she and her director, Ian Rickson, invited the actors to create fictitious characters who could thus be interviewed psychotherapeutically on the radio. This process offered listeners the opportunity to experience the psychological interaction without any violation of privacy or confidentiality.

I deeply enjoyed this conversation with Dr. Orbach, approximately half an hour in length, and, after having shared the tape with Oliver Rathbone, he intended to

DOI: 10.4324/9781003470090-4

post this interview on the Karnacology website as the launch podcast for the new "Radio Karnac".

But, alas, within days of having completed this important project, Oliver Rathbone received a rather unexpected offer from the Taylor and Francis Group, part of the "informa" business franchise – an internationally renowned rival publishing house – to purchase Karnac Books. Oliver agreed to this sale and, in due course, Taylor and Francis became the new owners of Karnac Books, the long-standing and esteemed psychoanalytical publishing firm. Regrettably, amid the hand-over, Oliver had to close down the Karnacology website and, in consequence, my conversation with Susie Orbach remained unused, collecting dust while archived on my computer.

It pleases me greatly that, since 2016, Taylor and Francis have enhanced their publishing venture enormously by having taken control of all of the classic backlist of titles once published by Karnac Books and now released through the long-standing imprint known as Routledge. Moreover, Taylor and Francis have continued to publish many exciting new books as well, thus enhancing their already well-established collection. Eventually, the old Karnac Books became absorbed by Routledge. But, in spite of this polite and mutually agreeable "take-over", Karnac Books did not disappear.

In 2020, Dr. Stephen Setterberg, a child psychiatrist and Jungian analyst, revived the old Karnac Books in collaboration with Jane Ryan, the Creative Director of Confer Limited – one of the United Kingdom's leading continuing professional development providers – and then, in 2023, Oliver Rathbone repurchased Karnac Books from Dr. Setterberg, and relaunched this important business yet again, in partnership with Kate Pearce, the founder of the iconic Phoenix Publishing House. In consequence, not only does Routledge continue to release many excellent psychoanalytical and psychotherapeutic books, but so, too, does the newly relaunched Karnac Books under the leadership of the experienced and creative Mrs. Pearce. Together, these two houses have made great contributions to the advancement of our professional base of knowledge.

While undertaking the editorial work for this special *Festschrift* in honour of Dr. Orbach, I unearthed the tape recording of our short, but informative, podcast interview, which I have now transcribed. And it pleases me that, although Karnac Books could not post the audio recording, as planned, on its Karnacology website, we can now include a transcript in this collection of essays. Alas, Susie and I barely had sufficient time to cover even one zillionth of her many contributions but, nevertheless, we did focus on her outstanding work as a pioneer in the expansion of media psychoanalysis, helping members of the public to access better mental health care in a safer and easier manner. Therefore, I can think of no topic more important and more timely than this one, thus providing newcomers with a very personal glimpse into the mind and the work of the woman whom we honour with this *Festschrift*.

In the pages which follow, readers will be able to enjoy Dr. Orbach's reflections and comments. In order to maintain the conversational nature, I have retained the original pauses as much as possible.

The Interview: 10ᵗʰ March, 2016

BK: Welcome to Radio Karnac. My guest today is the distinguished clinician, author, broadcaster, and social policy-maker, Dr. Susie Orbach. Welcome Susie.

SO: Very nice to be with you.

BK: We have so many areas that we might cover, but I really want to talk to you today about our profession – the psychoanalytical profession, the psycho-therapeutic profession – and the conflict we have that we are the most *private* community in the world, and yet, we also have an obligation to make our work known to the *general public*, so that people can be educated about us, so that people might find us, and so that people can use what we have to offer. And I think it's a real paradox and a real problem.

SO: I think I'm very lucky, because I moved back to England, which is my home, in 1976. And with Luise Eichenbaum, I opened The Women's Therapy Centre. Because I'd been in North America for a while, where therapy, certainly in the metropolitan cities, was something that was quite openly discussed, I didn't have any reservation about the fact that when we opened The Women's Therapy Centre, we would send out press releases, we talked to the local press, and we would appear on the equivalent of Radio 1. We wanted our service to be both known and, also, to be shaped by the people who came to it. So for me there's never been a distinction between the absolute privacy of the consulting room and the development of theory out of that – in that sense I'm a total Freudian – and the wish to share one's work and the insights of the consulting room, and to theorise – in the early days, of course, about women's psychology – with a wider public. And I've always felt that's part of the social responsibility of being a modern psychoanalyst.

BK: When you founded The Women's Therapy Centre – in 1976, I believe – might you have done so, in part, because your experience in America had given you the privilege and the authorisation, or do you think that it might have been your own personal courage and your pluckiness and your creativeness that allowed you to do something much more public than most colleagues had undertaken at that time?

SO: Well, I'm sure it was a combination, Brett. In America, there was a huge radical therapy movement. But I was also reading about what was occurring in the United Kingdom – R.D. Laing's work at the Philadelphia Association, for example. And I was also learning about the Arbours Association. And they were all publishing quite widely (e.g., Laing, 1960, 1971; Berke, 1977). So it didn't seem to me that I was being transgressive. Look, it was quite scary to do it and to proclaim ourselves as founders of The Women's Therapy

Centre. But Luise and I felt there was a real absence of theory and practice that addressed women's particular experiences. And we had been in study groups about psychoanalysis and women, around which there was some very interesting writing at the time (e.g., Mitchell, 1974). There was a lot of really interesting work, but we felt we had something different to offer. So, although it felt brave, because we were two young women and we had no money, and we were doing this, and we were *radicals* doing this, we wanted to open a therapy centre that was available to everybody, to women and their families. And that just felt like I was part of both a kind of British tradition, having read the Laing and the Arbours material, as well as the North American work. So, what felt plucky was that we were two young women daring to do it.

BK: And of course, very shortly after you opened The Women's Therapy Centre with Luise Eichenbaum, you published *F.I.F.I.*, the abbreviation for your classic book, *Fat is a Feminist Issue ...: The Anti-Diet Guide to Permanent Weight Loss* (Orbach, 1978).

SO: I did, but before that, which I think might be interesting, we started to learn about how therapy had to be *secretive*. The very fact that you went to therapy was secretive. Whereas therapy became a kind of discourse, both in intellectual and political circles. And within the first three months, we had a call from the clinic at the Institute of Psycho-Analysis in London asking us for patients.

BK: You became swamped with referrals.

SO: We were swamped with people referring themselves. That was one really interesting development. We answered the phone, so we knew what people wanted, or at least what they wanted consciously. But yes, you're right, in 1978, I thought, "I've learned so much at this point about women and their relationship to eating and their bodies and that I need to share this." And being of the generation of second-wave feminism, I thought, "Well, I'll write a pamphlet", that's what you do. But my partner at the time said, "You write a book." So I wrote a book, which I didn't really know how to do, and it touched a nerve and actually is still in print. And I've just done yet another introduction to it. So, that began my project, I suppose, of using writing as a way of making therapy insights public. But also putting together therapeutic understandings with the social structure – how does the outside get in and the inside get out – which is of course Luise Eichenbaum's and my first book, *Outside In ... Inside Out: Women's Psychology: A Feminist Psychoanalytic Approach* (Eichenbaum and Orbach, 1982).

BK: Absolutely. You've really taken the most private profession and I think you've found a way – rather creatively – to keep it both private *and* public at the very same time. I remember you saying once that, "Psychotherapy is not a spectator sport", and yet we have to find some way to let people have a glimpse of what it is we do.

SO: Over the years, I've had many, many requests to film therapy sessions, to write about the people who see me, and I've always been uncomfortable about that. And I suppose that culminated for me in 1999 when I published *The Impossibility of Sex* (Orbach, 1999), which is a series of imagined stories, from therapy, but what I chose to do in that was to imagine a therapist called "Susie", which is not such an odd literary device, if I dare compare myself to other literary writers who've used themselves as figures in their own fiction, and to explore the craft of what we actually do from the point of the therapist. The imagined patients, or the imagined people who come to see this imaginary therapist – who is a more clever or a more thoughtful version of me – whatever it is when you make stuff on the page as opposed to in the consulting room. It was a way to say there's something we want to share. I don't want to exploit the actual people. When I tell a story, I'm telling my story. I'm making theory out of what I've understood. I'm not actually telling the story of "John" or "Jack" or "Penny". Because they actually have a different story and the weighting of what they've understood is really different. I can only make the story from my perspective as an analyst, as a psychotherapist.

BK: This book, *The Impossibility of Sex*, is truly very remarkable, and I think it's really quite groundbreaking in the history of psychoanalysis, because I cannot think of another text that offers us such a privileged and detailed glimpse into the private mind of the practitioner while undertaking psychotherapeutic work. It's very fresh, it's very honest ... it's very *radical* actually.

SO: Well, I think it was a very radical act. And I would have written another whole series on that. I think it's akin to what you could find in the best of psychoanalytical writing in the United Kingdom at the time. I think it's akin to Christopher Bollas's (1979, 1987) work and Patrick Casement's (1985) work. But of course their cases were real cases. And that was the thing that made me uncomfortable, because the minute I changed something, the minute I fictionalised an aspect to change the person, I'm in Philip Roth territory, with Roth saying, "How dare you transpose me, a Jewish North American writer into an Italian painter", because you change everything that is completely central to who I am.

BK: I thought you had devised a deeply unique solution to several problems. First of all, at that time, you had already achieved a rather high public profile. And you had published many columns in *The Guardian* newspaper (e.g., Orbach, 1994a, 1994b, 1995), and had undertaken an enormous amount of broadcasting work, public lecturing, and so forth. Thus, I think it was essential that you did *not* write about your patients, because I suspect it would have given rise to a great deal of gossip, and I suppose that by having come up with these fictionalised characters, whom you treated as if they really were there ...

SO: Oh, they are still there. They're very real to me. And that's no different to this latest iteration, which is this series of broadcasts.

BK: Tell us about *In Therapy*.

SO: That was commissioned by B.B.C. Radio 4, and I chose to use actors, who were given a very limited scenario by the brilliant theatre director Ian Rickson. For example, you're a sixty-year-old trade unionist who's had two marriages that've gone wrong and you've been in therapy for eighteen months ... or you're a woman who's come from another country and there's some loss going on. So, actors were chosen to play these characters. Ian Rickson worked with these actors, whom he selected, to work out a "back story", and then these actors arrived at my consulting room as though they were coming for a session. I was given a little bit of the back story, but it was totally improvised. So I'm the therapist ... in a way, like in *Impossibility* ... who is surprised by what comes through my door. And I thought it was an interesting way to move from *Impossibility* to actually show a little bit about the process; in other words, "She said, he said", or "She said, he didn't say". If you listen to the broadcast, there's quite a bit of silence. Not dead silence ... I think a very "held" silence if I can put it that way.

BK: I would agree.

SO: But I wanted to show the intricate workings, neither from a scripted fashion nor from a real session, because that does feel to me too intimate. I do respect the intimacy of the consulting room and the privacy. But I wanted to have the feel of what the two of us are struggling with, hoping for, reaching for, sitting with, and feeling together.

BK: The programme has had a huge impact. This is a five-part radio series, right in the middle of the day, and transmitted on the British Broadcasting Corporation service. And *millions* of people listen to these shows. I do not know how many of our colleagues in the mental health field appreciate how much outreach that provides for our profession. Thankfully, people are engaging with it. I do know that on the day after the first programme went out, not one ... not two ... but *three* of my patients in a row said, "Oh, my God, I heard Susie Orbach's programme yesterday, did you hear it?" It proved really extraordinary that so many people engaged with it. What do you think has been the initial impact? I appreciate that the programme has only just come out.

SO: I think people are really thrilled to learn that psychotherapy is not mumbo-jumbo. That these are conversations of a different nature that speak to those parts of ourselves that literature does, that drama does, that art does, that religion in its best form can do. It's about ... I think the impact it has had is that people have understood that we're not *technicians* moving bits around the jigsaw, moving minds around. But we're there with our beating hearts, with our irritations and compassions, and with our intellect, trying both to be on the side of the people that we're working with, while dividing ourselves in such a way that we have minds that can float widely enough to think about their circumstances, their psyches, their histories, their social class, their moment in history. All of that is what we bring to bear on our engagement, as we're involved in trying to help individuals or couples situate themselves inside of themselves in a different and richer way.

BK: I thought you spoke so beautifully, and although we could not see your facial gestures or your hand gestures ... we could see you in the silence. It was a very powerful silence. And your voice came across really beautifully, really touchingly, really warmly. But you never lost the analytical precision. I experienced it as a beautiful master class.

SO: If I had a chance, I would do it again slightly differently. Because you can always hear your own mistakes, and on radio you can't edit them out. The voice doesn't land properly with the mistakes excised. And of course, in the book of these sessions, I will put in some of the things that I couldn't do in that twelve-and-a-half-minute slot. We therapists are in the business of yearning for truths, authenticity, noticing the impossibility of connection, treasuring moments of connection, seeing the material structures of the mind as they are. So, there's a very physical sense in a session. And I think radio is a beautiful medium for the listener to imagine and bring his, her, or their own thoughts to that endeavour. The other thing I was really interested in, both in *Impossibility* and also in this, is that I think all of us who do this work know that there's an aesthetic to our work. It's not one from column "A" and one from column "B". The artistry that is required, the sensitivity, knowing when to come in and when not to, and the getting it wrong and then having to get it right after you've done it wrong ... those are all done, I think, with a high aesthetic sense. I know that's an odd thing to see, but I can say it to you, Brett, because you're a musician as well as a writer and a clinician.

BK: Well it touches on what I've always thought of as the "tonal qualities" of therapy, about which we speak really very little. I'm extremely interested in the quality of the psychotherapist's speaking voice. We know many therapists who talk quite extensively, yet whom I consider to possess very strident speaking voices ... they actually enunciate in augmented fourths. And I think that your voice came across really rather beautifully, and I think that if I were looking for a therapist, I would have rung you straight after having listened to the programme.

SO: Well I'm afraid they did. There is a lovely American therapist whose name escapes me. Steven ... ?

BK: Steven Knoblauch?

SO: Yes, Steve Knoblauch (2000). And of course, he is a musician ... a saxophonist ... and I think he and you and I are very interested in these different aspects of tonality.

BK: Because what you have been able to convey on the radio, I think, has been not only the vocal tone but, also, issues of speed, issues of timbre ... how one actually formulates one's sentences. Indeed, when we read written case studies, we do not have the opportunity to hear the spoken voice of the author ...

SO: But I suppose you and I are so interested in it from different perspectives, you, because you're such a superb musician and me I because I'm very interested in the body. And in my work, where I've tried to talk about "What is a body and how do we get one?", part of what interests me in the whole Cartesian duality is that speech, and speech production, is the perfect example of mind and body, and I'm thinking now of Anne Karpf's (2006) work on the voice.

You find a voice in the consulting room. It isn't actually the same voice for everybody. You have humour with some people. You discover you interrupt other people. Or you talk fast. You make a new relationship with everybody. It of course has something to do with who Brett is, who Susie is ... but it has to have that individual quality in which the timbre and the tempo can be communicated.

BK: That is very nicely phrased. If we think about the three projects that you initiated in an historical sense – The Women's Therapy Centre founded in 1976, *The Impossibility of Sex*, published just over twenty years later in 1999, and then, in 2016, these B.B.C. radio programmes, *In Therapy*, with Dr. Susie Orbach – that's a forty-year trajectory. And those are only three of the many public outreach projects that you have initiated. What would you say has been the shift in public attitude and public understanding from the days of The Women's Therapy Centre in 1976 to the launch of your recent radio series in 2016?

SO: It's a very good question, but I think we'd need a whole other broadcast for that. I think that one of the big contributions of The Women's Therapy Centre was to make therapy public, long before the Tavistock Clinic did its series of talks. It's as though we picked up without even knowing it from Donald Winnicott's tradition.

BK: He was really the first public mental health broadcaster in this country.

SO: Exactly ... and the wisest, actually. So, I think we opened it up and we said, "Therapy is for everybody." So, the people who came to us ... there were women who'd been in mental hospitals. There were middle-class feminists. There were families in distress. There were women from other countries, such as Ireland, Saudi Arabia, France, Germany, the United States of America. A whole range. What happened historically? So now, whenever there's any kind of public emergency, we learn that counsellors or trauma specialists have been sent in. So I think that I've been part of that public conversation, partly through having *The Guardian* columns actually for all those years, and partly through other writings, of making therapy part of public life. The process may be behind closed doors, but the ideas that emerge from it, which need to take a place in public policy, in early childhood interventions, in Sure Start, in all of those ... I think that those things have begun to permeate the culture in a very, very interesting way.

BK: We have always had, I suppose, within the broader mental health profession, a very cautious element, perhaps a very conservative element ... people who think that the work really needs to stay in the consulting room, and that the general public should not know what our practices are, what our fees are, how to find us, whether one has a website ... yet I must say from my work teaching younger psychotherapists, they have absolutely come on board with the idea that we must have a much better developed public outreach programme. But what can we all do as mental health practitioners to "raise our game", especially here in the United Kingdom where we have a much tinier community

than our colleagues in the United States of America? ... particularly as we
have come to therapy many years later.

SO: I think we're in difficulty. Although the N.H.S. provided quite a lot of therapy
at one point, we've had terrible cutbacks. And we've had the problems of
the delivery of something called "therapy" that *isn't* therapy. I think ... and
you only do this with collaborators ... but Susanna Abse and I both try to
work in the social public policy area. Other people do as well. So, those
would be my strengths. Look, we know that M.P.s go to therapy. They don't
just go for coaching; they actually go for psychoanalysis or psychoanalytical
psychotherapy. So, I think there's that kind of place to be working. There
are policy papers. I would like to see therapy back in the university. I think
there's been something very unhealthy about it not being a discipline that has
a kind of academic engagement. You and I have both spent a long time training youngsters.

BK: Indeed.

SO: And I've been appalled sometimes that people will read a paper and be
less able to comment on it, but only regurgitate it, rather than have a critical view, which they would have if they were reading a history paper, an
anthropology paper, frankly, a G.C.S.E. geography paper. You're entitled to
have opinions.

BK: Yes.

SO: And that has been something that's been quite contentious in the training.

BK: Well, if you think about the history of our profession, we started out in
Freud's consulting room. We started out as private guilds. So, on both sides
of the Atlantic Ocean there has been quite a lot of banging on the doors to try
to get psychotherapy trainings and psychoanalytical trainings affiliated with
universities. I think we've gone *some* way towards that ...

SO: We have but we've lost ground, because with psychiatry in the United
States ... you had to do psychoanalysis after the war, didn't you? That's
now been changed because notions of mental distress have become biolo-
gised. And the fact that you and I have probably had young psychiatrists in
our practices doesn't mean that they've got the power to change the whole
shape. So, I think we have to work where we can, and each of us is working
in different places. And I'm very delighted that the youngsters want a more
public profile. I just hope they don't go "superficial" with it. And I don't see
why they should. Therapy isn't the easiest of things. It's incredibly reward-
ing but ...

BK: It's hard work.

SO: But it's hard work.

BK: It's very hard work. Absolutely. So, Susie, tell us about the next steps for you?
I know you're now working on a book-length version of the *In Therapy* radio
broadcasts. When might we expect to see that on our shelves?

SO: You will see it either at the end of this year, 2016, or, probably because of the
exigencies of the book trade, in January, 2017.

BK: Well, we look forward to that very much. We are so grateful to you for speaking to us here on Radio Karnac. I feel we've only just scratched the tiniest of surfaces, so you must come back and speak to us again quite frequently. Thank you very much.

SO: Thank *you* so much, Brett.

References

Berke, Joseph H. (1977). *Butterfly Man: Madness, Degradation and Redemption.* London: Hutchinson of London / Hutchinson and Company (Publishers).

Bollas, Christopher (1979). The Transformational Object. *International Journal of Psycho-Analysis*, *60*, 97–107.

Bollas, Christopher (1987). *The Shadow of the Object: Psychoanalysis of the Unthought Known.* London: Free Association Books.

Casement, Patrick (1985). *On Learning from the Patient.* London: Tavistock Publications.

Eichenbaum, Luise, and Orbach, Susie (1982). *Outside In ... Inside Out: Women's Psychology: A Feminist Psychoanalytic Approach.* Harmondsworth, Middlesex: Penguin Books.

Kahr, Brett (2016). *Tea with Winnicott.* London: Karnac Books.

Kahr, Brett (2017). *Coffee with Freud.* London: Karnac Books.

Kahr, Brett (Ed.). (2018). *New Horizons in Forensic Psychotherapy: Exploring the Work of Estela V. Welldon.* London: Karnac Books.

Karpf, Anne (2006). *The Human Voice: The Story of a Remarkable Talent.* London: Bloomsbury / Bloomsbury Publishing.

Knoblauch, Steven H. (2000). *The Musical Edge of Therapeutic Dialogue.* Hillsdale, New Jersey: Analytic Press.

Laing, Ronald D. (1960). *The Divided Self: A Study of Sanity and Madness.* London: Tavistock Publications.

Laing, Ronald D. (1971). *The Politics of the Family and Other Essays.* London: Tavistock Publications.

Mitchell, Juliet (1974). *Psychoanalysis and Feminism.* London: Allen Lane / Penguin Books.

Orbach, Susie (1978). *Fat is a Feminist Issue ...: The Anti-Diet Guide to Permanent Weight Loss.* London: Paddington Press.

Orbach, Susie (1994a). The Third Party Liabilities. *The Guardian Weekend.* 8th January, p. 21.

Orbach, Susie (1994b). Why Tongues are A-Wagging. *The Guardian Weekend.* 19th February, p. 44.

Orbach, Susie (1995). The Hidden Signs of Insecurity. *The Guardian Weekend.* 4th February, p. 8.

Orbach, Susie (1999). *The Impossibility of Sex.* London: Allen Lane / Penguin Press, Penguin Books, Penguin Group.

Orbach, Susie (2016). *In Therapy: How Conversations with Psychotherapists Really Work.* London: Profile Books.

Orbach, Susie (2018). *In Therapy: The Unfolding Story.* London: Profile Books / Wellcome Collection.

Part II

Orbach in the Consulting Room

Chapter 3

Shame and Shamelessness

Jane Haberlin

Having coasted through university and squandered many rich intellectual opportunities on offer, it was with delight that I discovered my psychoanalytic psychotherapy training seminars were to be led by Susie Orbach – someone whose work I had read and admired. Alongside a traditional curriculum in Freud, Klein, and British object relations, Susie introduced us to papers from an emerging theoretical perspective: relational psychoanalysis. Susie's great generosity in setting aside such valuable time and energy to teach us came with clear, high expectations: first and foremost was the requirement for close reading and rigorous thought. We read papers from relational psychoanalysis and compared them to classical texts – passive acceptance of orthodoxy was unacceptable as was any evangelical adoption of this new reframing. Instead, she required us to understand the concept discussed. Could we see the nuanced difference in what was being proposed? Did we agree or not? Could we imagine how the concept studied manifests in clinical practice? Susie Orbach was a formidable, challenging, and inspiring teacher and it was under her tutelage I discovered the hitherto entirely elusive pleasure of intellectual hard work.

Susie Orbach's (1978, 2009) work has expanded psychoanalytic theory through her work around eating problems and her theory as to how we acquire a bodily sense of ourselves. In *Understanding Women: A Feminist Psychoanalytic Approach* (Eichenbaum and Orbach, 1983), Orbach, together with Luise Eichenbaum, applied a feminist lens to psychoanalysis, thereby emphasising the lack of due attention that had been given to the subjectivity of the mother and the critical role of the mother-daughter relationship in the making of femininity. Such thinking undoubtedly influenced relational psychoanalytic theorising of the central importance of the subjectivity of the therapist – a development which marked a paradigm shift from a one-person to two-person psychology requiring the therapist to position herself in the field of analytic enquiry so that the material in the room for analysis is understood to be an expression of the psyches of two people in the consulting room and thus co-created (Orbach and Eichenbaum, 1999). Their work also illuminated the pernicious and enduring influence of internalised misogyny on women's psychology: how oppression is, in part, perpetuated by women's felt sense of shame at being thought inferior, messy or weak; how unentitled women feel to have their

DOI: 10.4324/9781003470090-6

emotional needs met, especially the need for dependency; how the way in which we carry a critical internal eye so that how we see ourselves in the eyes of others shapes our interpretation of the world and guides our actions; how it drives us forward; how it holds us back.

I greatly admire the way in which Susie weaves seamlessly in her mind between the intrapsychic and the interpersonal; making meaning only after having situated someone in a social, cultural, and political context. This capacity has underpinned Susie's success as a stellar ambassador for the field of psychotherapy; her column in *The Guardian* newspaper, "Shrink Rap", ran for over ten years, from 1989 to 2000, during a period of accelerated change in British societal norms, such as the deinstitutionalisation of those with mental and physical disabilities, the findings of the Macpherson Inquiry, and the lowering of the male homosexual age of consent. During this time, Susie used her column to promote understanding and encourage reflection as to how we internalise racism, homophobia, cultural and class inferiority. She illuminated how our internal worlds are not dry, mechanistic places as often portrayed by psychologists or neuroscientists, but are passionate, lively, lyrical places where our dreams and longings struggle for expression.

As an homage to Susie Orbach, the theme of my paper – shame and shamelessness – is beautifully pertinent. Shame continues to be an emotion powerfully employed to control women, and Susie has tirelessly campaigned to push back against the shaming of women's desires, positing instead the need for separated attachments so that a woman is not isolated as she dares to break the internalised taboo for a connected autonomy. She has also fought against the beauty, food, and fashion industries, as well as advertising, and media pressure, which have created such debilitating dissatisfaction and shame in women about their physical appearance.

In this paper I explore the social co-construction of shame and the relational psychoanalytic concepts of the mutual bi-directionality of psychotherapy and the significance of the subjectivity of the therapist, namely, how we use our own self – our history and associations as well as our use of language – idioms and idiosyncrasies, tone, and vocabulary to co-create relationship and co-construct meaning.

* * *

One of the ways that society regulates itself and marks its boundaries is through the emotion of shame. The markers which attract or mobilise shame are neither fixed nor universal: developments across time, and changes in the content of what causes shame, have far-reaching effects upon society. In Britain these markers have changed significantly in recent years and those with liberal sensibilities would celebrate much of it as progressive, for example, the amelioration of the felt shame of children born outside of legally-sanctioned marriage. But there have been bigger swings away from privacy, modesty, and ideas of honourable behaviour, and I am interested in exploring how these changes manifest in the consulting room and what challenges they present for psychotherapy. Particularly, how do we understand shame and shamelessness from a relational perspective? How is this experience felt and understood in the consulting room and what is there to be learned about the efficacy of different clinical approaches to working with shame or shamelessness?

Many theorists from self-psychology, attachment, and developmental research perspectives have expanded the Freudian psychoanalytic notion of shame as a reaction-formation against drives and therefore an exclusively intrapsychic phenomenon. Instead, they locate the affect of shame as the manifestation of the infant's response to non-responsiveness or missteps in the mothering person. Beebe and Lachmann (2002), Schore (1991), Stern (1985), and Trevarthen (1977) have each shown the importance of early attunement – by which they mean when a child's spontaneous gestures are recognised and sympathetically responded to the micro-adjustments in facial mirroring, the breaking of eye contact, the downward cast of the eyes, the burying of the baby's face, and the moving closer in and out. Kohut (1971) theorised that when the mirroring object (the baby's primary caregiver) accurately, promptly, and sensitively gives to the baby what it needs, then the baby has the feeling that it is right to have these needs gratified and develops a grandiose self. Conversely, where there is a consistent lack of attunement the child must make adaptations and submit to the out-of-tune signals of the parent, thereby stimulating the proto-experience of *"I got it wrong"*, which in turn undermines the baby's emergent sense of self. There is extensive literature and debate surrounding the phenomenology of shame, but, in broad terms, what developmental psychologists suggest is that we can track the emergence of the emotion of shame from this experience of an empathic break between our mirroring object and our grandiose self. In such moments we evidence the beginning of one important aspect of shame, the management of appropriate closeness and distance. As we develop and mature, we are made aware that what we do and how we appear matters to others; we learn to regulate ourselves and judge what to share and what to keep private. In this way, shame is constructed and negotiated; it serves as a regulator, to motivate and to inhibit. The experiential power of shame is typically accompanied by an excess of bodily stimulation: blushing, sweating, tears welling up, creating the paradoxical experience of the body drawing attention to oneself when one wants to be hidden. This is apparent in the idioms habitually employed to describe the experience of shame from *"wanting the floor to swallow me up"* to *"Kill me, now!"*

At the polarities of the shame continuum, we have shame-proneness; where the people live in fear of their failings being exposed or found out, and we have shamelessness where any need for a loving, praising relationship is denied, where the approving eyes of the other are no longer sought. However, shamelessness can also carry the positive connotation of having liberated oneself from society's intolerance and disapproval. *Shameless* is the name of a Canadian young women's magazine which reaches out to readers who are often ignored by mainstream media: "freethinkers, queer youth, young women of colour, feminists, artists, intellectuals and activists". In this context, shamelessness is equivalent to a call for guiltlessness – doing nothing of which to be ashamed, or entitlement – a claim that one's behaviour is, or should be, shame free. But we also have the television programme *Shameless* where the protagonists' refusal, not necessarily an active or knowing refusal, to comply with societal norms or live within its boundaries produces grotesque dystopian comedy.

We are living through a time of contradictions where the gears and levers of shame and shamelessness act as force and counterforce. We have seen the proliferation of social media usage where everyone is in charge of their own P.R., where selfies are perfected by posing from the most advantageous angle, augmented by the application of extreme contouring make-up and judicious filters, so that the public self is admired, and the private self is protected. Juxtaposed to this is an increasingly intrusive media which has escalated our appetite to enjoy the shame of others such as the *Daily Mail*'s rolling sidebar of shame where an actor's cellulite, spotty skin, and dishevelment fuel a delight in click-bait material. Another point on the shame / shamelessness continuum is the emergence of an abundance of politicians seemingly impervious to shame: Donald Trump's many and various breaches of widely accepted norms of what to expect in our leaders regarding honour, honesty, and wisdom did not reduce him in the eyes of great swathes of the United States electorate and in the United Kingdom, and this is matched by the popularity of Boris Johnson and Nigel Farage which remains undented despite abundant evidence of their incompetence or dishonesty. But we also have to understand the meaning behind the media's successful employment of images of Edward Miliband inelegantly eating a bacon sandwich to shame him publicly and powerfully strip him of gravitas in the run up to the 2015 general election. How do we reconcile the incongruity of this evidence regarding society's assessment of what constitutes shameful behaviour?

Is one answer that the preceding decade of rapid change in our notions about shame played a significant part in creating an environment into which a shameless protagonist such as Trump could succeed? – a decade in which the media continuously pushed at the boundaries of sexual mores and what was acceptable for public display. I offer two incidents which sizzle in my mind as examples of an acceleration of a public desire to shame, against which shamelessness might be a defence: the first, where David Cameron, at a time when he was on the cusp of becoming Prime Minister, was asked during a television interview by Jonathan Ross whether he used to masturbate to images of Margaret Thatcher as a youth. The second was only partially unfocused, namely, the broadcast of a female contestant on *Big Brother* masturbating with a wine bottle. These years also saw a marked increase in exhibitionism and exposure with societal approval seeming to matter less and less, particularly to large sections of youth where shamelessness can be understood as a positive active challenge to existing orthodoxies that need challenging. For example, simultaneous with the introduction of Anti-Social Behaviour Orders in 1999 came the manufacture and selling in Camden Market of hooded sweatshirts with A.S.B.O. printed on them – the label, which was intended to shame and humiliate the perpetrator being reclaimed and mastered by the young as a symbol of cool. Similarly, the racist warehousing of a disproportionate number of black males in the American penal system, and the humiliation of being deprived of their belts upon incarceration, was taken up and transformed by street fashion in which young men of all races and ethnicities wore their jeans oversized, low-slung, and showing their underpants. These adaptations suggest that a refusal to cower under society's cosh of shame had been mobilised and paradoxically created an appetite to cheer on those such as Trump or Johnson who surf over the opprobrium from the establishment.

Undoubtedly, an area of accelerated loosening of societal constraint has been around sexual mores. Early twentieth-century societal norms regarding acceptable sexual expression were narrowly confined with sexual appetites outside of these limits considered perverse and, by implication, shameful. Ideas of perversity rapidly changed with the publication of the Kinsey reports on sexuality and sexual practices (Kinsey, Pomeroy, and Martin, 1948; Kinsey, et al., 1953), previously considered to be within the repertoire of a minority, were identified as mainstream behaviour. Today it is a pertinent question about what behaviours, if any, we consider perverse. Muriel Dimen (2003, p. 290) reflects, "If perversion can coexist with health, if its status as illness varies with cultural time and place, then conversely, any sexuality may be symptomatic – or healthy." She challenges: "Perversion may be defined, after all, as the sex you like and I don't" (Dimen, 2003, p. 259). Whilst I find myself in intellectual, theoretical agreement with Dimen, I am interested in the feelings that are evoked when working with someone whose behaviours or values extend the boundaries of what we personally find acceptable. How then does the subjectivity of the therapist and our values, beliefs, prejudices, and ignorance affect the therapy?

* * *

My patient "Mark" is a highly educated and successful professional. His reason for coming to therapy was that his relationship was in crisis; his partner was demoralised in the same ways as previous lovers had become dissatisfied; they had complained as she had that Mark refuses to engage with her when she raises any issue which carries the merest hint of criticism. His response to her complaints – complaints which seem to me fairly reasonable, such as arriving home much later than he had said – oscillate between an aggressive symmetry: "Well, what about when you were ..." or, conversely, to withdraw completely. His parents, in particular his mother, were people of high expressed emotion who expected compliance, dutifulness, and diligence. When he fell short of their expectations, he would be severely punished, cruelly ridiculed, or ignored. He understood that he had carried this internal working model into his current relationship as well as previous relationships. And he acknowledges that he overacts but nevertheless feels unable to control his defensiveness.

In the early months of therapy, Mark worked hard to create a benign atmosphere so that, I theorised, no real kind of intimacy would occur. I understood that this spoke to his fear that I would discover him, find him wanting, and respond in the same way as his mother. One of the most essential, but hardest, things we can do for our patients is to reveal their destructiveness to them. When they ask, "What is the matter with me?", they want two different responses. They are defended and want to be reassured that there is nothing wrong with them – that there was a failure in their environment or in the way they were parented, but they also want us to tell them authentically what it is about the way they have adapted to that early failure that now creates the problem for them in their relationships with others. The most valuable thing we have to give them is a report of how it is to be in a relationship with them, especially when we have an *in vivo* experience of what it is that can happen that leads others to withdraw / reject / disappoint them.

One issue which Mark brought in a proud, almost boastful, way was that he professed to be sexually shameless. He was a habitual user of internet pornography, visiting extreme sites which involved simulated violence and many images which elicit what Muriel Dimen (2005, p. 1) has labelled the "Eew!" response in the therapist. He has a wide circle of male friends with whom he shares downloaded imagery, and with whom he discusses pornography with the intensity of connoisseurs discussing wine. He experiences his lack of shame as a good thing; he has thrown off the shackles of shame, and sex has been given the status of any other act. As an intellectual, he borrows an argument from Freud that because shame impels the individual to conceal some of his urges, fantasies, and deeds from others, it easily leads to hypocrisy. Freud objected vigorously to the many effects of the cultural shame of his time and emphasised honesty and openness. Freud proposed that psychoanalysis should reduce the strictness with which instincts were repressed and that correspondingly more value should be given to truthfulness. My "sexually shameless" patient is very attached to such a distinction and values truthtelling very highly. I struggled with my "Eew!" response; I wanted to appear openminded and curious, respectful of difference, but in truth I disapproved broadly of pornography and specifically about some of the areas he explored. I had resolved to bide my time until we had created a stronger therapeutic alliance before I broached a subject which I judged was likely to evoke shame.

One paradox of psychotherapy is that the patient brings to us the injuries they wish to heal and that despite our best efforts to approach these wounds sensitively, we are bound at times to cause hurt and pain. To this point, psychotherapy holds great potential to shame the patient, even if the therapeutic goal is to make the patient's destructive impulses conscious and therefore less likely to be acted out. The psychotherapeutic task is how to cast light sensitively onto those aspects of the patient's self which keep to the shadows without causing debilitating shame.

At the time of seeing this patient, my consulting room was in a street controlled by a Residents' Parking Scheme and consequently inconvenient for my patients as well as myself. While looking out of the window, in a break between sessions, I saw my patient park up outside of the house. As he arrived at the door, I cautioned him that he would be ticketed. He assured me he would be fine and, as we walked into the room to begin the session, he began to tell me that he had a disabled badge. Perplexed that I had known him for some time and was unaware of any disability,

I asked him, "How so?" He explained that he had bought it from a man in a pub for fifty pounds and that it has revolutionised his life – he can park wherever he wants. "I'm "Access All Areas", Jane." It was flirtatious and out of character for him to speak to me in this way and I wondered whether the interaction happening on the cusp of the session allowed some part of him a voice that was usually inhibited and monitored once the door had closed and the boundary was drawn. The comment was sexual but also carried connotations of going where perhaps he should not, of being omnipotent and in control. However, the expression "Access All Areas" was a badge of honour from my youth – a thing to assert one's superiority – to flaunt one's proximity to the band at a gig, to have free drinks – it was about hierarchy and competition and at that moment some of what I felt was the taint of being left out, inferior, having to scrabble for a parking place. In parallel, I also felt a rush of opprobrium at the criminality that had led to him having this permit. My mind spinning, we settled into our chairs and I began to deconstruct and distil the myriad possible meanings of what had been said, deciding in what manner I could most valuably take up this disclosure.

Patient: You don't approve?

My patient's voice brought me prematurely out of my reverie. The truth was I did not approve. I felt a blush of shame that I had revealed this on my face which my patient now scrutinised. Side-stepping the question, and too quickly gathering my thoughts, I drew a familiar link. My patient's limited ability to be empathic with others and make vivid his experience was something that had brought about impasse and disappointment in other relationships and I thought it could be useful to look at how he splits off in this respect. However, any vestige of usefulness was immediately obliterated as I offered up a sermon about the subjectivity of the disabled driver, and shared my fantasy that their car had been broken into, and spoke of the distress and inconvenience caused, observing that in order for him to enjoy the permit he did not imagine the experience of the other.

My patient retorted angrily that this was an act of ordinary delinquency, claiming "loads of people do it", and he accused me of trying to shame him. Indeed, he came at me with various denunciations about me being a sanctimonious reader of *The Guardian* as well as a polemic about the iniquities of Islington Council and their parking policy. I noticed that I felt off the hook, and a familiar feeling of righteous indignation began to soothe me; and the feeling of shame ebbed away.

Therapist: I think you do indeed feel shamed by me and that the feelings are so unbearable that you need me to carry them for you. It is I who must stand accused of getting it wrong, of transgression, of causing injury to another's feelings.

Clearly stung, he broke eye contact, shielded his face, and retorted angrily.

Patient: You'll be delighted to know you sound like my mother! I'm sick of women telling me off!

In Jessica Benjamin's (2017) model of intersubjectivity, breakdown is understood as a collapse into the complementarity of "doer and done to", typified by rapid oscillations, a ping-pong dynamic, in which reciprocal actions lock in the possible response of the other. Authorship and agency fail because one feels reactive rather than free to formulate intention, and one feels that one must blame rather than be responsible, and that one feels controlled rather than recognised.

Witnessing my patient's shame as he fixed his gaze to the floor brought me to my senses. I had become the eyes that had to be avoided. Hot visceral feelings of shame then flooded my body, but a realisation of what was happening allowed me to regulate myself and slowly recover my capacity to think and restore empathic contact with my patient. In every therapy there will be sessions when we miss our patient; we fail to attune; we reflect back to them some disowned aspect of themselves and the reflection is harsh and painful. Usually the patient can leave the session troubled, angry, shocked, and affronted, but the therapeutic alliance holds firm enough that they can go away, reflect, recover, and return curious as to why we said what we did. This process itself often represents the most significant breakthrough in the therapy; patients have rendered themselves sufficiently open and vulnerable to let us become important; they take the risk of bringing back to us these taboo feelings which in itself marks an embryonic belief that we are robust enough to hear about them and our relationship resilient enough to endure.

Therapist: That was pretty awful what happened between us wasn't it? Let me see if I can explain. I think I found your smugness provocative and then felt ashamed of your perceiving correctly that I didn't approve. I'm sorry, I'm horribly aware I sounded like your mother – I sounded like my mother!

He raised his eyes and looked at me and laughed. The invitation to look into the workings of my mind, to witness the aspects of myself that were less than lovely, and to experience me taking responsibility for my failings, gave my patient an experience of not being left alone to carry the "extruded malevolence" (Davies, 2004, p. 727) as he had done as a child.

Indeed, he returned to the issue of the parking permit with genuine curiosity about how he had squared it with himself, and this established a point of entry into my more boldly exploring his use of pornography. I was able to make conscious that my desire to be thought accepting of sexual behaviour unfamiliar to me inhibited my exploration of his pornography usage. I thought I knew what he meant by "regularly masturbating", perhaps daily, perhaps morning and night. It was only once I asked for the *specific* specifics that my patient could reveal that his usage sometimes caused him to miss deadlines or that he often made his penis and testicles sore. Such revelations allowed us to inch from his presenting "sexually shameless" self towards allowing me to know how addicted he was and to bear witness to the terrible shame he felt at this dependency being exposed.

Relational theory asks us to accept that we will be unconsciously drawn into enactments of early ruptures; this enactment provides us with an opportunity to differentiate ourselves from the original relational configuration; and not to respond in a familiar, feared, dreaded way. The therapist will be experienced as, and transformed into, a characteristic bad object, but becomes, if satisfactorily worked through, a different sort of object. This point in the therapy marked a significant improvement in Mark's capacity to bear criticism or feedback from his partner when he disappointed or upset her and he came to therapy with a growing confidence that he could bear me "finding out" about him. I delighted in the rich complexity of his language: "finding out" denotes curiosity or discovery as a precursor to getting closer, but "finding out" also carries the connotation of being "busted" – that is, having exposed those aspects of himself he felt were bad and which must remain concealed. Indeed, the success of this therapy was in large part because Mark came to express and to have validated his defence against dependency needs which the dependency on pornography had stood for.

* * *

Relational psychoanalysis does not suggest that it is necessary for there to be ruptures in every therapy but rather that we can come to see in retrospect that the patient needed to recreate a past relational configuration. When therapists are able to regulate themselves and not respond in a familiar, feared, dreaded way, the patient's relational world opens up; they have new experiential data. For example, not everyone is as harsh, volatile, cruel, or contemptuous as their mother or father or primary caregiver.

Acknowledging the potential to be drawn into enactments with our patient enlivens our notions about shame; we have to become both the shaming other and transform the experience. However, the projective processes involved in the shame defence can cause the therapist to resonate with our patient's shame so powerfully as to feel ashamed ourselves, either consciously or unconsciously. This risks our attention shifting away from containing and metabolising the patient's experience as we turn inwards in an attempt to regulate our own feelings of shame.

My patient "Alice" was brought up in a rarefied bohemian family. Alice was one of six children; her parents were internationally distinguished in their field and subsequently often absent because of professional demands. The home environment was one in which high expectations regarding achievement were explicitly stated and the requirement for the children to build a certain kind of character and personality was emphasised. To a great extent, the children fell into line and responded to these expectations by becoming exceptional, precocious learners. Little attention was paid to their emotional life and any problems were solved with efficient pragmatism; indeed, her parents would be scornful of failings and brooked no weakness. Her brothers would often taunt and humiliate her, and she learned to conceal and eventually split off from distress, perpetuating the dynamic in turn by humiliating her younger siblings. Alice received very little physical affection but bathed herself in her parents' warm approval of her academic distinction and her emergence as a young scientist. Shortly after university, she married another brilliant, rising star of whom her family approved and whose career ascendancy they promoted. They were a dazzling young couple, but the marriage was more cerebral than sexual. Alice's life seemed to be going very well until her late-twenties when her husband left her for another woman – a woman who was glamorous, sexy, and warm. Alice's incredulity that her intellect, status, and capacities did not trump the charms of the new woman tormented her. Neither could she fathom that her husband was prepared to "endure exile from Eden" for his transgression: "how could he give up access to all this? ... why would he take a hammer to his life?" Undone by impotent fury and bereft of understanding, Alice withdrew into obsessive rumination and self-harm, which eventually led to a depressive breakdown requiring a hospital admission. Alice spent several weeks in hospital and consulted me for psychotherapy three months after discharge when, though much better, she still had not managed to return to work.

As you may imagine, this was not a difficult therapy to which to bring insights and ideas. In the beginning, Alice would speak passionately and quickly and was eager to relate, one mind to another. Her breakdown had brought about a crisis in which she reviewed her childhood and began to see the shortfall in her parents' approach. As she began to discover these imperfections, so too she began to experience terrible embarrassment when she was away from me; she would be persecuted by an image of my face sneering at her. Similarly, she would look through the window of the front door as I approached to open it and would "see a look of disdain on my face". She petitioned me to be "more smiley" when we met at the door. I replied that whilst I could try to do that, I thought that it would be useful to understand why she saw disdain in my countenance rather than to seek a solution that reassured her. Alice, who had always used her fine mind to think her way through any obstacle or difficulty, responded to my invitation to allow room for these feelings with consternation. Why would I want to do that? Within weeks she had grown contemptuous. She began to respond to my observations and interpretations with retorts of "And ...?", "How does that change anything?", or she would do a précis of all the thoughts and links I had made and rattle them off with incredible oral dexterity like a psychoanalytic tongue-twister. Then, full of feeling, she would fall into silence and, short of swinging her legs and chewing gum, give a perfect impression of a stroppy adolescent. Any enquiry as to what she was feeling, or thinking, would be met with "I'm bored ... it's pointless ..." As I opened my mouth to speak, she would roll her eyes and sigh dramatically. I tried to reach her with suggestions that she was trying to give me an experience of what it was like to be humiliated and taunted by her family, but to no avail. I proffered that she found it unbearable that I could formulate an understanding of her before she could get to it herself. I acknowledged how frightened she must be to need to defend against me so fiercely, whilst continuing to speak of what unconscious meaning the defeating of my best efforts might carry. Alas, my sense of being useless intensified. I found myself feeling that I had emptied my mind of every intelligent thought to chisel her out of her resistance, and I began to experience terrible dread as she continued to come three times a week. When I enquired why, if I was so useless, she continued to come, she replied that she could not bear to fail and with a tone of arch sarcasm: "I presume at some point you'll break through."

And here was the knot. If she found me useful, let me in, it would mean I must be more capable, more potent than her – she would have to feel all of her defended against inferiority. The more she verbally insulted me, and I carried on doing an adequate impression of not being annihilated, the more ashamed she felt that she could not match my capacity to bear what she supposed I must be feeling.

Whilst I had some understanding of what might be happening for Alice, I was unable to comprehend fully what was happening for me. My shame at my lack as a therapist to transform this dynamic was enormous and I found myself experiencing the most extreme countertransference reaction of inadequacy. I would experience genuine relief on recovering my thoughtful, competent, and articulate self when in the presence of my next patient who attended only ten minutes after Alice had left. This rapid regulation reinforced my understanding that something powerful but outside of my conscious awareness was occurring between Alice and myself that needed to be understood and attended to, but this knowledge similarly bore down on me creating only heat and pressure rather than light. I would arrive at supervision full of self-mortification at my apparent ineptitude and leave with my confidence temporarily restored only to feel bereft of understanding and capacity once back in session with Alice. In order to regulate myself and survive, I dissociated at times, feeling like a voice simulator, unable to access myself fully. The therapy eventually ended when Alice concluded that "we've gone as far as we can go."

In a traditional psychoanalytic psychotherapy, we may understand what happened as a negative therapeutic reaction, where accurate insight and helpful interpretations lead to an exacerbation of feelings, or represent the therapist's failure to manage malignant projective identification. I included it in this paper on shame because I think it illustrates well the difficulty of working with the shame defence. A traditional psychoanalytic psychotherapist would approach this impasse by examining the feelings which disabled their ability to respond to their patient in order that they may be neutralised so as to clear the field of study in order to understand what unconscious processes were at work inside the patient. However, a relational psychotherapist does not assume that unconscious processes are one-sided and therefore this impasse cannot be meaningfully explained solely by reference to the patient's history or relational incapacities. Instead, an explanation is sought involving an acknowledgment that it is in a particular relational configuration that such intense feelings are provoked or mobilised, mutually constructed, and regulated or dysregulated.

This particular slide into the complementarity of "doer / done to" was harder to step out of because of the force with which Alice defended against feelings since her recent hospitalisation. The unconscious solution she had found was to re-defend and accept feeling unreal – but able to function – than risk feeling real and breaking down again. "Why would I want to do that?" is a quite understandable and poignant response to my invitation to connect with her feelings when we consider that she had endured a hospital stay relatively recently because these very feelings had left her feeling maddened and overwhelmed. Significantly, only one sibling visited Alice in hospital – her parents and grandparents and other siblings stayed away, claiming that it would be too shaming *for Alice* to be seen in such a place.

Only sometime after the therapy had ended did I began to understand that I had not been able to recognise Alice's deep feelings of shame. When she would retreat into silence and stare at the floor, I would read her response as a shaming gesture towards me. My contribution to the situation was my own self-criticism – partly a result of identifying with her criticism of herself and her criticism of me – but mainly my own feelings of dissatisfaction and inadequacy surrounding my psycho-therapeutic work with her. Symmetrically she became for me the shaming other.

Alice came from generations of privilege; her considerable intellectual confidence, along with her upper-class accent, activated my class hurt and the wound of being the scholarship girl. The psychoanalytic tongue-twister I described earlier, and the fact that I lack the facility to repeat it for you – still sends a frisson of humiliation through my body. The unconscious anxiety at the heart of shame is abandonment – a fear that we will be dropped, rejected. The affect in Alice's presence that I was not able to regulate was that of the felt shame of inferiority I carry, passed onto me by my mother. As a poor Irish immigrant, she sent me out into the world with the maxim: "Better to keep quiet and be thought a fool than to open one's mouth and remove all doubt." As Alice began to ridicule my thoughts, the meta-language of psychotherapy and my estuary accent, I did indeed begin to identify with the fool and collapse into a complementarity out of which it felt impossible to climb.

As I write, I notice that the thought of sharing this clinical vignette provokes shame for me. I am painfully aware that I have gone against my mother's maxim; I imagine her asking me why I have shared clinical material which is so exposing. Why not encourage an idealised professional self? Two answers: the first is about that profound experience, recognisable to clinicians who read this paper, whereby relationships with some of our patients continue to be explored or negotiated long after the actual therapy ends. My therapy relationship with Alice continues in my mind; and I believe I now understand things which were obscured to me at the time. The second thought is that sharing our clinical experience is not only how we learn about ourselves, our limitations, and our flaws, but also about how to be more effective as psychotherapists in the consulting room. In this respect, I learned, and continue to learn, a great deal about how to work with the shame defence from my relationship with Alice. In the words of a brave Irish man, Samuel Beckett: "Fail, Fail again, Fail better."

I hope to have demonstrated what I have learned from Susie Orbach about how to be a psychotherapist; what it demands of both therapist and patient – the mutual commitment required to go beyond symptom reduction to characterological change; the humbling honour of being entrusted with another's deepest vulnerabilities; the requirement to feel and hold their pain; the joy of watching another's sense of self being restored and revitalised. My capacity to be and endure as a therapist is in immeasurable part enhanced by my great, good fortune in knowing Susie Orbach. She is a formidably wise colleague, wonderfully generous in her encouragement, provision of delicious meals, and sourcing of hair products. She is a dear, loyal, and loving woman who I marvel is my friend.

References

Beebe, Beatrice, and Lachmann, Frank M. (2002). *Infant Research and Adult Treatment: Co-Constructing Interactions*. Hillsdale, New Jersey: Analytic Press.

Benjamin, Jessica (2017). *Beyond Doer and Done To: Recognition Theory, Intersubjectivity and the Third*. London: Routledge / Taylor and Francis Group, and Abingdon, Oxfordshire: Routledge / Taylor and Francis Group.

Davies, Jody M. (2004). Whose Bad Objects Are We Anyway? Repetition and Our Elusive Love Affair with Evil. *Psychoanalytic Dialogues*, *14*, 711–732.

Dimen, Muriel (2003). *Sexuality, Intimacy, Power*. New York: Analytic Press.

Dimen, Muriel (2005). Sexuality and Suffering, or the Eeew! Factor. *Studies in Gender and Sexuality*, *6*, 1–18.

Eichenbaum, Luise, and Orbach, Susie (1983). *Understanding Women: A Feminist Psychoanalytic Approach*. New York: Basic Books.

Kinsey, Alfred C., Pomeroy, Wardell B., and Martin, Clyde E. (1948). *Sexual Behavior in the Human Male*. Philadelphia, Pennsylvania: W.B. Saunders Company.

Kinsey, Alfred C., Pomeroy, Wardell B., Martin, Clyde E., Gebhard, Paul H., Brown, Jean M., Christenson, Cornelia V., Collins, Dorothy; Davis, Ritchie G., Dellenback, William; Field, Alice W., Leser, Hedwig G., Remak, Henry H., and Roehr, Eleanor L. (1953). *Sexual Behavior in the Human Female*. Philadelphia, Pennsylvania: W.B. Saunders Company.

Kohut, Heinz (1971). *The Analysis of the Self: A Systematic Approach to the Psychoanalytic Treatment of Narcissistic Personality Disorders*. New York: International Universities Press.

Orbach, Susie (1978). *Fat is a Feminist Issue*. London: Paddington Press.

Orbach, Susie (2009). *Bodies*. London: Profile Books.

Orbach, Susie, and Eichenbaum, Luise (1999). Relational Psychoanalysis and Feminism: A Crossing of Historical Paths. In Moisés Lemlij and María Rosa Fort Brescia (Eds.). *At the Threshold of the Millennium: A Selection of the Proceedings of the Conference*, pp. 175–181. Lima: Sidea.

Schore, Allan N. (1991). Early Superego Development: The Emergence of Shame and Narcissistic Affect Regulation in the Practicing Period. *Psychoanalysis and Contemporary Thought*, *14*, 187–249.

Stein, Ruth (1997). The Shame Experiences of the Analyst. *Progress in Self Psychology*, *13*, 109–123.

Stern, Daniel (1985). *The Interpersonal World of the Infant*. New York: Basic Books.

Trevarthen, Colwyn (1977). Descriptive Analyses of Infant Communicative Behaviour. In Heinz R. Schaffer (Ed.). *Studies in Mother-Infant Interaction*, pp. 227–270. London: Academic Press.

Chapter 4

Embodied Intimacies

Sarah Benamer

In thinking about how Susie Orbach's work has influenced me as a clinician, it felt like I was trying to unpick my therapeutic (and personal) D.N.A. The issues she explores in her extensive portfolio of literature, including feminism, power dynamics, and the cultural context of embodied experience, not to mention her commitment toward the demystifying and accessibility of therapy, are matters close to my heart.

Perhaps of the greatest importance is to see theory postulated from the ground up of contemporary times, which far from becoming complacent evolves as new information makes itself known. Her pioneering work offers a vital integration that unashamedly refuses to "know its place" by bringing together psychoanalytic and attachment theory, with insight and appreciations of societal trend, from the real world experience of a participant observer.

I will concentrate for the most part upon Orbach's theoretical contribution relating to embodiment. Her mapping of the cultural terrain "outside in – inside out" has provided an alternative voice to the mainstream, affording a safety in returning to meaning.

Through her lens the previously "difficult" or "pathological" individual is understood as part of a society, in a place in time, in a family that is the agent of that culture. In an era where we are entranced by the quantitative, whilst not losing sight of research, Orbach reminds us that the essence of being human is a qualitative relational experience.

As an advocate working in the National Health Service (N.H.S.) psychiatric system, I met "Mia". In her increasingly tenuous relationship with the world she had ceased to eat, she hardly moved, and she communicated infrequently. Mia's reed-like limbs seemed barely substantial enough to resist gravity. In the psychiatric institution (where she was detained under section), the locked doors held what was left of her physicality while her mind dissociated. Being with Mia made me feel fiercely protective. I wanted simultaneously to hold my breath and to breathe out for us both.

I was troubled by the institutional response to Mia, and to the predominantly female inpatients whose language of pain included their bodies. From ingesting hair and picking at themselves, to purging or refusing to eat, it seemed to me that

DOI: 10.4324/9781003470090-7

these women were trying to resolve something beyond the concrete. However what was being communicated was apparently unbearable for all concerned. Sadly there appeared to be a stereotypical way in which these patients were understood: the word that I most heard was "manipulative", with the perception that they were doing something to us rather than to themselves, and that far from being a cry of pain this was "attention seeking". Treatment was medically orientated and focused largely upon the behaviour and symptom, and held vague ideas that you could "grow out of it", suggesting that to involve one's body was somehow infantile.

As a young community worker, my femininity contorted by Margaret Thatcher's Britain, where the media was using the Princess of Wales's bulimia to scorch the earth salaciously, I was experiencing conflict between my feminist ideals and true feelings about my own body, and I wanted answers for Mia and myself. I found my way to *Fat is a Feminist Issue* (Orbach, 1978) and to *Hunger Strike: The Anorectic's Struggle as a Metaphor for Our Age* (Orbach, 1986), and to ideas of personal meaning framed by patriarchy. If "Our anorectic and bulimic sisters inscribe on their bodies the conflicts that can't be told in other ways yet" (Orbach, 1986, p. xxii), what was the whispered scream of Mia's body narrative?

With the overlay of this insight I was able to appreciate more fully that Mia sought a resolution to her unnamed trauma through consciously and unconsciously using her body-self, internalising her workings out as any "good girl" is raised to do. Piecing together the fragments of her verbal and nonverbal narrative over a year, I was to discover that underlying her restriction of food was terror of what she had already taken in. A young self had been force-fed, feeling meals beyond capability or palate. This was a story of early separation and abuse in the context of a society where a girl shaping her body was a legitimate pathway.

Mia's body had been her only constant and yet she could not trust its boundaries to contain the feelings and trauma she had already experienced – she needed to stop things getting out. She could not tolerate the need for others that left her yearning for more, or trust her body's boundaries to guard her from the emotional and physical violations that the world of attachment to others contained – she had to stop things and people getting in. Lockdown of the pathways in and out was the only protection available.

To label this control is to minimise the terror that Mia was creatively trying to bear, and to demean the self that she was attempting to have despite multiple psychic atrocities. This young woman had seemingly returned to a preverbal state, was fed by an umbilicus through a nasogastric tube, in total power of the psychiatric system on section. Her story was being told in fragments, and her relationship with the staff and the institution held both the repetition of the original trauma (overwhelming attention to the physical rather than the emotional force, and powerlessness) and the possibility of something different, perhaps in an unconscious attempt to reconfigure a breakdown that had already happened. The atrophying of the self had held the hope of a new beginning. Maybe this time baby could be borne in mind, nourished, and contained? As encapsulated in *Hunger Strike: The*

Anorectic's Struggle as a Metaphor for Our Age, "The eating problem is not the problem, it is the solution" (Orbach, 1986, p. xxvi).

In contrast to the medical or community care environments with which I was familiar, on training as a psychotherapist I found myself immersed in a place where the splits were configured differently. Here the pull was all to "mind", and the lived-in body (as I understood it) was at best neglected. There was an apparent recapitulation of the psyche-soma split, with the therapist ostensibly having arrived at the psyche, a place to which the soma-embedded client could aspire.

Discussion of the therapist's body seemed to be held apart from being one of "them". Principally orientated around how we are *seen* – what we wear or how we cut our hair – or coming into focus at times where we could no longer hide our bodies (as if this were possible and we should!) – such as pregnancy or illness, or in the context of the taboos of touch or sexual enactment, it was as if bodies were optional and the appreciation of embodiment as an ordinary part of how we understand ourselves was largely absent.

Clients' bodies were regarded as the repository of unprocessed feeling from which they could emerge via catharsis and the capacity to symbolise. Whilst feelings that initially defy integration for whatever reason may, of course, become lodged in the body, ideas of symptom and cure seemed to maroon clients who had experienced complex trauma, for whom working through this trauma did not illicit what Susie Orbach (2009, p. 14) describes as a "peaceable body" lying dormant underneath.

In terms of the body-to-body relationship between the therapist and the client, as two individuals sharing intimate space over time (as distinct from touch) it appeared that influence was unidirectional. The therapist's body was a receptacle for the client's feelings: objective and clearly delineated.

Whilst seductive, the sense of having transcended my body was not how I experienced myself, personally or professionally, or something I felt was feasible or desirable for my clients.

The power dynamics of gender and racial difference, and of ageing or living with disability as embodied, were (and often still are) relegated to the realm of equal opportunities policies rather than integrated into therapeutic response. It seemed as if the entanglement of attachment-based clinical practice, of the repeated fathoming of bodily sensation, and the "me-not-me" dilemmas of long-term developmental relationships were not encompassed by this.

Then, at the John Bowlby Memorial Conference in 2003, Susie Orbach (2004, p. 28) suggested that there was "No such thing as a body" but "only a body in relationship with another body" (Orbach, 2004, p. 28), undercutting the familiar given with the simplest of statements. "Them and us" collapsed into the revelation of the co-creation of bodies within an interpersonal and cultural context. Her challenge to the profession was to move beyond our historical reluctance and to see the "body as body", not just as a dustbin for the mind. It seemed we could no longer retreat to the safe haven of the body of the other, the baby body, the symptomatic or perverted body; we were talking about all of *our* bodies! The day-to-day reality of our desiring, failing, multifaceted bodies as they were engaged in our lives and work: beginnings that have not diminished in their relevance.

Orbach's work imparts that our sense of embodiment is not homogenous but comes about as a result of other processes. The story of our bodies (of fat or thin) is a feminist issue, an issue of attachment to one's family, to oneself, and to society. Security or insecurity is embodied.

In order to make this developmental journey to our own body and mind we need the felt bodies *and* minds of our closest attachments. In the right caregiving circumstances we learn to ride out the phenomena of our feelings and to differentiate some of what we would call emotion from bodily sensation. Slowly, with practice and support over time, we internalise this capacity, and in combination with acquiring verbal symbolic capability we are able to contain our feelings. In parallel, respectful and attuned physical responses from others afford us an experience of embodiment, of inhabiting space, of understanding where we begin and end, and of boundaries that can be trusted without defence.

If this apprenticeship does not happen, if we are not held physically or emotionally, are delegitimised or shamed or experience repeated misattunement, or are abused, neglected or traumatised, the way in which we are able to show ourselves and our feelings can be impaired and constructed in a way that incorporates these intrusions or absences.

This is also written into the script of our embodiment. Orbach's work describes how these patterns may be unconsciously inscribed through families, and to the intergenerational transmission of attachment she adds the intergenerational transmission of bodies (Orbach, 2009). Our perception, handling, use of our own body, or the bodies of others, is inextricably relational and attachment-bound.

As any clinician brings his or her own subjectivity to therapeutic practice, and each client relationship is inherently different, I cannot know if I work in the way that Orbach would, but it is in some of her questions about our corporeality that I continue to find my clients and myself. Orbach's mapping of the culture at large, her appreciation of body narrative, how we get a body, and how we maintain one, are crucial to my understanding the embodied intimacies that emerge in my clinical work.

In contrast to previous N.H.S. advocacy work, I now have the relative luxury of working long term in private practice as a relational attachment-based psychoanalytic psychotherapist. Indeed, I see clients who, as an aspect of their overall mental health picture, conform to many of the diagnostic labels that describe a stereotype but which rarely convey the individual.

My frame for working with *all* psychic distress, not just that which is concentrated upon the body, relies upon the idea that everyone's relationship with the body holds particular elements of what it means to be them. The way in which we inhabit, use, and experience our bodies, or the moment-by-moment mutual influence between bodies is part of, not set apart from, the narrative of who we are. Consequently, it is essential to include the language of bodies in how we understand what is happening in therapy.

Once the idea of the pathological body is despatched we are free to explore and learn: to be open to the story being conveyed by an individual's body and behaviour. What I have witnessed in my consulting room are the multi-layered ways in which clients relate to their bodies (and to mine). Of particular interest is the way in which the body may be engaged in the service of attachment, or as a place to express usurped desire. The searching for and perfecting of the body as object often masks a need to grow in a family or cultural environment that is not receptive to that person's subjectivity. This preoccupation proposes a means of keeping self and desire alive in a state of hopelessness.

The emotional nuances of our past may be unconsciously mirrored in our handling of our body selves – for example, bulimia incorporating the trauma patterns of anticipatory dread, punishment, numbed aftermath, and yearned-for absolution. We can use our bodies as a covert arena in which to express or bury pain, rage, or perceived badness that might, if projected outwards, threaten our place in the world. As Orbach (1986) illuminates in *Hunger Strike: The Anorectic's Struggle as a Metaphor for Our Age*, underlying the starvation of body is a response to relational negation that is paradoxically compliant and rebellious.

Unlike intimacy with another person, to use our body in the service of relational development is to have an available other seemingly within the scope of our power. However, adoption of this system is not without damaging consequence in the long term and cannot take us beyond what we already know.

As well as exploring the symbolic, communicative, or relational aspects of embodiment, I understand that there are some things that are just of the body: the concrete of our being is also the cradle of the unknown.

In addition to reconfiguring embodiment *per se*, Orbach's recent work identifies that contemporary times are unprecedented in regard to the power mankind has over the evolution and construction of bodies. She names that, "There is now a crisis about the body itself" (Orbach, 2009, p. 11), and that our "body can no longer be relied upon as something essentially stable" (Orbach, 2009, p. 11).

Perhaps in reflection of this I am increasingly seeing clients for whom the crisis of embodiment goes beyond nutrition and image to encompass their entire physicality. Here the person's search for a self extends to desire for certainty and control over *all* the visceral systems underlying bodily functioning. The unknown of the body is itself a source of terror.

It seems that I am encountering the psychological hangover from the reframing of the body as a constantly evolving commodity. As she describes, "The body is turning from being the means of production to the production itself" (Orbach, 2009, p. 6). Here, echoing those with eating disorders where the relationship with body is a way of being, an objective aim commensurate with cultural and societal expectations, and a subjective communication of the very personal experience of the relational world, the body as work is all consuming, but the body that is yearned for is not only a certain size or shape (Orbach, 1978, 2009). This longed-for fantasy body is in essence an object or a machine rather than an organism, something completely certain, totally comprehensible and possible to control to the micro level.

One such client is "Zoe".

Whilst as clinicians we might wonder with every client if we are the right therapist to meet that person's need, from the moment I hear Zoe's soft Scottish accent on the telephone my introspection takes a particular form. As well as the usual curiosity and fantasies of who she is and what might be required of me, on the barest of information my mind has crowded with questions of my substance, namely, whether I am strong enough? Do any physical vulnerabilities preclude our working together? What seems to have arrived in the feeling-scape are questions of a particularly concrete bodily nature. Not "is this therapy viable?" but "am I viable?" Will I last the course?

In supervision, I talk out this powerful "arrival", unpicking the personal and professional before we actually meet. So far I know that Zoe was diagnosed with obsessive-compulsive disorder (O.C.D.) at the age of eleven. She is now in her thirties and has been on medication for all but a year since that time. She has recently decided to come off her medication again. She is now in search of what she hopes will be a "sustainable" way forward, hence seeking therapy. The original manifestation of the O.C.D. was around a fear of needles, blood, and contamination with H.I.V. / A.I.D.S. Zoe has a long-term partner, full-time work, and a support network of friends and family.

In terms of therapeutic "viability", there is a concrete meeting of fear and actuality that has already had to occur in my body and mind to welcome Zoe in. A medical condition requires that I carry emergency injections at all times. In sitting in therapy with me, Zoe will be unknowingly in close proximity to something she fears.

When we meet, Zoe sits birdlike on the edge of my couch. It is as if every part of her is being held aloft so as not to intrude too much upon the space. She is earnest and determined and yet apparently swiftly derailed by self-doubt. She rarely uses the personal pronoun, saying instead "you" and "You feel this when this happens don't you ... ", rather than "I". As I ask her about her history, she frequently compares herself unfavourably with others, minimising her world view or the difficulty of her life experience, her sentences tailing off dismissively with a hint of self-directed anger and shame. She looks down as she tells me what a "burden" she feels herself to be to her partner and her family because of her O.C.D. These attachments are clearly current and important to her sense of place in the world. She needs to know that our work will be about understanding, not blame.

In profound contrast to my initial feelings, when Zoe and I encounter each other in person the notion of my lacking viability gives way and I feel solidity in my body. Something as old as time, akin to being the granite of the Cornish cliffs, both worn by the sea and influencing the swell. There is an urgency flirting around the edges of my consciousness competing with a need to take things slowly and not startle. We agree to meet once a week.

Zoe has had psychiatric involvement from the time she made her family aware of her symptoms, having had several family therapy sessions as a child and, latterly, cognitive-behavioural therapy as an adult, including exposure therapy. The original treatment of Zoe's condition prescribed that her entire support network should "not engage" when she talked about any health or physical matter that could be deemed as compulsively seeking reassurance. The extreme of which meant that when Zoe was twelve years old her mother was instructed by the psychiatric team to leave the family home for some time as she "could not be trusted" not to respond to, or reassure, her daughter. Sadly, this separation confirmed Zoe's original fears and sense of omnipotence that she was responsible for the family's coherence and safety, and that no one could soothe her.

Unfortunately, the continuance of this embargo introduced a daily "Still Face Experiment" (Tronick, et al., 1978; cf. Brazelton and Cramer, 1990) into her life. Believing that they were helping, those closest turned away from her when she was most in need. Consequently, Zoe was left with nowhere to reality-check what may be "normal" fears, as if fear itself was not to be contemplated. This inevitably increased her disturbance, as there was not a reliable mirror that could ground her in both body and mind. In this treatment model thoughts were meant to conquer feelings much as in her original survival strategy actions were meant to conquer feelings.

Zoe's background could be described as aspirational working class. She is among the first in the family to be university educated, and in many regards has progressed beyond what her parents know. Throughout Zoe's development, O.C.D. symptomatology has been the continuing language of distress. Her attachment-seeking behaviour includes offering up a task to be solved. Asking "Is that damp patch blood?" or "Does that paper conceal a needle?" is the concrete that can be named.

Zoe describes her mother as having high expectations, and hints at control around cleanliness and food. She sees her father as avoidant of feeling and straightforward, but at times blunt. Emotions were habitually dealt with through diversion into action, taking oneself away, or with alcohol. Any unhappiness perceived remained largely unexplained. Bodies were tools. Physical proximity, day-to-day involvement in each other's lives, and practical support were the primary markers of closeness.

As our work develops, I learn that Zoe has engaged in protective rituals for as long as she can remember. Underpinning many of her here-and-now fears about her body are feelings she has always carried. I hear of this young child pulling out a small amount of hair from her favourite soft toy every night and scattering it around her pillow as a means to protect her family whilst she slept. Her fears of being alone when she moved bedrooms as a small girl were transformed into a belief that she was the sentinel for the rear of the house; responsible for listening for the back door and alerting the family of danger, the guardian of the rabbit in the back garden.

I hear of washing rituals that resulted in her being banned from the upstairs bathroom in the family home, of her being a "good girl" – an identity founded upon compliance, and self-imposed rigid homework patterns. High levels of academic achievement offer little nourishment to her self-esteem and are all too easily disavowed as application rather than intellect. At times in adult life, when her O.C.D. symptoms lessened, a tyrannical work ethic, exercise regimes, and food restriction combined with psychological and practical "no go" areas, masked a need to assuage the constant onslaught of emotional furies.

Although anecdotes are emerging, I have much more of a sense of Zoe's later childhood than I have been able to garner of her infancy. Perhaps this is in protection of the parents to whom she is close, but for the moment also allows her to avert the powerlessness that infancy represents, and to maintain the illusion that she has always had agency and responsibility.

By the time she was eleven years old, Zoe's terror around contamination and H.I.V. / A.I.D.S. had become so overwhelming that she was scrubbing her skin raw and living in constant fear of encountering used needles. It is perhaps no coincidence that the crisis point was at the key time of adolescence with all the cognitive, endocrine, and developmental challenges that represents. The particular symptomatic emphasis could be seen as linked to the developmental task of incorporating adult sexuality (confused by media representations) into existing attachment structures at a time where those structures were a source of confusion and uncertainty themselves rather than a place of consistency and comfort.

Zoe's parents experienced significant bereavements and her sibling became life-threateningly unwell with a mysterious illness around this time. Her father's heavy industry job entailed long hours, yet, despite his diligence, was unpredictable with money worries rife. Zoe remembers hours of her mother's loud sobbing at night with no daytime explanation. Her ill sibling would cry out in pain and Zoe would provide comfort, finding solace in companionship for her own night-time fears. The usual approach to any hardship was to "put a smile on your face", and to work hard and search for answers.

To a young Zoe, the instability and unsustainability of bodies was underscored in every direction. This family endured many crises, facing illness, deaths, industrial decline, and the limitation of their hitherto coping mechanisms, framed by a world in which fear, blame, and damning personal accountability predominated in the media and in the public response to H.I.V. / A.I.D.S. The public health television adverts of falling tombstones were co-opted into the warning parable of her fear of contamination. In combination with the bodily changes of adolescence, this demanded that she find a self-sufficient way to carry on being psychologically adept in spite of apocalyptic levels of terror about what was happening *to* her and *around* her.

What began as a means of self-soothing has gone rogue, leaving Zoe trapped in a perpetual state of searching. Her underlying need for a survival strategy was not addressed by the original treatment that she received. In focusing upon the behaviour and not appreciating her specific relational and sociocultural environment, Zoe remained alone with her fears and was shamed for not being able to master the symptoms with her mind.

Consequently, the paralysing anxiety around needles has mutated into a more elaborate form. Zoe's body in its entirety is now the locus of her terror, sometimes described as somatic O.C.D., and this variant of her original diagnosis means that she is in a constant state of hypervigilance, scrutinising visceral bodily functions (swallowing, blinking, bowel movements), looking for something to explain her feeling that she is in danger, and that there is something fundamentally wrong with her (now most consistently cancer). Repeated ministrations by public health bodies that the key to cure and survival is finding something "*early*" have bolstered Zoe's belief system that if she does not maintain her vigilance, she will be to blame for all the loss and hurt that both she and others will experience. As often described in regard to people who experience high levels of anxiety, in this system, not to do something holds equal weight with what is done (Seif and Winston, 2014). She is always on the cusp of failure; and the dichotomy of ill and well is a precipice to fall off at a moment's notice with only herself to blame.

This shifting range of symptoms and related fears have resulted in repeated visits to Zoe's general practitioner. This in turn has brought about a cornucopia of referrals to consultants, as well as medical investigations examining her brain, nervous system, bowel, reproductive and sexual organs, skin, throat, and eyes. The tests are consistently clear, which provide her with momentary relief before she begins to scrutinise what has been said. A consultant's written or verbal reassurance is examined for ambiguity; terms and phrases such as "reasonable" or "keep an eye on it" often re-ignite the original fear, or in perverse irony the intrusive medical investigation that the symptom demanded becomes the hub of her anxiety. Satisfaction that a particular symptom is not the signifier of a greater threat is always short-lived as the terror manifests itself with a fresh focus.

Zoe apparently has little capacity to suspend disbelief and hold onto the idea that "it will be all right". To say whether Zoe's dilemma is a crisis of psyche or soma is seemingly impossible. She has in essence failed to acquire a body, has no sense of stability in her physicality, and engages her mind in pursuit of this. In parallel, she does not trust her thoughts or feelings and looks for answers in the concrete of a body she does not experience as reliable.

Zoe inhabits this fragile terrain between the mind and body in a trauma state to which her whole being is orientated. The precocious omnipotence that allowed her some sense of agency as an overwhelmed child now has her stuck holding tight to the belief that she alone can know it all, work hard at it, and acquire cast iron assurance to her existential viability.

Our work together begins with my encouraging Zoe to tell me the detail of her feelings and fears around her body. In the wake of psychiatric treatment, she fears my judgement and is acutely sensitive to being shamed, so it takes her some time to "confess" the ways in which covert avoidance, scrutiny, and checking have been incorporated into her life.

Over time, I have come to understand the complex belief system that underscores Zoe's pursuit of absolute answers for existential terror. Gradually, I have noticed with her how feelings such as anger, uncertainty, and anxiety propagate new obsessional searches, or how avoidances generate what she originally feared, but in regard to her body rather than where they began. For example, Zoe is afraid of being alone in the house at night. As her partner is away on business she thinks it will be better to stay with her parents. Alone in her old bedroom in their house that night she begins worrying about dying of stomach cancer and, after using the toilet, searches through her faeces for blood. Talking this through together, Zoe and I unpick the pattern, the feelings that she cannot bear, and the actions she takes to escape them. In unwittingly choosing evasion, rather than soothing, the fear re-emerges in regard to her physicality. Her overwhelmed psychological world demands a concrete mirror. Her attachment behaviour and fears are framed as an urgent search for cancer.

Zoe becomes used to my slowing the pace, and to looking for the feelings that have gone awry; disenfranchised emotions in the here and now have become heightened by signals of what is developmentally missing and unresolved from the past and which find a place in her relationship with her body. She sits more firmly on my couch. My soothing challenges her omnipotence and lack of trust in others, and the deep down feeling that only she can really know begins to give a little. I support her to distinguish "normal" feelings, and where these tip over into trauma for her and begin the cycle of preoccupation, trying gently to expand the anxiety she is able to bear so that she is better able to go on being without jumping immediately to action. She now invites me in and we navigate crises together. We meet more frequently. At times the feelings of futility and emptiness inhabit us both. Our rhythm is established.

Then one day Zoe opens a session with the words "I'm pregnant." A therapeutic triad begins.

Zoe's relationship with her pregnancy is complex. In contrast to some women with whom I have worked therapeutically, there is little sense of the child growing inside her. There is an absence of fantasy, hopes and fears, or dreams that relate directly to either the baby or becoming a mother. She is in survival mode. As her abdomen grows I am conscious and concerned about this, wondering when the little one will make an entrance. I name that motherhood can be a particular trigger for O.C.D. in women who have not previously experienced it, and we talk about how it might be for her, but the space compresses quickly.

However, Zoe's feelings about her changing body begin to take on a particular character and urgency. She has become acutely aware of her head, face, and eyes, and she is hypervigilant to any change in her vision. She talks about her fear of a tumour growing inside her – an idea of this "thing" in her head that she will fail to identify, or get help for soon enough and which will kill her off.

I begin to see that Zoe's pregnancy is becoming psychologically routed along the practised pathways. Her concern that the tumour may overtake her are the concrete expressions of what motherhood means for her fragile self. The body she has barely mapped in normality is populated and unfamiliar. As her child grows inside her, Zoe understands the undifferentiated sensations of physical and emotional change as danger signals; and the experience in her body requires bodily "solution". I tentatively name how these two parts of her experience may be connected, integrating how hard it is for her, barely knowing her feelings or body to encompass these new sensations or ideas of identity.

And so we have continued through pregnancy, to birth and motherhood. Zoe's daughter "Amy" is now included in our sorting through which feelings belong where. Zoe is a sensitive mother who does not want her child to be impacted upon by her fears, something that motivates her in our work together. Notably, when faced with actual illness (her own or her child's), Zoe's responses are proportionate and finite. Anxiety about Amy does not necessarily reveal itself as such, once again being channelled via the familiarity of distress in regard to Zoe's own body. For example, weaning Amy results in refreshed terror of swallowing and throat cancer for Zoe.

Zoe's burgeoning curiosity for understanding her daughter as a person, and pleasure in their intimate connection, expands alongside our enlarging of her interest in her own feelings and adding flesh to the bones of her story of herself. In responding to Amy, Zoe is able to comprehend with immediacy the non-verbal, and the confusion of the physical and emotional. The simplicity of a body-to-body soothing response is alive. At a time where there is no escaping the fragility of life, our relationship provides an additional membrane to the maternal bubble where the unquantifiable is more safely contemplated. For example, through introducing the idea that when Amy cries this might not solely be a reflection of physical need but an expression of her feelings and desire for contact, Zoe can encompass that she too might require comfort from another but has not felt legitimate in the need for emotional soothing.

As Orbach's work underlines the sociocultural terrain in which Zoe and I find ourselves could be seen as counter to our therapeutic task. Zoe's idea that she can take complete responsibility for her body, or that precise certainty is attainable, are ones that are mainstays of the twenty-first century. For many who have absorbed the contemporary references for embodiment, this all-consuming quest can be framed as "normal".

We are sold the idea that we can, through making certain lifestyle choices, or the right purchases, take total command or control of our bodies and evade pain, illness, entropy, and perhaps, ultimately, mortality. Whilst this may, if we view our bodies as objects or products, seem possible, the psychological toll of internalising this doctrine without an understanding of its limitations is writ large in Zoe's daily life.

A cultural precedent of insatiable desire to be other, or to possess another, reduces us to the sum of our parts: to a cliché with no depth or meaning. With the body as an ever-evolving product, it seems the self can find no rest. We become stranded in the searching phase of the mourning cycle. Acceptance, loss, limitation, and enduring discomfort are not encouraged in the western capitalist agenda.

At a conference in 2015, I asked Susie Orbach if it were actually at all possible to have body security in contemporary times, to which she replied, "yes", and that this was like "an anti-viral shot", a vaccine against the hostile onslaught our bodies must currently endure. This resilience is what I would hope to impart to Zoe, in our co-creating a body that she can rely upon to face the world. The "shot" or needle that remains undisclosed in my bag is a talisman of what Zoe's therapy requires of me. This goes to the heart of my body narrative, of my story as a person. Supporting Zoe calls to my subjective journey toward securing a body.

There is no doubt that my body security is earned, which perhaps unlike a base level of security from birth means that I am conscious of the shifts and milestones that took place along the way to a sense of stability in my physical self. The needle I carry, whilst symbolic of the cusp of life and death for us both, has an additional payload of hope for me. It is also emblematic of a relationship with the prevailing medical culture, but one that ultimately does not provide any definitive solution to the fragility of my own life. Generally this falls into the backdrop of my mind. The existential is normalised in a way that Zoe cannot currently imagine.

Through a process of understanding my own body narrative, and surrender, not achieving control, I have come to a place of acceptance that my body is contingent. In this there is intimacy and freedom. Whilst this may not be the body that I yearned for it is the one I fully inhabit. Orbach's policy work advocates for the "Two for the price of one" model in regard to the intergenerational transmission of bodies from caregiver to child, and how through supporting mothers effectively it is possible to influence profoundly the body security of their offspring (Orbach and Rubin, 2014). With the B.O.D.I. group, she has developed a protocol that affords us greater insight into the nuanced ways in which caregivers' body-selves impact upon their children (Baker-Pitts, et al., 2015). Echoing this, in the collaborative process in our consulting rooms, our bodies are needed for our clients to grow beyond what they already know. In Orbach's (2004, p. 31) words, "They use our bodies just as they use our psyches." Zoe is feeling and internalising my bodily responses to her, regardless of the verbal content of our sessions.

When Zoe tells me of scrutinising her urine or faeces in search of blood, or extensive Internet searches for answers about the latest symptomatology, I do not belittle or dismiss her with platitudes. Sitting in the uselessness is at times difficult to endure. The enormity of her existential anxiety calls to my body self. Once again the feelings of lacking longevity or viability return, and I feel ephemeral and flimsy. Unease frays at my edges. What if she does have a horrible disease and I have sat in this with her not raising the alarm? What if I die on her? In these moments I return to the unfathomable body as body. I sit squarely in what I cannot know.

My powerlessness is the counter to her omnipotence, my faith in not knowing the balance to her need for proof. These are the things that my mind and body contain as we go on being together. I cannot give her the specific reassurance she craves, that she and those she loves will not come to harm. I can hold onto my subjective experience of inhabiting a body over time and make this body available to encompass the feelings of terror with her. This may calm her enough to uncouple the feeling from the symptom and from the need for immediate activity to avert impending doom. This is the unworded, co-created body that contains what we both bring.

In the verbal domain I name the uncertainty that we must all bear. I support Zoe to name what she feels, and to find the places in her past where some of these feelings deeply belong. Zoe asks about my relationship with the detail of my body. She searches for norms she can trust in my concrete reality.

It is also necessary that I identify that what we are doing together is a different project to the one we are sold: that we cannot completely know our bodies. We are animal not machine. Certainty cannot be bought, and our minds cannot ultimately conquer matter as we are so frequently told. We do not know how or when we will die, we just know we will, and there is no balm for that truth.

The failure to accept what we are and grieve accordingly is, I feel, of dire consequence, and a reflection of a wider societal pain. Whilst in the endless pursuit of an impossible dream, we are increasingly unavailable to the more grounded possibilities of truly intimate connection and ill-prepared for the inevitable milestones of the human lifecycle. I have come to appreciate that it is only in this process of accepting our limitations, of surrender to what we cannot control or know, that we can come to terms with our own organismic degradation, and secure a body – if only for a limited time.

In the privacy of our homes and consulting rooms we experience the pain of lost and disenfranchised body-selves. In an age where the constant curating of self extends beyond the camera phone to the surgeon's knife, and where the unstable body "commodity" is a collective baseline, there are so many questions for psychoanalytic theory and clinical practice. Grounding ourselves physically in the face of the "unprecedented attack" described by Orbach (2009, p. 14) is essential.

For the psychotherapeutic and related professions, Orbach heralds a need to commit to ongoing reflection about our embodiment. The discovery of mirror neurons upholds that we feel before we see: whatever we may or may not disclose by our shape and size, our clothes, and so forth, our clients feel our bodies as we do theirs. As my work with Zoe illuminates, and as Orbach (1999) notes in *The Impossibility of Sex*, every relationship with every client calls to different aspects of our physicality. From the maternal to the erotic, countertransference is felt body to body.

In *Hunger Strike: The Anorectic's Struggle as a Metaphor for Our Age* (Orbach, 1986), our attention is drawn to how the interplay of the professionals' relationship with food and weight, and those of the client can become muddled. In this specific cultural moment this can perhaps be extended to body awareness as a whole. In the pursuit and maintenance of a body, we are in no way immune to the pressures of the modern age. Like a family is an agent of culture, so is a therapist.

With this in mind I am curious as to how the psychotherapeutic profession can better attend to the implications of our body security or insecurities to the benefit of the work. In fast moving times, this project relies upon a willingness to tread softly, but also tenaciously, as we attempt to catch our theories up with technological and medical advances and the needs of a society where there are both greater bodily freedoms and possibilities for bodily harm.

Power dynamics around race, sexuality, gender, and ability are in part seen and felt matters of the body, and it is in these areas that the psychotherapeutic endeavour has often found its nemesis. Complacent invisibility of our own bodies may mean that our clients are rendered other in the intersubjective space, or that traumatic enactment finds a niche in wilful ignorance. Should it be possible to have a therapy or supervision where the body is not mentioned? In the same way that a white therapist should not place the responsibility for race on the shoulders of a black client, what does the recognition of ordinary embodiment mean in regard to the therapist's obligation to include all of the bodies in the room?

How we engage with the culture is of import. If a therapist has plastic surgery, this personal is not just political but it is an act of meaning for our working relationships. In this I am not endorsing a puritanical stance but suggesting the need for ease in talking about bodies and power. Education about embodiment, from biology to culture, and the exploration of the practitioner's body identity and narrative is vital to the foundation of our work so that we may best facilitate the client in this regard.

To reframe one's body as subject, not object, is to swim against the cultural tide for therapist and client alike (Baker-Pitts, Bloom, Eichenbaum, Garofallou, Orbach, Petrucelli, Sliva, and Tortora, 2015). As such it may be seen as inherently political. As we age, or our bodies "fail us" through illness, if we are seen as outside or unacceptable to prevailing norms, or if we cannot or simply choose not to comply to body as product, we are marginalised in the mind's eye of contemporary times. This is a painful hinterland to wander without hope of finding home. Compliance without awareness can leave us equally lost.

Finding voice for disturbed bodies may mean that psychotherapists must renounce the idea of the objective analytic body, and risk owning our place on the continuum, at the very least to our supervisors and ourselves, and sometimes in the embodied intimate space of the therapeutic dyad. I trust that in naming physical realities we are not subjugating the space for our clients' journeys but ensuring a relevant secure base for their travels.

In Susie Orbach's intrepid exploration of embodiment, her reading of modernity, and her challenge to the mainstream, she makes this psychotherapeutic endeavour a little more possible for all concerned.

References

Baker-Pitts, Catherine; Bloom, Carol; Eichenbaum, Luise; Garofallou, Linda; Orbach, Susie; Petrucelli, Jean; Sliva, Victoria; and Tortora, Suzi (2015). The Acquisition of a Body: Establishing a New Paradigm and Introducing a Clinical Tool to Explore the Intergenerational Transmission of Embodiment. In Jean Petrucelli (Ed.). *Body-States: Interpersonal and Relational Perspectives on the Treatment of Eating Disorders*, pp. 302–315. New York: Routledge / Taylor and Francis Group.

Brazelton, T. Berry, and Cramer, Bertrand G. (1990). *The Earliest Relationship: Parents Infants, and the Drama of Early Attachment*. Cambridge, Massachusetts: Addison-Wesley Publishing Company.

Orbach, Susie (1978). *Fat is a Feminist Issue*. London: Paddington Press.

Orbach, Susie (1986). *Hunger Strike: The Anorectic's Struggle as a Metaphor for Our Age*. London: Faber and Faber.

Orbach, Susie (1999). *The Impossibility of Sex*. London: Allen Lane / Penguin Press, Penguin Books, Penguin Group.

Orbach, Susie (2004). The John Bowlby Memorial Lecture 2003: The Body in Clinical Practice. Part One. There is No Such Thing as a Body. In Kate White (Ed.). *Touch: Attachment and the Body. The John Bowlby Memorial Conference Monograph 2003*, pp. 17–34. London: Karnac Books / Karnac (Books).

Orbach, Susie (2009). *Bodies*. London: Profile Books.

Orbach, Susie, and Rubin, Holli (2014). *Two For The Price of One: The Impact of Body Image During Pregnancy and After*. n.p.: Government Equalities Office.

Seif, Martin N., and Winston, Sally (2014). *What Every Therapist Needs to Know About Anxiety Disorders: Key Concepts, Insights, and Interventions*. Hove, East Sussex: Routledge.

Tronick, Edward; Als, Heidelise; Adamson, Lauren; Wise, Susan, and Brazelton, T. Berry (1978). The Infant's Response to Entrapment Between Contradictory Messages in Face-to-Face Interaction. *Journal of the American Academy of Child Psychiatry*, *17*, 1–13.

Part III

Orbach in Politics and Society

Chapter 5

Therapists as Consultants

Experts, Relationals, Visionaries, Antidotes, Fools ... and Leaders[1]

Andrew Samuels

One Susie Orbach

There is only one Susie Orbach. I look up to very, very few people in my profession or in my life. I have chosen the paths of the maverick or contrarian. But I do look up to Susie Orbach and have massively valued our co-operations within the profession and outside in the explicitly political sphere. As Orbach (2010, p. 185) has written (in my own *Festschrift*), "It is an odd cooperation. Andrew and I rarely plan or agree on what we will do and yet from our different backgrounds and milieux we end up thinking along pretty similar lines and are often involved in the same actions."

This chapter has the explicit programme of confirming, expanding, and critiquing Susie's position (Orbach, 2012, n.p.) that "psychoanalytic ideas have something special to offer [to society] if we can do the hard work to clarify what exactly that is, put it into concepts that others can grasp, and not be arrogant about our knowledge, nor too humble."

Holding this position has been far from easy and this is the moment to praise Susie Orbach's courage when she is attacked and threatened, from inside the profession and from outside it, as she has been. These words of Maya Angelou's apply to her: "Courage is the most important of all the virtues, because without courage you can't practice any other virtue consistently. You can practice any virtue erratically, but nothing consistently without courage" (quoted in Stedman, 2006, p. 224.)

The specific focus assigned to me in this chapter is on the relationship between therapy, including psychoanalysis, and social and public policy. In this regard, Susie has a long track record. She has worked as a consultant to the World Bank, for the Department of Health and with the National Health Service. The assigned focus means I will not be writing about her contributions to feminist and psychoanalytic theory and practice. Nor about her work on bodies and eating, or on what happens in therapy. One particular loss is not to be able to write about how those of us who write on male psychology have been making use of some of the concepts that Susie and Luise Eichenbaum developed in relation to women, particularly the idea of "separated attachment".

DOI: 10.4324/9781003470090-9

History and Ethics

The project of linking therapy thinking to social and political issues is not a new one. Sometimes, the outcomes are not at all progressive and humane. On the more progressive side, the Critical Theory of the Frankfurt School is the best known example and psychoanalysis figured prominently in the work of the School in the 1930s before and after its enforced move to New York. Then there is the whole range of activities referred to generally as Freudo-Marxism.

But in Susie's case (and in my own), it is very specifically a move from the consulting room to public policy. This is new, and important, and very difficult to pull off. The translation from the clinical work with individuals to the level of generalisation needed for social policy is intellectually risky.

There are also ethical issues to consider. If you engage as a therapist with politicians and civil servants, you sometimes have to pay attention to the ethics of it and eat with a very long spoon. And there is precious little loyalty to be given in return by our clients. "Put not thy trust in princes", it says in the Psalm.

Consultancy in the social and political fields can be problematic for analysts of a left-wing or – these days – even of a mildly progressive political outlook. One might have to help deal with the psychological consequences of reductions in staffing levels and pay cuts. This may mean taking a capitalist road, no matter how robustly our contribution is stressed as being humane and for the betterment of staff and workers. As I have worked for corporations (a large supermarket chain, a manufacturer of cell phones), and as I also identify as a person of the left, I have had to wrestle with some tough questions. For me, ambivalence about corporations may involve personal transferences, stemming from the complex intergenerational dynamics of my own mercantile family and its business vicissitudes.[2]

There is nearly always an economic shadow (Samuels, 2015). I take most of the work I am offered because I need the money and because, usually, the task is to provide input to an intractable situation where the managers or political leaders in question have already decided that the issues are human ones. So the therapeutic consultant is often understood by those hiring him or her to be in an ameliorative role. Nevertheless, one cannot avoid the fact that the work may, no matter how slightly, increase the profits of the corporation in question.

But all of us in clinical practice know how off-putting some of the values and behaviours of our clients can be. We do not usually decline to work with them on those grounds. In addition, we need to bear in mind that not all consultation is with corporations. Much of my own work here has been with the leading National Health Service think tank, or with politicians in several countries with whose positions I can feel comfortable. I would conclude that, to avoid *trahison des clercs*, the therapeutic consultant needs to undertake regular self-monitoring, if not, in fact, attend political re-education.

Something else to mention in this chapter is the relative usefulness of therapists doing this kind of work individually, or in small groups and organisations of therapists (such as Psychotherapists and Counsellors for Social Responsibility or the Mental Wealth Alliance). This is an important question. Of course the answer is "both", but the "how" is quite difficult. The big therapy organisations like the United Kingdom Council for Psychotherapy find it difficult to take the government to task whilst maintaining privileged access to the corridors of power. But the smaller organisations are ... well ... small.

Individuals can of course do what any citizen can do but, without access, cannot do a lot more. Susie's unique strength is to have found manifold ways to gain the necessary access.

Utility

There seem to be very few studies of the efficacy of interventions such as those described above. For the therapeutic consultant, customer satisfaction is way more prominent than establishing an evidence base. Those who hire such consultants are often hard-nosed, bottom-line types and they will not come back for more if they are not satisfied. Certainly, when working for politicians seeking election, I have felt far more at risk of being dropped when my utility has been found wanting than ever I do with an individual client.

My own experience as a consultant is that the usual psychoanalytic approach of listening and relating to the client before moving into what might lie "behind" or "underneath" remains intact. But the positioning is quite different. The person who hires the consultant is like the initial presenting surface material in the individual clinical situation. It is often when you get to meet the team or group that you have been hired to work with that the "deeper" stuff comes to the fore. So there can be a fascinating tension between the initial interviews out of which a contract for work emerges and what the actual work throws up. In fact, I would claim that it is almost invariably the one who hires, and hence provides the initial information, who turns out to be part of "the problem". Unconsciously, the hirer may know this. Then working to heal their narcissistic bruising as the team (or even the entire company) turns on them may be a big part of the work.

The main obstacle to being useful to the employer is sticking too closely to one's preferred theories. But, close behind, comes the problem of having no theories at all.

"How Psychoanalytic Theory can be Used in Social Policy" – Susie Orbach

In this section, I will summarise Susie's account of how six themes derived from the clinic can be employed in connection with the creation of social policies. It stems from her paper "How Psychoanalytic Theory Can Be Used in Social Policy" (Orbach, 2012) which is a good example of her thinking.

She is writing about what "the technologies of psychoanalysis can bring to the conversation about social distress" (Orbach, 2012, n.p.). She is interested in both the formation of public policy and research into social and political issues.

Her "cases" in this piece were the banking crisis of 2008 and the 2011 riots in Tottenham, London.

Here are her six themes:

(1) The capacity to listen.
(2) Exploring disavowed feelings.
(3) Unconscious motivations and behaviour.
(4) Bringing developmental theory into any attempt to link psychoanalysis and social policy.
(5) Inevitably, the therapist addressing a social policy issue needs to have transference, countertransference, and enactment in mind.
(6) Susie emphasises that research and policy require the use of self by the researcher or politician.

I will go through the six themes in turn.

(a) *The capacity to listen.* This was absent in both cases of the banks and the riots. Or, Susie says, people knew but turned a blind eye – something we know from therapy work.
(b) *The exploration of disavowed feelings* – for example, the profound anxieties and insecurities of the bankers about which neither they nor the politicians wanted to know.
(c) *Ways of understanding unconscious motivation and behaviour.* Here, Susie makes a point that should be highlighted in every training in analysis, psychotherapy, and counselling. We need to remember how the contents of the unconscious come into being. We must "take account of the fact that our psyches are structures formed … as a result of the economic, social, caste and gender we are introduced to from infancy on" (Orbach, 2012, n.p.). As an example, I will mention very briefly the culture of masculinity, and how our current confusions, delusions, denigrations, and idealisations about it contribute to the ongoing structuring of our psyches.
(d) *Bringing developmental theory into any attempt to link psychoanalysis and social policy.* This means, especially, but not only, early life factors. Susie has always been interested in how unmet needs for nurture and relationship and insecure attachment undermine authentic independence.
(e) *Inevitably, the therapist addressing a social policy issue needs to have transference, countertransference, and enactment in mind.* Joseph Sandler's (1976) term is apt in this context of psychoanalysis and social policy. The psychoanalyst allows himself or herself to be assigned (so to speak) a role emanating from the patient's internal world. He or she responds to the part (role) that the patient assigns him. It is a difficult experience but extremely useful clinically and in consultancy. Just allowing oneself to be what the organisation or government department in question wants one to be. Sounds easy but requires enormous discipline.

(f) *Susie emphasises that research and policy require the use of self by the researcher or politician.* This idea is on relational psychoanalytic theory. We are in the work not outside it. We are all wounded researchers as well as wounded healers (Romanyshyn, 2013). And, when it comes to politics, we are part of "the street".

Six Roles for Therapists in the Creation of Public Policy

Clinical work, as Susie knows, depends on context, personal style, and performance / performativity. You can hear this vividly in the B.B.C. broadcasts that became published in book form as *In Therapy: How Conversations with Psychotherapists Really Work* (Orbach, 2016). It ain't what you do, it's the way that you do it – and that's what gets results.

Hence, for this chapter, I have worked up a model of the ways therapists can do consultancy work. You can call these six styles, types, forms, personifications, in which the therapist can function in relation to public policy. The consultant can choose a style, or a combination of styles, according to personal preferences (and limitations), and according to the situation. Maybe, over time, a consultant will operate in all of them. Later, I will invite readers to explore this question of consultant style for themselves. Here is the list: experts, relationals, visionaries, antidotes, fools, leaders.

Let us now work through these in turn.

(1) *Experts* are hired for their knowledge and skills. A bit like an organic psychiatrist of the old school who tells and prescribes. Ones who know! Or are supposed to know, anyway. For example, experts on the psychodynamics of organisations are needed right now by the National Health Service. The King's Fund work on staff burn-out demonstrates this clearly. But the experts position themselves *outside* the problem being addressed. At the lecture on which this chapter is based, I illustrated this point exaggeratedly and metaphorically via an image of Dr. Walter Freeman performing a lobotomy using an instrument.

(2) *Relationals.* A relational consultant works interactively and intersubjectively with the people involved in political or social activity, more like today's relational therapists. For example, in bringing a therapeutic perspective to human rights activism. Or to environmental and ecological activism. Or in relation to organisations working with refugees and asylum seekers. The question is always how committed and passionate the consultant should be. It is easier if there is a similarity between their beliefs and those of the group they are working with. I learned this working with Friends of the Earth. But such alignment is not a necessity.

(3) *Visionaries.* Therapists who contribute to public policy as visionaries try to think outside the box. That is what visionaries do. They are prophetic and prescient. They are not restricted by the *Zeitgeist* but challenge it. In this, they are fuelled by their sense of human potential, a kind of idealism, a denial of

the realities of time, space, and then place, denying the social and political realities of power. I call this personification the Trickster role, undermining the existing social order. The image is of the classical figure of the Trickster, the Greek god Hermes, tricking the dominant and powerful Apollo by stealing his cattle and walking them away from their shed backwards, so the tracks do not help the pursuers. (For a full account of Hermes and Tricksters in politics, see Samuels, 1993, pp. 78–102).

(4) *Antidotes*. By referring to therapists in the public arena as antidotes, I mean more than a play on the title (Antidote) of the campaign for emotional literacy in the public sphere that Susie and I started twenty years ago. I mean outright opposition and contrariness, something allopathic. Always sceptical, always questioning, always seeking to rectify an imbalance. Examples would be the ways in which therapists consider the imbalances that underpin intractable political problematics. An example would be the situation between Israel and Palestine. Or the pressing issue of economic inequality which dominates Western politics right now.

(5) *Fool*. When the public policy therapist is a fool, it means accepting – Susie's words – the caricatures of "theories about penises, phalluses, cigars and hysteria". When you work as a fool you have to accept that there will be massive disbelief and even ridicule. Yet remember what Theodor Adorno (1974, p. 49) wrote: "In psychoanalysis nothing is true except the exaggerations". Lear's fool also knew a thing or two about power and the powerful.

(6) *Leader*. When a therapist engaging with social policy is in role as a *leader*, there is direct, committed, passionate, and highly personal involvement in which the consultant has views, opinions, and ideals. A good example of this is Susie's work as a leader with AnyBody and the whole problem of body tyranny.

I write more about leadership than about any other style of consultancy because it is, for me, the most suggestive and challenging way to be a consultant. My notion on consultant-as-leader stems from working with political leaders in the United Kingdom and United States. There is also a practical aspect in that, for someone as *recherché* as a therapist or psychoanalyst to find consultancy work, the point of access is often quite high on the company tree. The hirer may be a leader in the organisation. Be that as it may, there is something frankly numinous for many of us in working with significant figures in leadership roles whose decisions will affect the lives of millions (if one is working for a political party or a senior politician running for office, as I have done).

I want to look at one specific contemporary problem for organisations: the problem of hierarchical, heroic leadership. Organisational and political theory and practice has assumed there are two main approaches to leadership. There is hierarchical and heroic leadership based on (male) authority (sometimes operated by female leaders: think Meir, think Thatcher, think Gandhi). Such leaders used a "masculinist" approach to knowledge that assumes there is but one objectively true social story. In this model, there are good leaders and there are bad leaders, and we all have our lists of them. For contemporary corporations, this kind of leader is often their problem.

A second approach is much more collaborative and non-hierarchical, involving a kind of "sibling" take on leadership. But, although appealing and sometimes usable in community projects, sibling leadership is just too demanding on people who work in corporations and organisations to be in operation all the time. People duck dive for cover; they do not necessarily mean to become bystanders, but they do not see any other way to manage the burden of being collaborative leaders.

So, there is heroic leadership and there is collaborative leadership and, over time, companies and organisations may invoke one to rectify the problems induced by the other in a distinctly unhelpful swinging from one extreme to the other. It is to handle situations like these that, for many years, I have been advocating a third kind of leader – what I call "the good-enough leader" (Samuels, 2001, p. 75). I have found that many organisations take to this notion which obviously draws on therapy thinking about the family. Donald Winnicott said that parents and babies have to find a middle way between the baby's idealisation and denigration of the parent. There is a natural tendency in the infant to idealise the parent, but when things go in a less than perfect way (as they surely will), it flips over into denigration.

Sound familiar from the perspective of an organisation or even a country? An initial idealisation, then a failure to deliver things perfectly, then denigration? It is meant to sound familiar because this is how organisations respond to leaders, first by passively following the idealised leader then by seeking out their feet of clay. What can we do about such a pattern which causes huge stress and distress on organisations? Sometimes, this is why the denigrated leader of an organisation seeks, in a mood of bewilderment and betrayal, for assistance from a therapeutic consultant.

We might try to change how we position "success" and "failure", and I think the therapies can assist us here. Our training has allowed us to acquire a tolerance for ambiguity and confusion that is useful in an arena that prizes certainty and quick results. The word "failure" hurts people's feelings because it is so in-your-face. Failure means falling short, being imperfect, fallible, only passable, fucking up – an all too human lack of potency. Yet maybe what we need nowadays are "can't do" executives, impotent managers – they are that, anyway, are they not? – as the financial crisis shows us.

Maybe being only and always "in control" is not always valuable. Winnicott (1971) argued that the parent fails the baby, but in the baby's own way. I would add that failure by a top manager paves the way for greater contributions and more autonomy on the part of the workforce. The manager fails the workers, but in the workers' own way.

Bob Dylan nibbled away at the success-failure binary when he sang "There's no success like failure and failure's no success at all." Experienced politicians engage ruefully with the same theme. For example, in July, 2008, Bill Clinton spoke of the "inevitability" of failure in politics. I believe it was the first time he had ever done that. When Harold Macmillan, the British Prime Minister, was asked by a journalist in 1963 what had brought him down, he replied in accepting vein, "Events, dear boy, events." The Sufi poet Rumi wrote that "failure is the key to the kingdom". Good-enoughness always involves failure. The key thing is how to manage failure, even to see failure as an art, follow Beckett, and try to "fail better". Disappointment is difficult, for sure, but it, too, has to be managed.

So, the good-enough leader-manager can receive consultancy that facilitates the acceptance of the likelihood of failure, in a post-heroic take on business leadership. But there's a head-heart problem here. In our heads, we often know that the old-style leaders are dangerous, but in our hearts and guts we feel we need the fatherly protection they offer. In our souls, we are in love with the heroic leader whose *Führer*-eroticism turns us on. In our heads, we agree with Brecht's *Galileo*, who former American Senator Bill Bradley used to quote many years ago: "Unhappy is the land that has need of heroes." Could organisations and corporations become more aware of their abusive love affair with heroic leaders? Is achieving that not a critical task of the therapeutic consultant?

So far so good (-enough). But what happens to these good-enough managers when things get really difficult ... when the shit hits the fan? This is where the good-enough take on leadership appears to hit a rock. What happens when there is a perfect storm or when the oil gushes forth from a wrecked ship? Where does good-enough leadership leave us with respect to major crises like that? Do we not need straight and traditional masculine virtues then? Do we not need paternal security and a corporate father's protection then? The hell with this liberal guff about good-enough leadership!

My answer to this question is that the good-enough leader needs to know where to hire the hard-hitting, militaristic talent to deal with the crisis that affects people's security. But he or she does not need to be a generalissimo as opposed to knowing where to find one.

Consultancy-Style Exercise for Readers

Imagine you are a therapist, either alone or with others, called upon to contribute to a matter of social or public policy. Maybe you have done so, in which case use your experience. Which of the six options listed above would suit you in your role as a therapist engaged with social and political issues and questions of public policy? Which ones might be beyond your capacities? Can you imagine these as being your cutting edge as a consultant, and to strive to do what you cannot at present do very well?

Theory and Practice: Putting Imagination to Work

Everyone notes that consultancy is different from clinical work with individuals and small groups. And everyone who offers consultation tends to ignore this in practice, often with unexpectedly positive results, at least in my experience. For example, I was asked by a large supermarket chain to help them with a gap that had opened up between the main board and the group of executives immediately below board level. The company was losing far more of these up-and-coming types than they were comfortable with – and rightly so because these would be the next leaders of the company. The first thing I noticed when meeting the two groups – board and just-below-board – was the substantial age gap between them, the junior people palpably being very much younger than the seniors. Although this was totally obvious, it had not been factored into their in-house attempts to understand what was happening. So I showed both groups some extracts from Pasolini's (1967) *Oedipus Rex* film in order to "naturalise" or "normalise" the idea of intergenerational conflict within the organisation. I was, perhaps incorrectly from an intellectual point of view, using a model derived from an individual's psychology of their (internal) family to address an organisational problem.

Both groups "got it" pretty well and understood more clearly the perspective of the other group. I also had in my mind something populistically Jungian like "the archetype of competition" but that was not the language I used – I kept it to the algebra of family members that psychoanalysts are used to. In the discussions that followed over several months, there was a good deal of personal sharing about relations with parents, focusing on competitiveness and rivalry.

One practical outcome was that this company decided to follow my advice and introduce a form of "reverse mentoring". In its most extreme form, reverse mentoring involves very young staff members being assigned as mentors to the most senior executives and the board. The rationale is that the seniors have lost touch with a rapidly changing contemporary cultural scene. Here, nothing quite as extreme was needed. But, having in mind that the resolution of Oedipus involves the recognition of mutual dependence and interdependence, the introduction of reverse mentoring came to seem sort of an obvious thing to do.

Of course, there is by now a massive body of psychoanalytic work on organisational dynamics, much of it derived from the Tavistock Clinic or from Wilfred Bion. Whilst there is much to learn from this literature, I find it lacks stress on the inherent potential of organisations to heal and improve themselves. There is too much suspicion, too much pessimism, too much fear of hope and joy. Moreover, there is an unhelpful emphasis on clarity and boundary that tends to keep the consultant outside the swamp. Relational psychoanalysis has established by now that being in the swamp is far from being only an abject place. Finally, as I argue elsewhere (Samuels, 1993), the use of models of parent-infant interaction to understand organisations is neither politically nor ethically neutral, particularly if the workers in an organisation are placed into the baby role.

To rectify these defects in much psychoanalytic organisational theory emanating from Britain, you have to consider turning to the humanistic psychologies and, to some extent, classical Jungian theory. To a psychoanalytic eye, these approaches can seem technique-heavy. Think of Gestalt and the empty chair technique, or of the manoeuvres of transactional analysis, or of asking people to choose which Greek god or goddess they respond to. Personally, I think the situations in which therapeutic consultants find themselves call for fresher techniques than these which are time-worn and tedious, even if the ideas behind them are still alive. But I definitely think there is a need for such techniques – usually called "exercises" – in therapeutic consultancy work and, when I describe what I do to clinical colleagues, they often respond that I am being a whole lot more active than any one-to-one clinician would be. The task is to devise exercises which are theory-based *au fond* – but are also relevant to the problem at hand and suitable for the participants.

The goal of such exercises is *to put the imagination to work*, and I think a stress on creativity is often what organisations need. Putting imagination to work is not exactly the same as putting the unconscious to work (which would be impossible) – but the idea does rest on a conception of the unconscious as not only nasty and brutish, but as being also a rich reservoir of ingenuity and fresh approaches to difficulties.

One psychoanalytic idea that I have found useful in therapeutic consultation work is free association. Jung extended this to embrace "directed association" which is equally useful. Now, obviously, free or directed association in analysis is different in many ways from "blue skies thinking" in a workplace. But there are some key similarities with regard to the problems of achieving the "free" bit. *In an organisation, it is very dangerous to say whatever comes into one's mind with regard to a problem.* One might look stupid, lose advancement, be stigmatised as a trouble-maker. It is not likely that people will experience one as the "mystic in the group", to use Bion's self-congratulatory phrase. Sometimes, I have found that you get freer results if you use an arts therapy medium. For example, our work on the brand image problem of an international fruit and juice company was greatly enhanced by the use of sand tray techniques using small models to elicit what employees, current consumers, and consumers who had ceased to use the company's products associated to the brand. On other occasions, I have used movement and drama.

Maybe it was more Jung's notion of "directed association" that helped me here, in which the analyst facilitates the associative process, not denying his own desire and knowledge. It was possible to photograph the sand trays the participants made and show them to the senior management who had commissioned the study. Amusingly, they then asked to do the sand trays themselves. I doubt I am the only consultant to have found that many politicians and business people are creative and curious people.

The move I seek to set in motion is away from superegoic rigidity towards a more chilled and spontaneous managerial style. A further example of summoning up imagination often occurs when the brief is to try to unstick a stuck organisational dynamic. When power or other political themes are prominent, I ask people to do a "political memory" exercise to kick things off. Participants are asked to recall the first time they became aware of something "political" – someone called the Prime Minister, elections, war, insiders and outsiders, haves and have-nots, whites and non-whites, etc. This is an amazing exercise. Asking for the first political memory rather than the biggest makes people dig a bit deeper and, in dialogue with me and the others in the room, it is possible for them to get a bit more of a handle on how they perform in terms of office politics. After this exercise, all discussions of the bedevilling dynamics are more reflective and less focused on what happened in the past week or so. We see *Nachträglichkeit* (deferred action) at work here, as new meanings and approaches out of the "facts" from old times.

I believe that therapeutic consultants have to take office politics seriously – not only as an unnecessary excrescence on the organisational body but as part of the whole, and a valuable and potentially useful part at that. All too often, people dismiss office politics as dirty or tricksy, whilst at the very moment of indulging in office politics. To the contrary, this kind of consultancy work retrieves something from the organisational shadow – the part the organisation would not want to be – and mines it for whatever hidden gold there might be therein.

To give an example, when I was working with a European cell phone manufacturer on a revision of their global values, we found that the regions of the company's activity had internalised a hierarchy with Europe at its peak and the other regions arranged below Europe. This was an organisational shadow and affected everything. But when we got all the regions to make presentations of their versions of the global values in their own cultural forms and images, we were able to get people to talk about this nationalistic hierarchy in a new way so that the value of local perspectives could emerge. Up to then, to be proud of working in one of the Asian offices had been very difficult. Succinctly, the company was implicitly and institutionally racist and could not accept the fact. When all of this tumbled out at a vast meeting with people from over fifty countries present, the chief executive officer burst into tears and said it was the most moving day of his life in the company he had joined straight from college.

A Concluding Reflection: the Benefits of Consultancy in Clinical Work

The clinical project of the therapies may gain as much from experiences in the organisational consultancy field as it gives. To say this is to reverse the conventional order of things in which the clinical project comes first, and then, after processes of alloying and dilution, gets applied in other contexts. No, I have found that my work with organisations and politicians has refreshed my clinical work in unexpected ways. The first and most apparent is that I am much better attuned to what people tell me about their experiences at work. There is a downside to this, though, in that I can see myself sometimes knowing too much too soon and even, as Patrick Casement puts it, getting into clichéd understandings of what the client is telling me about experiences at work.

The second gift to the clinician from organisational consultancy concerns the management of my heroic tendencies in the work. It is not enough just to junk the heroic. As I wrote, the good-enough leader needs to know when and where to hire a fierce soldier. Similarly, the therapist needs to be able to access the heroic themselves when that is what the therapeutic relationship calls for. But understanding the ubiquity of failure, and the pressing need to find imaginative and satisfying ways to manage it, is something I have brought to my office from the "real world".

Finally, less apparent, but perhaps more profound, is the impact on my consciousness of how interconnected things are in the life of my client and in my own life. We bring personal complexes to our work, that is for sure. But our work contributes to the formation of who we are as persons at the deepest level. And how we are as persons and how we are as workers contributes to how we are politically ... as citizens.

Notes

1   My use of the terms "therapy", "therapist", and "therapeutic" on the one hand, and of the terms "psychoanalysis", "psychoanalyst", and "psychoanalytic" on the other, is careful and deliberate.
2   For an overview of my consultancy work, see: http://www.andrewsamuels.com/organiz ational-consultancy-telos/

References

Adorno, Theodor W. (1974). *Minima Moralia: Reflections from Damaged Life*. Edmund F.N. Jephcott (Transl.). London: New Left Books.

Orbach, Susie (2010). Unpicking. In Gottfried Heuer (Ed.). *Sacral Revolutions: Reflecting on the Work of Andrew Samuels – Cutting Edges in Psychoanalysis and Jungian Analysis*, pp. 184–191. Hove, East Sussex: Routledge / Taylor and Francis Group.

Orbach, Susie (2012). How Psychoanalytic Theory Can Be Used in Social Policy. Centre for Crime and Justice Studies. [https://www.crimeandjustice.org.uk/resources/how-psychoa nalytic-theory-can-be-used-social-policy; Accessed on 7th April, 2024].

Orbach, Susie (2016). *In Therapy: How Conversations with Psychotherapists Really Work*. London: Profile Books.

Romanyshyn, Robert (2013). *The Wounded Researcher: Research with Soul in Mind*. London: Routledge.

Samuels, Andrew (1993). *The Political Psyche*. London: Routledge.

Samuels, Andrew (2001). *Politics on the Couch: Citizenship and the Internal Life*. London: H. Karnac (Books).

Samuels, Andrew (2015). *A New Therapy for Politics?* London: Karnac Books.

Sandler, Joseph (1976). Countertransference and Role-Responsiveness. *International Review of Psycho-Analysis*, *3*, 43–47.

Stedman, Graham (2006). *Diversity: Leaders Not Labels*. New York: Simon and Schuster.

Winnicott, Donald W. (1971). *Playing and Reality*. London: Tavistock Publications.

Chapter 6

Bodies as Profit Centres

Orbach's Work in the Context of Performance

Roanna Mitchell[1]

I first met Susie Orbach at an Open Space event at the Royal Central School of Speech and Drama in London in 2009. Focusing on the theme of "The Actor's Body: Identity and Image", this event brought together actors, directors, casting agents, costume designers, and actor-trainers, along with Orbach as chair, offering insights from a psychoanalytic perspective. It provided space for one of the first public discussions in the United Kingdom – if not worldwide – to acknowledge body anxiety in the context of the acting profession as a legitimate and important concern. The intersection between the insights that Orbach's work is able to offer and my own work with actors would go on to provide a rich space of discovery over the next nine years, during which I have worked closely with Orbach as a fellow body-activist and mentor.

My profession, as a pedagogue and performance-maker who specialises in actor-movement, entails close and often sustained encounters with actors' bodies. It is from this vantage point that I explore and attempt to untangle the politics of the body in the acting profession, and the anxieties and strategies to manage these that they entail. As Deborah Dean (2008, p. 161) eloquently argues in relation to female performers' access to work, the way bodies are treated and employed in the performance industries is "a manifestation of [the actor's] position as formal and informal proxies for women's experience in wider society". In other words, the microcosm of body politics in the acting profession can tell us much about the role and status of bodies in the broader social context, and vice versa.

These politics are deeply enmeshed with the personal, as the actor's work is fundamentally embodied. The actor's transformation into other worlds and other characters is in constant dialogue – and often in tension – with the demands and expectations their everyday life places on their bodies (Mitchell, 2014). My research since 2008 has been concerned with how this tension affects the actor's work and wellbeing. It examines the way actors are able to engage with the labour of care necessary to preserve themselves and their craft in the face of competition, individualism, and the labour of production which, as Orbach (2009) sees it, now includes the production of the body itself.

In the following, I will trace through the various ways in which I perceive Orbach's work to be in dialogue with the world of performance and performers'

DOI: 10.4324/9781003470090-10

bodies. I will begin by drawing a link between performance as a space predicated on the ability to act and Orbach's central impulse towards action, which will allow me to share and document the role of body activism in her work.[2] I will then discuss aspects of Orbach's work in relation to actors' bodies specifically, and finally, will bring both strands together to reflect on the future, examining key challenges presented by the notion of self-care as it is currently traded in performance and activism.

Creative Activism

Orbach's approach to the anxiety, discomfort, and shame that many of us experience in relation to our bodies, is twofold. On the one hand she offers astute observations, reflections, and approaches for how each of us as individuals might work through this discomfort, and does so by encouraging greater trust in our bodies and listening to the signals of our appetites and needs – whether these be emotional or physical (Orbach, 2002, 2006). On the other hand, she has always, from *Fat is a Feminist Issue* (Orbach, 1978) onward, situated our discomfort with our bodies in a social context, knowing that a neoliberal narrative of individual self-improvement will not resolve the inequalities and exploitations that feed so fundamentally into body anxiety.

This situating of personal experience within socio-political contexts provides the activist impulse within Orbach's work. Never content with identifying and discussing structural inequalities, those of us who have worked with her are familiar with her inevitable question: "So what is the action?" How can we shift, nudge, shove, and gnaw at the binds of complex industry and policy networks that have learned to exploit body anxiety for all the money and docility it is worth?

In this search for action Orbach has consistently joined forces with artists and creatives. Indeed, insisting on the question of what the action is in some ways already aligns Orbach with the world of performance, which is predicated on "doing", or more specifically, "showing-doing" – "pointing to, underlining, and displaying doing" (Schechner, 2013, p. 28) – which in an activist context can provide vital opportunity for critical reflection and to imagine change creatively. Performance and activism have long gone hand in hand, and feminist activism in particular has a well-documented history of using performance as part of its strategies of resistance. In the Anglophone context, this history spans the realist suffrage plays of the early twentieth century, used to promote pro-suffrage messages in private homes and local theatres (Holledge, 1981; Finnegan, 1999), as well as the feminist performance practices emerging from the 1960s onward, in which the body and lived experience were used to disrupt or refract the male gaze and as ways to articulate things that cannot be put into words (Mulvey, 1975; Phelan, 1993; Diamond, 1997). But this dialogue is of course not simply history: performance and activism are in an ongoing, living exchange, constantly evolving to include new technologies and engage with new feminist challenges (Bissell, 2011).

Image 6.1 AnyBody UK Workshop at BodyKind Festival, Totnes, 2017.

Graphic Recording by Jo Harrison.

Orbach's work in activism shows that she has a real sense of this dialogue and its powerful potential to engage and to articulate. The centralising of body and lived experience in feminist performance practice arose out of the consciousness-raising work of the late 1960s and 1970s, a time during which Orbach herself was working intensively to raise women's consciousness about their bodies, their relationships, appetites, and needs. It was during this time that she founded The Women's Therapy Centre with Luise Eichenbaum, and published *Fat is a Feminist Issue* (Orbach, 1978), the volume that would define a key trajectory of her work for the next forty years. It is perhaps unsurprising, considering the context from which her work first sprang, that in her activism Orbach continues to seek out the views and perspectives of artists to convey a sense of what is wrong with the world; to interrogate and imagine differently; and, as director Eugenio Barba (2010, p. 185) puts it: "caress a wound in that part within [us] which lived in exile".

Raising Awareness – Making Change

I began work with Susie Orbach in 2010, preparing for a summit that was titled "Endangered Species", following the premise that the woman who loves and accepts her body, and is able to live from it freely and without fear, is an endangered species. The idea for the summit was born out of the decision of Susie Orbach, Luise Eichenbaum, and Carol Bloom to "have a great big meeting to draw attention to the hurt that is done to women's bodies" (Mitchell, 2011, p. 20).

A multi-locational event, with live-streamed gatherings in London, New York, Buenos Aires, Melbourne, and São Paulo, the 2011 summit was designed with the aim of both creating networks of mutual support among grassroots activists, and to engage as many as possible of the stakeholders that have interest in, duty of care for, critique, and influence our bodies and through them our identities. To encourage the latter, representatives from advertising, education, healthcare, media, film and performance industry, and government were invited to speak. Their contributions responded to, and were placed against the context of, the voices of grassroots activists, the great majority of whom used artistic expression to provide an embodied understanding of the issues at stake. As Sara Ahmed (2017, p. 30) writes, "Feminism involves a process of finding another way to live in your body", and thus performance, videos, and artwork framed and underlined the message of the summit, centralising the body not only as theme, but also as a visceral, living presence.

At the London Summit, individuals and groups from the United Kingdom, Peru, Mexico, Argentina, and New York were joined by representatives from initiatives across Europe to showcase their ongoing work with and about young women – from projects in schools, colleges and communities to web-based groups and campaigning organisations (see Mitchell, 2011, for a full report on the summit).

In this moment of coming together the event fulfilled the task of communal consciousness-raising, creating a "feminist catalog" (Ahmed, 2017, p. 30) to reveal "that this or that incident is not isolated but part of a series of events: a series as a structure" (Ahmed, 2017, p. 30), and illuminating the structural complexities of the issues at stake. As Orbach noted in her opening speech: "Our aims are not modest. They are ambitious. We want every girl to grow up feeling a matter-of-fact right to her body. Without attack. Without self-criticism. Without being watchful" (quoted in Mitchell, 2011, p. 20).

Image 6.2 Emilia Telese, *Perfect 10* – 2006–2010.[a] Performance installation, dimensions variable.

Photograph: Marcus Haydock.

a Perfect 10 was a site-specific performance and installation by Emilia Telese exhibited at Leeds City Art Gallery in 2006, Rochester Art Gallery in 2010, and subsequently shown as a video documentary piece at the Endangered Species Summit, at the Royal Festival Hall, London, and in Buenos Aires, Argentina. In it, the artist made use of over 1,500 items of makeup and grooming implements collected by her between 1990 and 2006. The work deals with body image obsession and the concept of "fitting in" by trying to achieve unattainable ideals of beauty perpetrated by contemporary media.

While these events in themselves were deeply hopeful, creative, and imaginative, in retrospect they can be seen to mark a sea-change in the degree to which body activism would go on to form a part of mainstream debate. I argue that they contributed as a significant catalyst to magnify, and propel forward, the work that had been done for decades by committed feminists, including Susie Orbach, Jean Kilbourne (1979), Naomi Wolf (1991), Susan Bordo (2003), and many others. Many topics raised at this event – such as the sexualisation of girls and women in media and advertising, the hierarchies of value placed on bodies in regard to race, ability, and shape, or the pernicious exploitation of health discourse and associated morals by the diet and pharmaceutical industries – are now more present in popular consciousness than ever before, and have undergone significant change in the way they are responded to, as the following examples will show.

Satisfactory solutions for the extensive structural inequalities that attack women's bodies – and, increasingly, all bodies – are far from being achieved. Nevertheless, clear lines can be drawn from the work surrounding the Endangered Species summit to events we see occurring seven years later. One example of this has been the announcement of new rules by the British Advertising Standards Authority (A.S.A.) in 2017, which banned advertising that perpetuates sexist stereotypes (Sweney, 2017). Viewed against the context of the preceding decade, this announcement has reflected the tireless work and activist voices of many. I touch here on only a few instances which I believe led, eventually, to the A.S.A.'s new rules, to illustrate the potential impact of bringing various groups into dialogue.

In 2009, Liberal Democrat M.P. Jo Swinson, and fellow delegates, called for a ban on airbrushed images which create "overly perfected and unrealistic images" of women in adverts targeted at children" (Mulholland, 2009, n.p.), and formed policy "calling for cigarette-style health warnings by advertisers for the adult market which "tell the truth" about the use of digital retouching technology" (Mulholland, 2009, n.p.). As a consequence of promoting this agenda, Swinson and the then Equalities Minister of the Conservative-Liberal Democrat coalition Lynne Featherstone, both co-founders of a government-backed "Campaign for Body Confidence",[3] were invited to attend the Endangered Species summit. In their speeches, both emphasised the government's recognition of the problem and their dedication in supporting the groups who are making active change, a significant endorsement for the grass roots. At the same time, A.S.A. representatives were also present at the summit and raised awareness of the A.S.A.'s system for reporting false or damaging advertising.

Body activists who had attended the summit then proceeded to amplify this awareness-raising in subsequent campaigns, promoting the mechanism of reporting false or damaging advertising as one possible action that any individual might take to push back against images that they find damaging or misleading. Returning to the present day, the A.S.A.'s new ruling not only responds to these complaints, but also shows a developed understanding of the issues, recognising that not only "unrealistic images" are damaging, but also those that sexualise and objectify. The

A.S.A.'s statement on their new standards highlights the role that the voices of many have played in forming this decision:

> The ASA receives many complaints about the depiction of women in a sexual or objectifying way in advertising, and in recent years the ASA has also received a number of complaints about ads that sexualise men, or portray men as objects, though these remain in the minority (A.S.A., 2018).

The voices of many are also more and more frequently heard in response to the aims and strategies of the weight-loss industry, such as Weight Watchers' announcement of a new programme to include membership for individuals as young as thirteen, with the aim to develop "healthy habits at a critical life-stage" (Weight Watchers, 2018, n.p.).

The giant corporation's new programme was met with a remarkable wave of resistance, including the Twitter campaign #WakeUpWeightWatchers. In this campaign members of the public highlighted the damaging nature of Weight Watchers' programmes in tweets such as this: "Dieting is not a rite of passage into adulthood. It's a set up for a lifetime of anxiety, confusion, and body dissatisfaction." (Toler, 2018, n.p.).[4] Here we see the long-standing argument for a stance against the diet industry –put forth by Orbach, by the Association for Size Diversity and Health's "Health At Every Size" movement, and others – gone mainstream. This is further illustrated in Teen Vogue's reporting on the events. Its headline "Weight Watchers is Offering Teens Free Membership and People Aren't Happy" is followed by the subtitle quote, "This is certainly not the time to then put the body on a diet" (Weiss, 2018, n.p.).

While the work that contributed towards this shift in consciousness is that of many dedicated health professionals and activists, and too large a topic to cover here in full, in the context of this *Festschrift* it is worth noting that it is a gratifying result for Orbach – who in 2012 gave evidence against Weight Watchers and Slimming World in a United Kingdom All Party Parliamentary Inquiry on Body Image – and fellow activists (A.P.P.G. Report, 2012). Orbach's testimony inside the Houses of Parliament was characteristically accompanied by performative

Image 6.3 Ditching Dieting Campaign-Logo.
Design: Jo Harrison.

Image 6.4 Ditching Dieting Protest in London, January, 2012.

Image: Ruth Johnston.

grassroots action, in this case a Ditching Dieting protest in Parliament Square in which large yellow bins, marked with toxic waste signs composed of images of scales, invited individuals to "bin" their diet books, magazines, and other diet paraphernalia. The report that finally emerged from this inquiry included a recommendation to "Reframe health messages from a focus on weight-loss to health-enhancing behaviours and adopt weight-neutral language" (A.P.P.G. Report, 2012, n.p.), and to review "the evidence-base to support the long term efficacy and safety of diets" (A.P.P.G. Report, 2012, n.p.).

The activists standing in the cold around those yellow bins did not know what impact these and various online actions might eventually have on public consciousness, but they did have hope. As Rebecca Solnit (2017, n.p.) reminds us "To sustain [resistance], people have to believe that the myriad small, incremental actions matter. That they matter even when the consequences aren't immediate or obvious". Solnit (2017, n.p.) goes on to describe what I perceive to be Orbach's main gift to fellow activists: The belief that, in persisting, "you may change the story or the rules, give tools, templates or encouragement to future activists, and make it possible for those around you to persist in their efforts."

Orbach's talent to gather and to galvanise has played no small part in the growth of Endangered Species into the local-global activist organisation Endangered Bodies. The organisation now has chapters in Argentina, Australia, Brazil, Germany, Ireland, New Zealand, the United States, and the United Kingdom.[5] Maintained by volunteers with little to no funding, it runs on hope, good will, and determination, as well as substantial organisational skills.[6] Campaigns are run both globally and locally in response to country-specific needs, and continue in the vein of the 2011 summit by harnessing the artistic skills of members into creative activism. While provision of details about each campaign lies beyond the scope of this chapter, a summary of the areas tackled by Endangered Bodies campaigns underlines Orbach's statement that, "Our aims are not modest" (quoted in Mitchell, 2011, p. 226).

Areas that have been covered by Orbach and her colleagues, while by no means exhaustive, include:

Image 6.5 Susie Orbach Opening the 2011 Endangered Species Summit in London.
Image: Eilidh Mcleod.

The fashion industry: Using Stephanie Ifill's *Model Meter* installation to underline the narrow physical parameters by which the clothes we wear are imagined and designed. The installation was used extensively between 2012 and 2018 as part of AnyBody Argentina's campaign makes a greater range of clothes sizes available in Argentine stores (Endangered Bodies, 2012a).

The beauty industry: In co-creating the Dove Campaign for Real Beauty, Orbach – some say contentiously – harnessed Dove's economic clout to encourage diversity of bodies in advertising. The campaign went on to provide support for parents navigating body anxiety in their daughters in the form of resources and school workshops (Orbach, 2005; Dove, 2016).

The diet industry: Organising the Ditching Dieting campaign and associated online and live actions (Endangered Bodies, 2012b).

The cosmetic surgery industry: Giving evidence as part of a *Review of the Regulation of Cosmetic Interventions* (Keogh, 2013). The consequent report recommended that the government establish a clear regulatory framework to ensure high quality care, comprehensive public information, and accessible resolution and redress in the event of complications. It also asked that "Existing advertising recommendations and restrictions should be updated and better enforced" (Keogh, 2013, p. 8). These recommendations have since been taken forward by Health Education England (Bruce and Jollie, 2014).

Education: Running the "Shape Your Culture" programme in British schools, universities, and community groups to raise awareness and facilitate a sense of agency in the face of body anxiety (Shape Your Culture, 2014).

Mothers and babies: Conducting training for midwives and health visitors under the auspices of the "Two for the Price of One" project (Orbach and Rubin, 2014).

Social media: Conducting the successful "Fat is Not a Feeling" campaign, which convinced Facebook to remove the "I feel fat" emoticon from its options and positioned Endangered Bodies as an expert resource for Facebook with regard to body image and eating disorder prevention (Endangered Bodies, 2015).

Gaming: A global campaign demanding more effective rules from Apple, and its software programme, iTunes, and Google to make plastic surgery games aimed at children unavailable. This campaign has persevered, having gleaned over 100,000 signatures in a supporting petition (Endangered Bodies, 2017), having been endorsed by the Nuffield Council of Bioethics in their 2017 report on cosmetic procedures (Edwards, 2017).

Actors' Bodies

I now want to shift the focus of this discussion to examine aspects of Orbach's work in relation to the actor's body specifically. As highlighted by her presence at the above-mentioned Open Space on "The Actor's Body: Identity and Image", Orbach has played an important part in legitimising the discourse around body anxiety in this field among many others. Bringing into focus the risk which body anxiety poses for the actor's wellbeing continues, however, to be a challenging process. The acting profession has long been concerned with the actor's appearance as a primary ingredient of the actor's popularity. In 1750, John Hill wrote in *The Actor: Treatise on the Art of Playing*:

> Tell people that there is a new actress to appear upon the stage such a night, the first question they ask is, Is she handsome? And 'tis ten to one, but they forget to enquire at all whether she has any merit in the profession (quoted in Cohen and Calleri, 2009, p. 22).

Athene Seyler, one of the first pupils of the Royal Academy of Dramatic Arts, tells how when she initially applied, around 1909, she was told that she had "no qualifications for the stage" (Hollege, 1981, p. 12) because she was "very plain" (Hollege, 1981, p. 12). In 2010, meanwhile, an online response to Richard Schechner's proposal for "casting without limits" states:

> Why is it so hard to accept that acting is one of the few professions in which one's physical appearance is central to the job? If that seems unfair, it is. You are also free to choose another profession (quoted in Schechner, 2010, n.p.).

These narratives indicate that the actor's body has long been their "calling card" (Orbach, 2009, p. 5). However, whereas a century ago a certain appearance might have proven the end of an actor's career, today's actor lives in a world where technologies to modify the body proliferate: failure to produce a body that is marketable then becomes the fault of the individual, implying lack of commitment to their profession as is typical of a neoliberal context. As Orbach (2009, p. 5) notes, assessing the status of the body in the twenty-first century, "Whatever the means, our body is […] vested with showing the results of our hard work and watchfulness, or, alternatively, our failure and sloth".

The watchfulness required here, and the sense of individual failing, are, I would argue, exacerbated for the actor by the fact that aesthetic modification and improvement has increasingly been normalised as an inevitable aspect of their profession. The voice of business is then generally accepted to be the voice of reason, where "by not making the changes that would be possible (losing weight, getting a blepharoplasty, being better groomed) I am being irresponsible. I know what the business requires and it's up to me to make myself as castable as possible" (quoted in Mitchell, 2014, p. 61). This occurs despite compelling arguments that a constantly watchful relationship with one's body is destabilising and reduces the actor's capacity for creative transformation (Mitchell, 2014). As the body has become "a series of visual images and a labour process in itself" (Orbach, 2009, p. 75), entangled with narratives that equate health with moral superiority (Shilling, 2010), it is often felt to be unreliable and a source of anxiety, rather than "generative and animated, as well as alive to ordinary discontents and longings" (Orbach, 2009, p. 76).

The actors, for whom the demands of business and art compete with the demands of the body, are thus caught in the paradox between defining themselves as a marketable product, fixed in an image, and being capable of transformation through their craft. The first often requires banning appetites and needs of the self, whereby listening to the body's voice is suppressed; whereas the second demands this very listening to the body – "being in touch with, and able to reflect on, somatic experiences and wider emotional meaning" (Park, Dunn, and Barnard, 2012, p. 91) – as a precondition for imagination to radiate out through the body, thereby to transform it for the eye of the audience. As actor-movement pedagogues Ewan and Green (2015, pp. 128–129) note, "Living in the now is an essential skill for the actor … For the actor to experience total transformation, the work must be both internal and external".

The transformation of the actor's body through their craft also involves the spectator, who completes the act through their own imagination. Umberto Eco (1989) argues that it is when the creative work is left open, when there are gaps left for the spectator's imagination to build into, that the spectator can become a creative partner. All too often, however, actors' bodies are hired, and their surfaces moulded in a different kind of transformation than that which they are capable of through their craft:

> I know there have been people who have been told by agents and casting directors that they should try to lose weight, or should not put on any more weight … people have their teeth, their nose or their boobs done (quoted in Mitchell, 2013, p. 167).

The aim of such surface transformations is to present a visual image that is a closed system, and this has an impact not only on the actors' own relationship to their bodies, but also on all of us who watch them. Eradicating signs of the socially abject – of age, poverty, appetite – from the visual landscape of the stories we tell, means that we are creating a smooth surface in which there are no gaps for the spectator's imagination to insert itself. How can we do the work of making theatre "for that part of [us] that live[s] in exile" (Barba, 2010, p. 185), when we simultaneously insist on a "distribution of the sensible" (Rancière, 2004) that bans the very flesh which speaks of those parts?

The aesthetic-emotional labour required of the actor[7] is of course a precondition for this closed system, in which existing images are reflected against one another. It mirrors the aesthetic labour required of all of us in relation to the post-industrial body that Orbach describes, and in turn returns the image of its product back to us as an achievement to be celebrated and a reality to be believed.

The message underlying this experience is that, in order to regulate one's being-in-the-world, judgement from those around us is more reliable than inner sensation. In the context of actor training this message is something akin to Frank Camilleri's (2009, p. 28) notion of "ideological" training systems for actors. These are defined as structures in which the responsibility to make rules and define boundaries – whether these pertain to the body or other aspects of labour – is handed over to the training institution. It is not far-fetched to compare this notion to the way in which rules and boundaries pertaining to the body are defined by, for example, diet plans and fashion trends.

The opposite to this is what Camilleri (2009, p. 27) calls an "ethical" training approach, where such responsibilities are worked out in a relational manner by listening to the embodied self in dialogue with others, comparable to Orbach's (2002) notion of intuitive eating. As Camilleri (2009, p. 31) notes, such an "ethical" approach often stands in conflict with economic imperatives and the desire to benefit from the swing of market forces, reinforcing the paradox of the actors' bodies as caught between the responsibilities toward business, art, and self (Mitchell, 2014). The question of whether an actor would agree to body modifications such as weight loss in exchange for a desirable part is an example that clearly illuminates this paradox:

> I don't think it would necessarily be a healthy thing, because I think the shape that I am now is probably the shape I'm supposed to be, but ... that kind of goes to show, for something like that, if it was plausible to do, then I would probably try (quoted in Mitchell, 2013, p. 153).

There are of course, and have been for years, performers and performances that seek to disrupt the closed system of reproducing idealised images – although, significantly, this most frequently occurs on the fringes of the industry, where fewer financial stakeholders are involved. Feminist theatre's acts of "active vanishing" (Phelan, 1993, p. 19), where expectations are intentionally subverted in order to

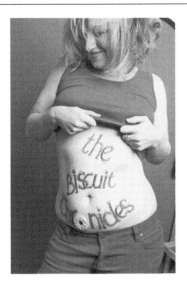

Image 6.6 Amy Godfrey, *The Biscuit Chronicles*, 2014.

Image: Penny Dixie

disrupt the male gaze, are one example of this (cf. Solga, 2016, for an excellent overview), as are performances that explicitly take the complexities of body anxiety as their subject matter. In Amy Godfrey's (2014) *The Biscuit Chronicles*, for instance, a one-woman show intelligently explores the body's inevitable failing in the push-and-pull between personal experience and neoliberal narratives.

Increasingly frequent forays into both experimenting with casting against type and across gender are further examples. In 2016, theatre critic Lynne Gardner (2016, n.p.) remarks that *The Tempest*, directed by Phyllida Lloyd, the final production of the all-female Shakespeare trilogy at London's Donmar Warehouse, gives "a glorious reminder that genuine diversity on stage offers astonishing creative benefits." She argues that it is evidence that "there is a growing critical mass of gender-blind casting" (Gardner, 2016, n.p.), when only in 2012 "cross-gender casting was still perceived by some as a novelty" (Gardner, 2016, n.p.). The productions she lists to emphasise this are in mainstream houses: "Glenda Jackson is playing King Lear at the Old Vic and Anna Francolini is Captain Hook at the National Theatre, where Tamsin Greig will soon play Malvolio" (Gardner, 2016, n.p.).

This growth in performance opportunities across the gender, race, and age spectrum is certainly an important step to alleviate actors' anxiety about the need to change their body – and it is a slow one, which has been long in the making and relies on continuous campaigning by artists and activists.[8] However, as Jessa Crispin (2017, p. 85) reminds us, doing well within an oppressive system – "one that values consumerism and competition, that devalues compassion and community" – risks still maintaining that system. Including a greater diversity of bodies and voices in the stories we tell will not, in itself, resolve the fact that the performance industry continues to thrive on the self-exploitation of its participants, and values the labour of production – and the self-sacrifice this entails – far higher than the labour of care. Further, it does not necessarily do so overtly; in fact, the labour of care, and especially narratives of self-care, are increasingly promoted by the same frameworks that also rely on self-exploitation. It is by examining the complexity at play here that I want to conclude this chapter.

Actors, Activists, and the Next Action

In searching for solutions for systemic change, both the field of body activism and that of the acting profession are faced with the challenge of circumventing the neoliberal appropriation of what it means to practise self-care – to find ways of looking after ourselves in the face of debilitating body anxiety and, simultaneously, to look after others by continuing to challenge the structures that exacerbate and exploit this anxiety.

Once upon a time, the invitation to dare to be confident in the body that you are living in was in itself a radical and empowering proposal, and seemed a positive first step toward change. It was on the basis of this principle that Endangered Bodies launched its 2011 guerrilla campaign, disseminating stickers in public spaces which read, "Join the resistance: Love your body". It is also on the basis of this principle that actors are enjoined to strive for confidence as a goal, grounded in the assumption that being "confident communicators, who say 'this is me, this is what I look like, this is who I am, here I am and I am fit for purpose'" (quoted in Mitchell, 2013, p. 138) will make them more resilient in dealing with body anxiety.

However, while the call to "love your body" has become a staple of what is now often called the "body positivity" movement, it has also been swiftly appropriated back into the systems that seek to exploit body anxiety. As illustrated in Gill's and Elias's (2014) critique of "Love Your Body" discourse, the notion of self-care has become ever more comprehensively commodified, flattened, and diluted. The neoliberal logic of self-care put forth by media and advertising industries has shifted all focus away from communal action and systemic critique, instead suggesting that discomfort with their bodies is something that women, and men, do to themselves, and that therefore the power to *stop* doing so is in their hands (ideally by spending money on tools that can help them love themselves more). Failure to achieve body confidence has then become just that – another thing at which the individual might fail.[9]

Thus, even though Britain has a government-backed "Campaign for Body Confidence", and although a large proportion of resources available for dealing with body image in young people is funded by the Dove "Self-Esteem Project", encouraging body confidence as a goal in itself is problematic and insufficient. Where troubled relationships with the embodied self have become "dislocated from their structural determinants in patriarchal capitalism and shorn of their psychosocial complexity" (Gill and Elias, 2014, p. 188), the encouragement to "love your body" is at best an "ameliorative sticking plaster on the wounds of injustice" (Ledwith, 2007, n.p.). At worst, it leads to further insidious self-exploitation, as it is often assumed that any practices that will give the individual a feeling of confidence are by default caring practices, and therefore benign.

Psychologists Crocker and Park (2004, p. 407) make the case that threats to achieving self-esteem can in fact lead to behaviours that are destructive or self-destructive, and conclude that, "The pursuit of self-esteem interferes with related-ness, learning, autonomy, self-regulation, and mental and physical health". While *having* self-esteem has many benefits, there is thus a high cost to *aiming for* self-esteem as a goal – a cost which becomes apparent when we examine "what people do to achieve boosts to self-esteem and avoid drops in self-esteem in their daily lives" (Crocker and Park, 2004, p. 393). As this student actor notes, "If I knew I had to be on stage in underwear, I would go and lose weight and tone up, so that I could be confident in my performance" (quoted in Mitchell, 2013, p. 96).

Resilience certainly plays an important part in being able to survive, resist, and create change – however, the great social justice movements around the world have taught us that nothing builds resilience more than being part of a community that is working towards change. While we do live in a world where accepting our bodies' appetites and needs is radical, it is through dialogue with others that we learn to dis-tinguish between "the ordinary discontents and longings" of life and work (Orbach, 2009, p. 76; cf. Orbach, 2008) and the structural inequalities that are making it impossible for many of us to live fully in and from our bodies. It is through the sup-portive presence of others that our feelings of guilt or failure can be contextualised and accepted as part of the messy, unruly process of self-actualising in the face of ongoing discriminations and exclusions:

> I do believe that the work of loving our selves and our bodies also requires the work of other people showing us that this is possible through loving us and our bodies. It isn't always work we can do alone, the way that "Love Your Body" rhetoric suggests (Luna, 2016, n.p.).

Importantly, being part of such a community should not mean uncritically sur-rounding oneself with people whose opinions and beliefs support our own. As Eichenbaum and Orbach (1987, p. 178) discuss in *Between Women: Love, Envy and Competition in Women's Friendships*, finding ways to disagree productively and navigate the feelings that disagreement raises are a crucial ingredient for col-lectively re-imagining more just and equitable structures: "Creating the balance between autonomy and connectedness is becoming ever more critical, both socially and psychologically".[10]

Finally, as Margaret Ledwith (2007, n.p.) argues in her call for "reclaiming the radical agenda" in community development, activists must "be vigilant and stay critical if we are to prevent our practice getting distracted … We need to reclaim our radical agenda from attempts to hijack and dilute it into a rhetoric of self help"

(Ledwith, 2007, n.p.). A focus on practical considerations can be both illuminating and helpful to carry this agenda forward. In the context of the acting profession, we might begin by interrogating whether the ecologies in which self-care is being promoted to actors actually provide opportunities to practise that self-care. Where training institutions promote a nutritious, varied diet, is such food available?[11] Where relaxation and mindfulness are encouraged, is this taken into account when planning actors' working hours? Where emotional risk-taking is encouraged, are strategies to regain emotional equilibrium disseminated and given time and space to be enacted? Where greater diversity in casting is celebrated, is this extended beyond colour-blind and cross-gender casting to include fat bodies, disabled bodies, bodies that do not conform to gender or class expectations – and is this paired with greater diversity among those who write, direct, design, produce, and review the stories we tell? Are the significant institutions and bodies of the performance industry providing space in which to reflect critically on the industry's glamourising of self-sacrifice for business and art? Are stakeholders who claim concern for actors committing, through action, to being part of a community of change regarding actors' bodies?

The #MeToo movement is one example of activism that has forced the performance industries to begin to engage with some of these questions practically. Started by Tarana Burke in Harlem in 2006 to "spread awareness and understanding about sexual assault in underprivileged communities of colour" (Shugerman, 2016, n.p.), "Me Too" turned into a global movement in 2016 in response to the public airing of thousands of cases of sexual abuse, harassment, and exploitation in the theatre and film world and beyond.[12] The body was by default centralised in these discussions, and practices that had for decades been normalised are now questioned and critiqued, and countered with alternatives. The rise of a new profession, that of Intimacy Director, is one example of this, providing a professionally-guided approach to creatively choreographing scenes of sex and intimacy – as fight directors have long done with scenes of violence – rather than leaving actors and their bodies vulnerable to in-the-moment improvisation and the risks this entails (Sanderson, 2017; Talbot, 2017).

Much has thus happened through collective movements to defend our bodies as a place to live from, even though arguably, still, "our time and place are dire for bodies" (Orbach, 2017, n.p.). This project is not one that offers quick gratification; it requires time and the realisation that lasting change may not be achieved within our lifetime. It is a huge piece of work to dismantle what was long thought inevitable. It means a profound rethinking of everything, and even those of us who very consciously experience the oppressions that come with the markets of physical capital struggle to imagine what a different version of the world might look like. In 2011, when asked whether she thinks we will see real change in the way future generations relate to their bodies, Orbach (2011, n.p.) answers, "I am deeply pessimistic". But she also shows that for her, as for all of us, the strength to continue comes from working together with, and in relation to, others: "What choice do

Image 6.7 Occupy Your Body
Image: Sharon Haywood.

we have but to challenge the hurt and the vicious attacks on bodies? What gives me hope are the number of body activists out there – young, old, across cultures and class, who are insisting on something more humane in relation to our bodies" (Orbach, 2011, n.p.).

It is in the spirit of this collective persistence that the question must be asked, and then asked again: "What is the action?"

Notes

1   Dr. Roanna Mitchell wrote this chapter in 2018 as a special tribute for Dr. Susie Orbach's seventy-second birthday.
2   It should be noted that in both Orbach's work and the work of the performer, the ability to act also requires the ability to "listen", and that listening should be understood as an integral aspect of action. Orbach's description of this vital aspect of her therapeutic work resonates with considerations of relational dynamics in performance: "The therapist makes patterns and theories, but they are also reflecting on the words that are spoken, how they are delivered – in a staccato fashion, or flatly, or stop and start – and how the words, once spoken, affect the speaker and the therapist themselves [...] just as words reveal so, too, can they obscure, and this gets us to the listening and feeling part of the therapy" (Orbach, 2018, n.p.).
3   Following changes in government, this campaign continues to exist under the name "Be Real", although its partnership with cosmetics company Dove, and brief dalliance with "lifestyle" programme Slimming World, are testimony of the troubled relationship between activism gone mainstream and the profit-focused aims of stakeholder industries.

4 The campaign was initiated by the BALANCE Eating Disorders Treatment Center in New York City.
5 The United Kingdom chapter of Endangered Bodies, convened by Orbach until 2017, is called AnyBody UK. The confusing proliferation of names bears testament to the organic growth of a movement: AnyBody was first founded by Orbach and colleagues Jo Harrison, Karishma Chugani, Althea Greenan, Mary-Jayne Rust, Natasha Harvey, and others in 2002, as a lobbying group and blog site (now archived by the British Library). As other groups across the globe joined, the name AnyBody became problematic as it is also used by American pro-life activists, and so while the U.K. group retains the name locally, the global organisation is now titled Endangered Bodies.
6 The work of writer, editor, and body activist Sharon Haywood, based in Argentina, merits particular mention here, as a galvaniser and particular inspiration for the continuing work of the organisation.
7 Entwistle and Wissinger (2006, p. 786) argue that, "the effort required to keep up appearances is very much emotional and feelingful as well as physical and aesthetic". For actors this includes all manner of practices that will help them achieve an appearance likely to yield commercial success: "These might range from changes in hair-style and -colour or use of make-up through to more intrusive practices, such as diets that induce weight-loss or weight-gain, fitness regimes to build muscle which may be accompanied by protein-shakes or steroids, plastic surgery, Botox injections, skin-whitening or tanning, and re-shaping of the teeth" (Mitchell, 2014, p. 65).
8 An example of such activism is the U.K. organisation Tonic Theatre, which "supports the arts, theatre and creative industries to achieve greater gender equality and diversity in their work and workforces" (Tonic Theatre, 2011, n.p.).
9 As Jordan Kisner (2017, n.p.) points out, in the United States narratives of self-care can be traced back to "puritanical values of self-improvement and self-examination" and their use to justify who is or is not an "unfit citizen" (Kisner, 2017). In the twentieth century, this was countered by a reclaiming of the term by the oppressed, as in Audre Lorde's (2017, p. 130) statement that, "Caring for myself is not self-indulgence, it is self-preservation, and that is an act of political warfare". These two narratives continue to co-exist in constant tension with one another.
10 Although their discussion focuses on the particular historical moment of the women's movement in the 1970s, many aspects raised continue to be relevant today.
11 The consensus on what constitutes a "healthy" diet is of course in itself contested and is entangled with issues of attainability and class. As Orbach (2018, n.p.) wrote, "When you grow up absorbing the idea that food is quasi dangerous it is hard to know how to handle it. And there are no end of experts selling their wares whose books and products end up generating enormous profits".
12 The movement involved individuals who have experienced sexual assault or harassment responding with the hashtag or phrase "Me Too" as a sign of solidarity and to highlight the endemic nature of such experiences. The discourse and activism evolving from this has led to a number of activist developments, including the Time's Up (2017) movement.

References

A.S.A. (2018). Offence: Sexualisation and Objectification. ASA Advice Online. 2nd January. [https://www.asa.org.uk/advice-online/offence-sexism.html; Accessed on 13th March, 2018].
Ahmed, Sara (2017). *Living a Feminist Life*. Durham, North Carolina: Duke University Press.

All Party Parliamentary Group on Body Image (2012). Reflections on Body Image. 29th May. [https://issuu.com/bodyimage/docs/reflections_on_body_image?printButtonEnab led=false&backgroundColor=%2523222222; Accessed on 13th March, 2018].

BALANCE Eating Disorder Treatment Centre (2018). Weight Watchers Twitter Takeover: Are You In? *BLANCE Blog*. [http://balancedtx.com/blog/2018/2/8/weight-watchers-twitter-takeover-are-you-in; Accessed on 13th March, 2018].

Barba, Eugenio (2010). *On Directing and Dramaturgy: Burning the House*. London: Routledge.

Bissell, Laura (2011). *The Female Body, Technology and Performance: Performing a Feminist Praxis*. Doctoral Dissertation, University of Glasgow, Glasgow, Scotland.

Bordo, Susan (2003). *Unbearable Weight*. Tenth Edition. Los Angeles, California: University of California Press.

Bruce, Charles, and Jollie, Carol (2014). Review of Qualifications Required for Delivery of Non-Surgical Cosmetic Interventions. Health Education England. September. [https://www.hee.nhs.uk/sites/default/files/documents/Non-surgical%20cosmetic%20interventi ons%20-%20Report%20on%20Phase%201.pdf; Accessed on 14th March, 2018].

Camilleri, Frank (2009). Of Pounds of Flesh and Trojan Horses. *Theatre, Dance and Performance Training*, *14*, Number 2, 26–34.

Cohen, Robert, and Calleri, James (2009). *Acting Professionally: Raw Facts About Careers in Acting*. Houndmills, Basingstoke, Hampshire: Palgrave Macmillan.

Crispin, Jessa (2017). *Why I Am Not A Feminist: A Feminist Manifesto*. Brooklyn, New York: Melville House.

Crocker, Jennifer, and Park, Laura E. (2004). The Costly Pursuit of Self-Esteem. *Psychological Bulletin*, *130*, 392–414.

Dean, Deborah (2008). No Human Resource is an Island. *Gender, Work and Organization*, *15*, 161–181.

Diamond, Elin (1997). *Unmaking Mimesis: Essays on Feminism and Theatre*. London: Routledge.

Dove (2016). School Workshops on Body Image: Confident Me. Self-Esteem Project. [https://www.dove.com/uk/dove-self-esteem-project/school-workshops-on-body-image-confident-me.html; Accessed on 13th March, 2018].

Eco, Umberto (1989). *The Open Work*. Cambridge, Massachusetts: Harvard University Press.

Edwards, Jeanette (2017). Cosmetic Procedures: Ethical Issues. Nuffield Council on Bioethics. June. [http://nuffieldbioethics.org/project/cosmetic-procedures; Accessed on 21st March, 2018].

Eichenbaum, Luise, and Orbach, Susie (1987). *Between Women: Love, Envy and Competition in Women's Friendships*. New York: Penguin Random House.

Endangered Bodies (2012a). Model Meter: Its Origins. 8th December. [http://buenosaires. endangeredbodies.org/its_origins; Accessed on 13th March, 2018].

Endangered Bodies (2012b). What Does the Word 'Diet' Mean to You? Ditching Dieting. [http://london.endangeredbodies.org/ditching_dieting; Accessed on 13th March, 2018].

Endangered Bodies (2015). Fat is Not a Feeling. Endangered Bodies Blog. [http://www. endangeredbodies.org/fat_is_not_a_feeling; Accessed on 14th March, 2018].

Endangered Bodies (2017). Kids and Cosmetic Surgery: Not a Pretty Picture. Endangered Bodies Blog. [http://www.endangeredbodies.org/kids_and_cosmetic_surgery_not_a_pre tty_picture; Accessed on 14th March, 2018].

Entwistle, Joanne, and Wissinger, Elizabeth (2006). Keeping Up Appearances: Aesthetic Labour in the Fashion Modelling Industries of London and New York. *Sociological Review, 54*, 774–794.

Ewan, Vanessa, and Green, Debbie (2015). *Actor Movement: Expression of the Physical Being.* London: Methuen Drama.

Finnegan, Margaret (1999). *Selling Suffrage: Consumer Culture and Votes for Women.* New York: Columbia University Press.

Gardner, Lyn (2016). Shakespeare Trilogy Review: Donmar's Phenomenal All-Female Triumph. *The Guardian.* 23rd November. [https://www.theguardian.com/stage/2016/nov/23/shakespeare-trilogy-five-star-review-donmar-kings-cross-harriet-walter; Accessed on 14th March, 2018].

Gill, Rosalind, and Elias, Ana Sofia (2014). 'Awaken Your Incredible': Love Your Body Discourses and Feminist Contradictions. *International Journal of Media and Cultural Politics, 10*, 179–188.

Godfrey, Amy (2009). *The Biscuit Chronicles.* Performer and Director: Amy Godfrey. Tom Thumb Theatre, Margate, Kent.

Holledge, Julie (1981). *Innocent Flowers: Women in the Edwardian Theatre.* London: Virago.

Keogh, Bruce (2013). Review of the Regulation of Cosmetic Surgery Interventions. Department of Health. April. [https://www.gov.uk/government/uploads/system/uploads/attachment_data/file/192028/Review_of_the_Regulation_of_Cosmetic_Interventions.pdf; Accessed on 14th March, 2018].

Kilbourne, Jean (1979). *Killing Us Softly.* Directors: Margaret Lazarus and Renner Wunderlich. Producer: Cambridge Documentary Films.

Kisner, Jordan (2017). The Politics of Conspicuous Displays of Self-Care. *New Yorker.* 14th March. [https://www.newyorker.com/culture/culture-desk/the-politics-of-selfcare; Accessed on 21st March, 2018].

Ledwith, Margaret (2007). Reclaiming the Radical Agenda: A Critical Approach to Community Development. Infed. [https://www.infed.org/community/critical_community_development.htm; Accessed on 15th March, 2018].

Lorde, Audre (2017). *A Burst of Light and Other Essays.* Mineola, New York: Ixia Press.

Luna, Caleb (2016). The Hidden Problems with 'Love Your Body' Talk. The Establishment. [http://www.theestablishment.co/2016/09/24/the-hidden-problems-with-love-your-body-talk/; Accessed on 15th March, 2018].

Mitchell, Roanna (2011). Endangered Species: Report on the Summit. *Criminal Justice Matters, 85*, 20–21.

Mitchell, Roanna (2013). *The Body Politics of Acting in the Context of Training and the Performance Industry: Perspectives from Contemporary Britain.* Doctoral Thesis, University of Kent, Canterbury, Kent.

Mitchell, Roanna (2014). Seen But Not Heard: An Embodied Account of the (Student) Actor's Aesthetic Labour. *Theatre, Dance and Performance Training, 5*, 59–73.

Mulholland, Hélène (2009). Lib Dems Call for Ban on Airbrushed Photos. 19th September. *The Guardian.* [https://www.theguardian.com/politics/2009/sep/19/liberal-democrats-airbrush-ban; Accessed on 13th March, 2018].

Mulvey, Laura (1974). Visual Pleasure and Narrative Cinema. *Screen, 16*, Number 3, 6–18.

Orbach, Susie (1978). *Fat is a Feminist Issue.* London: Paddington Press.

Orbach, Susie (2002). *On Eating.* London: Penguin Books / Penguin Group.

Orbach, Susie (2005). Fat is an Advertising Issue. Campaign [Online]. 17th June. [https://www.campaignlive.co.uk/article/fat-advertising-issue/481078; Accessed on 13th March, 2018].

Orbach, Susie (2006). *Fat is a Feminist Issue*. London: Arrow Books.

Orbach, Susie (2008). Work is Where We Live. *Emotion, Space and Society*, *1*, 14–17.

Orbach, Susie. (2009). *Bodies*. London: Profile Books.

Orbach, Susie (2011). Navigating Our Culture's Body Anxiety and Finding Body Confidence: Q and A with Susie Orbach. The Centre For Eating Disorders at Sheppard Pratt. [https://eatingdisorder.org/blog/2011/09/navigating-our-cultures-body-anxiety-finding-body-confidence-q-a-discussion-with-susie-orbach/; Accessed on 15th March, 2018].

Orbach, Susie (2017). Keynote Address. *Food Is A Feminist Issue: Media, Bodies, Appetites*, *30 June*. York: York Medical Society.

Orbach, Susie (2018). How Can a Therapist Get the Most Out of Therapy? *The Guardian*. 14th January. [https://www.theguardian.com/lifeandstyle/2018/jan/14/how-can-a-therapist-get-the-most-out-of-therapy; Accessed on 13th March, 2018].

Orbach, Susie, and Rubin, Holli (2014). Two for the Price of One: The Impact of Body Image During Pregnancy and After Birth. Government Equalities Office. [https://www.gov.uk/government/uploads/system/uploads/attachment_data/file/317739/TWO_FOR_THE_PRICE_OF_ONE.pdf; Accessed on 14th March, 2018].

Park, Rebecca J., Dunn, Barnaby D., and Barnard, Philip J. (2012). Schematic Models and Modes of Mind in Anorexia Nervosa II: Implications for Treatment and Course. *International Journal of Cognitive Therapy*, *5*, 86–98.

Phelan, Peggy (1993). *Unmarked: The Politics of Performance*. London: Routledge.

Rancière, Jacques (2004). *The Politics of Aesthetics*. London: Continuum.

Sanderson, David (2017). 'Intimacy directors' on Set Could Protect Actors from Harassment. *The Times*. 21st November. [https://www.thetimes.co.uk/article/intimacy-directors-on-set-could-protect-actors-from-harassment-x26n79gk8; Accessed on 15th March, 2018].

Schechner, Richard (2010). Casting Without Limits: What if Theatres Stopped Using Actors' Gender, Age, Race and Body Type to Assign Roles? Theatre Communications Group. [http://www.tcg.org/publications/at/dec10/casting.cfm; Accessed on 14th March, 2018].

Schechner, Richard (2013). *Performance Studies: An Introduction*. London: Routledge.

Shape Your Culture (2014). About SYC. [http://www.shapeyourculture.org.uk/about-syc-2/; Accessed on 14th March, 2018].

Shilling, Chris (2010). Exploring the Society-Body-School Nexus: Theoretical and Methodology Issues in the Study of Body Pedagogics. *Sport, Education and Society, 15*, 151–167.

Shugerman, Emily (2017). Me Too: Why Are Women Sharing Stories of Sexual Assault and How Did it Start? *The Independent*. [https://www.independent.co.uk/news/world/americas/me-too-facebook-hashtag-why-when-meaning-sexual-harassment-rape-stories-explained-a8005936.htm; Accessed on 15th March, 2017].

Solga, Kim (2016). *Theatre and Feminism*. London: Palgrave Macmillan.

Solnit, Rebecca (2017). Protest and Resist: Why Giving Up Hope is Not an Option. *The Guardian*. 13th March. [https://www.theguardian.com/world/2017/mar/13/protest-persist-hope-trump-activism-anti-nuclear-movement; Accessed on 14th March, 2018].

Sweney, Mark (2017). Standards Body Unveils Plan to Crack Down on Sexist Advertisements. *The Guardian*. 18th July. [https://www.theguardian.com/media/2017/jul/18/new-measures-announced-to-crack-down-on-sexist-adverts; Accessed on 13th March, 2018].

Talbot, Elizabeth (2017). Consensual Creativity. *Theatrical Intimacy*. [https://www.theatri calintimacy.com/about; Accessed on 15th March, 2018].

The Actor's Body: Identity and Image (2009). *Open Space Forum, 25 September*. London: Royal Central School of Speech and Drama.

The Be Real Campaign (2018). About Us. [https://www.berealcampaign.co.uk; Accessed on 16th March, 2018].

Time's Up (2017). Time's Up. [https://www.timesupnow.com; Accessed on 15th March, 2018].

Toler, Melissa (2018). Dieting is Not a Rite of Passage into Adulthood: It's a Set Up for a Lifetime of Anxiety, Confusion, and Body Dissatisfaction. #WakeUpWeightWatchers. Twitter. 10th February. [https://twitter.com/MelissaDToler/status/962393059647545349; Accessed on 13th March, 2018].

Tonic Theatre (2011). About Tonic. Tonic. [https://www.tonictheatre.co.uk/#services; Accessed on 14th March, 2018].

Weight Watchers (2018). Weight Watchers Announces Strategic Vision to Make Wellness Accessible to All, Inspiring Healthy Habits for Real Life. Press Release. 7th January. Weight Watchers. [http://www.weightwatchersinternational.com/file/Index?KeyFile= 392090462'; Accessed on 13th March, 2018].

Weiss, Suzannah (2018). Weight Watchers is Offering Teens Free Memberships and People Aren't Happy. *Teen Vogue*, Nutrition. 12th February. [https://www.teenvogue.com/story/ weight-watchers-teens; Accessed on 13th March, 2018].

Wolf, Naomi (1991). *The Beauty Myth: How Images of Beauty Are Used Against Women*. London: Vintage Books.

Part IV

Orbach in the Media

Chapter 7

"Psychotherapy is not a spectator sport"

The Dissemination of Psychoanalysis from Freud to Orbach

Brett Kahr

"müßten wir unsere Abgeschlossenheit aufgeben und versuchen, geignete Personen in unsere Versammlungen zu bringen und an der Mitarbeit teilnehmen zu lassen." ["We must give up our seclusion and seek to bring suitable persons to our meetings and to let them take part in our work."]

Dr. Alfred Adler, addressing a meeting of the Wiener Psychoanalytische Vereinigung [Vienna Psycho-Analytical Society], 6th April, 1910 (quoted in Rank, 1910a, p. 424 [German Version] and in Rank, 1910b, p. 464 [English Version])

In 2005, the Hollywood actress Meryl Streep starred in a charming romantic comedy film entitled *Prime*: a story about Mrs. "Lisa Metzger", a Jewish psychotherapist, whose young female patient, quite unwittingly, begins to date Mrs. Metzger's son! Several years later, in 2011, Ms. Streep featured in three episodes of the American television series *Web Therapy* as "Camilla Bowner", a so-called sexual orientation therapist. And in 2012, Streep headlined yet another mainstream movie, *Hope Springs*, as a disillusioned housewife, "Kay Soames", who entreats her husband to embark upon marital counselling in order to restore some joy into their emotionally anaemic lives.

As the winner of three Academy Awards, and as a nominee for eighteen others, Ms. Streep may justly be considered the most venerated actress of modern times. In view of her position as Hollywood's premier thespian, Streep's portrayal as either a clinician or as a patient on no fewer than three occasions speaks volumes about the way in which psychotherapy has penetrated to the very core of popular culture.

Indeed, psychotherapy has become such a standard fixture of television dramas and sitcoms that one would struggle to find an ongoing series that does not feature mental health workers in seminal roles; and these include *Frasier*, *The Sopranos*, *Desperate Housewives*, *In Treatment*, *The Affair*, and *Shrinking* (cf. Kahr, 2011, 2012, 2014).

Hollywood royalty has certainly embraced psychotherapy and psychoanalysis, so much so that virtually every major celebrity from Judy Garland (Frank, 1975), Frank Sinatra (Kelley, 1984), and Marilyn Monroe (Spoto, 1993) to the

DOI: 10.4324/9781003470090-12

legions of more modern performers will have spent time on the proverbial couch. Extraordinarily, no fewer than three substantial books have appeared, devoted exclusively to the subject of celebrities undergoing psychoanalysis (Freeman, 1970; Stelzer, 1977; Farber and Green, 1993).

Not only have the stars of the screen championed psychoanalytical and psycho-therapeutic ideas but, so, too, has haematological royalty. As early as 26th June, 1934, His Royal Highness The Prince George (the future Duke of Kent), son of His Majesty King George V and Her Majesty Queen Mary, became the President of the Institute of Medical Psychology: for many years the governing body of the Tavistock Clinic in London. Indeed, a bust of Prince George, sculpted by the Hungarian artist Professor Kisfalud Sigismund de Ströbl, displayed originally at the Tavistock Clinic headquarters in Malet Street, in Central London (Dicks, 1970), now resides in the ground floor corridor of the Tavistock Centre's newer home in Belsize Park, in North West London. After the Duke of Kent's untimely death during the Second World War, the patronage of the Tavistock Clinic passed to his widow, Her Royal Highness Princess Marina, The Duchess of Kent, and, ultim-ately, to their daughter, Her Royal Highness Princess Alexandra, The Honourable Lady Ogilvy – first cousin to Her Majesty Queen Elizabeth II – who eventually became the guest of honour at the launch of the Freud Museum in London, in 1986 (Kahr, 2021, 2022–2023).

Other members of the British Royal Family have embraced psychotherapy and modern psychology even more enthusiastically. Famously, Her Royal Highness Princess Diana, The Princess of Wales, embarked upon a course of individual psy-chotherapy (Morton, 1992).

More recently still, on 16th March, 2017, Princess Diana's younger son, His Royal Highness Prince Henry of Wales, better known as Prince Harry, spoke as guest of honour at a conference on the mental health of veterans, organised by the King's Centre for Military Health Research, at King's College London in the University of London. On this occasion, Prince Harry pleaded, "We need to improve the conver-sation. We all have mental health, in the same way that we all have physical health. We worry about our physical fitness probably now more than we ever have before – but our mental fitness is just as important" (quoted in Prince Harry Joins Veterans' Mental Health Conference, 2017, n.p.). Since that time, Prince Harry admitted pub-licly that he, too, had undergone counselling quite successfully in order to deal with the trauma of the death of his mother. This announcement, revealed by *The Daily Telegraph* on 17th April, 2017, instantly became world news (e.g., Bloom, 2017; MacLellan and Chopra, 2017; Prince Harry on Diana Grief, 2017; York, 2017), thus contributing, one hopes, to the tremendous destigmatisation of psychological services.

On 23rd March, 2017, exactly one week after Prince Harry championed psy-chological wellbeing, his sister-in-law, Her Royal Highness The Duchess of Cambridge – subsequently elevated to become Her Royal Highness The Princess of Wales, and known more widely and affectionately as "Kate", the wife of Prince William – addressed a meeting of the organisation Best Beginnings, held at the

Royal College of Obstetricians and Gynaecologists in London, and spoke about the care of women suffering from postnatal depression. Both the Prince and the Duchess enthused about the importance of providing appropriate psychological therapeutic assistance to those in distress and did so in a completely normalising and unashamed manner.

Since that time, the younger members of the Royal Family have become even more vocal about the centrality of mental health (e.g., Anonymous, 2019), and continue to do so. In fact, the Princess of Wales, the daughter-in-law of our current monarch King Charles III, actually became the official Patron of the Anna Freud Centre in London in 2016, an organisation subsequently restyled as the Anna Freud National Centre for Children and Families, and, more recently and more simply, as "Anna Freud", thus linking the Freud family and the Royal Family together in this official capacity.

In contemporary Britain, psychoanalysis has insinuated itself so fully into the fabric of daily life that even the noted, popular actor David Tennant, best remembered for his role in the iconic British Broadcasting Corporation television series *Doctor Who*, married the granddaughter of the esteemed American psychoanalyst Dr. Harold Searles in 2011, namely Georgia Moffett, now known as Georgia Tennant. And, more recently still, David Tennant, a Scot by birth, has portrayed the sometime psychoanalyst Dr. Ronald Laing in the film *Mad to Be Normal*, released in 2017.

To my amazement, even the obscurities of Lacanian theory have now become part of popular culture. On 30th January, 2017, one of Great Britain's most durable television programmes, *University Challenge*, first broadcast in 1962, featured several bonus questions about the work of the famous French psychoanalyst Dr. Jacques Lacan in a quarter-final competition between Emmanuel College, of the University of Cambridge, and its rival, the University of Warwick. Broadcast on B.B.C. 2, and presented by Jeremy Paxman, the bonus questions for the team from Warwick included the following: "In Lacan's psychoanalysis, what French term refers to something that is desired but can never be obtained?" (quoted in *University Challenge*, 2016). In view of the fact that most non-Lacanian psychological *professionals* would not know the correct answer – namely, the "*petit objet a*" – (nor did the Warwick students who answered, incorrectly, with the phrase "*idée fixe*"), the inclusion of such a seemingly arcane question provides strong evidence of the sheer extent to which the specificities of French psychodynamics have now become part of our everyday British lives.

With supporters such as Meryl Streep, the British Royal Family, and even "Doctor Who", members of the mental health community might well breathe a sigh of relief, knowing that we have, at last, arrived. Psychotherapy has become, truly, a stalwart, even respectable, profession. Indeed, since 2020, due to the eruption of the coronavirus pandemic, mental health, including psychotherapy as a core ingredient, has emerged as an increasingly popular topic of conversation, indeed necessity, and no longer remains a "hushed" subject.

Sadly, however, in spite of the improvements in twenty-first-century mental health, the medical community and the general public have not always granted such a warm reception to psychoanalysis and psychotherapy. Our forefathers and foremothers in the mental health field certainly had to combat an immense amount of suspicion – even sadism – throughout most of the last century.

In 1965, the British comedian Ken Dodd quipped famously that, "The trouble with Freud is that he never played the Glasgow Empire Saturday night" (quoted in Anonymous, 1965, p. 10). One suspects that Mr. Dodd may have regarded Sigmund Freud as a somewhat stuffy curmudgeon, devoid of the humour so endemic to the stand-up performer. But Dodd's little dig represents only the tiniest of annoyances in the far more bloody campaign against psychoanalysis.

Throughout his lifetime, Freud and his disciples had to endure an immense amount of vitriol. For instance, on 27th May, 1906, the distinguished German physician, Professor Dr. med. Gustav Aschaffenburg (1906, p. 1798) of Köln, addressed a meeting of neurologists and psychiatrists in Baden-Baden, lambasting Freud's theories as little more than "bedenklich" – in other words, "alarming" – and, also, as "entbehrlich" (Aschaffenburg, 1906, p. 1798) – in other words, "expendable".

Many objected to the work of Freud owing to its overt emphasis on sexuality. When, in 1908, a young Italian medical student, Herr Edoardo Weiss, expressed an interest in meeting Freud, his teacher at the Universität zu Wien – the eminent neurologist Professor Otto Marburg – warned Herr Weiss (1970, p. 2) to beware of the founder of psychoanalysis, whom he regarded as nothing more than a "Casanova". Others spoke about Freud and his colleagues with even greater venom. When the young Hungarian student Ferenc Alexander – the future Professor Franz Alexander (1960, p. 55) – first embraced psychoanalytical concepts, his father, Professor Bernát Alexander, a noted philosopher, balked, regarding Freud's contributions as "simply a horror" and, also, as "a descent into a spiritual gutter" (Alexander, 1960, p. 55).

Herr Max Graf (1942, p. 469), the distinguished Viennese musicologist – better known as the father of Herbert Graf (the famous "Little Hans") – reminisced about the early hatred towards psychoanalysis, noting that, "In those days when one mentioned Freud's name in a Viennese gathering, everyone would begin to laugh, as if someone had told a joke". Indeed, as Graf (1942, p. 469) further recalled, "It was considered bad taste to bring up Freud's name in the presence of ladies."

In similar vein, Graf's Viennese colleague Dr. Hanns Sachs (1944, p. 73), an early member of Freud's inner circle, reminisced that contemporaries considered Sigmund Freud to be "a rather disgusting freak", and, likewise, regarded psychoanalysis as little more than ' "immoral" ' (Sachs, 1944, p. 85). One can certainly understand the suspicion of the Viennese towards Freud's new sexual psychology. As Sachs (1944, p. 24) explained, Vienna adopted a strict conservative code, and, thus, "The use of words like homosexuality or syphilis was still strictly prohibited in the daily papers and the strangest forms of circumlocution had to be employed, e.g. *Handarbeiterin* – "a woman who works with her hands" – for prostitute". He expanded this observation about the use of euphemisms by noting that "'Where babies come from' belonged to the unmentionable subjects about which adolescents whispered shyly in dark corners" (Sachs, 1944, p. 24) and, further, that in respectable Viennese households, novels such as *Nana* by Émile Zola would be kept hidden from ladies.

Other pioneering psychoanalysts, apart from Freud, also had to endure vicious attacks. When, in 1911, Dr. Sándor Ferenczi spoke to a group of medical colleagues in Budapest, a fellow physician – a hydrotherapist – arose from his seat in response to Ferenczi's paper, dismissing psychoanalytical work as little more than "Schweinereien" (quoted in Ferenczi, 1911a, p. 354), which might best be translated as "pig-like filth". At this very same meeting, a dermatologist reviled Freudianism, proclaiming that, "Die Analyse ist Pornographie; die Analytiker gehören also in den Kerker" (Ferenczi, 1911a, p. 354) ["Analysis is pornography; so analysts belong in jail" (Ferenczi, 1911b, p. 256)].

Undoubtedly, psychoanalysis posed an immense number of challenges to those physicians who treated neurotic and psychotic patients with either neglect, or, in more sinister fashion, with genital surgery and other forms of physical intervention. The psychoanalysts foregrounded sexuality – a dangerous strategy during the post-Victorian era – and, moreover, questioned the centrality of the conscious mind, claiming that a far more powerful force – the *unconscious* mind – governs our behaviours and thoughts. No wonder, then, that most people dismissed this dangerous, radical new set of ideas.

Much derided in the German-speaking countries, Freud fared little better in the English-speaking world. In 1917, for instance, Dr. David Thomson (1917a,1917b), President of the Medico-Psychological Association – the forerunner of the Royal College of Psychiatrists – derided Freud in print, as did the noted forensic psychiatrist, Dr. Charles Mercier, one of Great Britain's most famous mental health professionals, who delighted in referring to the Viennese progenitor of psychoanalysis not as Freud but, rather, as "Fraud" (quoted in Stoddart, 1940, p. 191). And in a scathing attack on psychoanalysis, published in *The British Medical Journal*, Mercier (1914a, p. 172) fumed against Freudianism, lambasting it as little more than "pornography", and that, moreover, "Phallic worship, under one disguise or another, perpetually revives from time to time, and is perhaps most sickening when it masquerades as science" (Mercier, 1914a, p. 172). In subsequent contributions, Mercier (1914b, p. 276) dismissed psychoanalysis as "obscene beyond belief" and he expressed a fear that psychoanalysis would "corrupt the rising generation" (Mercier, 1916, p. 900).

The pioneering British psychoanalyst, Dr. David Forsyth (1922, p. 1), noted that people accused the early Freudians of practising "charlatanry". And Dr. Ernest Jones (1955, p. 108) considered the hatred towards dynamic psychology as an expression of the prevailing "*odium sexicum*" – hatred of sexuality – in the first half of the twentieth century, which made discussion of delicate matters, even by psychoanalysts, rather compromising (cf. Kahr, 2009).

Although the Americans embraced psychoanalysis more fully than their Continental or British counterparts, many still regarded the Viennese Jewish sexual psychology with considerable trepidation. Even during the early 1930s – more than three decades after the publication of Freud's (1900) masterpiece *Die Traumdeutung* [*The Interpretation of Dreams*] – the medical library of the University of Chicago, in Chicago, Illinois, held no books at all written by Sigmund Freud. The psychology library did boast some Freud titles, but it kept these locked up in a back room and, according to the testimony of Professor Roy Grinker, Sr. (1979, 1985), one needed special permission to study these hidden texts.

Anti-psychoanalytical sentiments penetrated not only British and American medicine but, also, popular culture more widely. In 1921, the British author David Herbert Lawrence [D.H. Lawrence] published a book in New York entitled *Psychoanalysis and the Unconscious*, in which he spoke of Freud's work as "a public danger" (Lawrence, 1921, p. 10). He also described Freud himself as rather "sinister" (Lawrence, 1921, p. 10). This book appeared, subsequently, in an edition released in London (Lawrence, 1923); hence, Britons, too, would have had ample opportunity to read about Lawrence's suspicions towards Freud. Although Lawrence had not yet written *Lady Chatterley's Lover*, he had already published such impactful novels as *Sons and Lovers*, *The Rainbow*, and *Women in Love*; hence, comments from a noted public figure would have resonated widely (cf. Rapp, 1988, 1990).

Anti-Freudianism persisted throughout much of the first half of the twentieth century. During the Second World War, Dr. Millais Culpin (1940, p. 54), one of the most significant mid-century medical psychologists, commented that many physicians regarded psychoanalytical practitioners as nothing but "credulous cranks fooled by artificial neurotics". The venom towards Freud and his followers has ultimately spawned an immense literature; and one could readily cite a number of texts which either lampooned or eviscerated Freud and his work (e.g., Thornton, 1983; Eysenck, 1985; Torrey, 1992; Webster, 1995; Borch-Jacobsen and Shamdasani, 2006).

So, in view of the tremendous opprobrium towards psychoanalysis throughout much of the first half of the twentieth century and even beyond, how then did the so-called rantings of the ostensibly cocaine-addicted pornographer Sigmund Freud impact on our culture to the point where Meryl Streep, Princess Diana, and Prince Harry could all become cheerleaders of the talking cure?

How did Sigmund Freud and his early followers deal with the savage attacks upon their reputations and their systems of belief?

At the age of nineteen, while a young medical student, Sigmund Freud (1875a, p. 144) came to appreciate that, "Ein angesehener Mann, von der Presse und den Reichen unterstützt, könnte Wunder tun, um körperliche Leiden zu lindern" ["A respected man, supported by the press and the rich, could do wonders in alleviating physical ills" (Freud, 1875b, p. 127)]. But as Freud aged, he became increasingly suspicious about the prospect of collaborating with the press.

In 1910, Dr. Alfred Adler reported to colleagues in the Wiener Psychoanalytische Vereinigung [Vienna Psycho-Analytical Society] that various neurologists in Germany had agreed to boycott any clinics which treated patients psychoanalytically (Rank, 1910c). But Sigmund Freud (1910a, p. 231) waxed stoical, even somewhat jaded, to his disciple Sándor Ferenczi, and dismissed such interference as "Unheimliche Dinge, denen man mit Fassung entgegengehen muß." ["Sinister things, which one has to confront with equanimity." (Freud, 1910b, p. 152)].

In spite of Freud's fortitude and perseverance as a personality, he did not particularly enjoy engaging with the general public in a fulsome manner. After having established psychoanalysis as a profession and as a movement, he spent the vast majority of his time at home in Vienna's Berggasse treating patients, writing books and papers, attending to his voluminous correspondence, and entertaining colleagues. Famously, he rarely interacted with the "media" *per se* and refrained from doing so for good reasons. Indeed, Freud harboured considerable suspicion towards the reporters who often misrepresented him grossly. For instance, Freud had once granted a five-minute interview to the journalist Mr. H.V. Kaltenborn [Hans von Kaltenborn], which appeared in the *Brooklyn Daily Eagle* on 18th December, 1921, under the headline, "A Talk with Dr. Freud, Psycho-Analyst". Fallaciously, Kaltenborn reported that the greedy Professor Freud kept as many as thirty to forty people in his waiting room (Hale, 1995). Similarly, on 6th December, 1934, the American physician Dr. Joseph Wortis (1954), who went to Vienna in order to study psychoanalysis with its founder, told Freud that he had read an article in an American magazine quoting Freud's views on war. Apparently, Freud had no knowledge of this at all, and he regarded the article as a complete fabrication.

In spite of Freud's heaving ambitions for psychoanalysis, he retained a lifelong suspicion towards modern technology. As his one-time analysand, Dr. Adolph Stern, recalled, "He was rather shy and not given to public appearances easily" (quoted in Eissler, 1952, p. 2). Consequently, he turned down many opportunities to collaborate more publicly, having rejected the chance to serve as consultant to the feature film *Geheimnisse einer Seele* [*Secrets of a Soul*], which popularised psychoanalysis in a serious way (Freud, 1925a; Chodorkoff and Baxter, 1974; Ries, 1995); and, moreover, he had refused to meet with the American film mogul Samuel Goldwyn who wished to discuss a cinema project with Freud about the great lovers of history (Jones, 1957). As a man who loathed the telephone and who almost never listened to the radio (Freud, 1957), the father of psychoanalysis regarded invitations from film producers as rather vulgar; indeed, as he explained to his younger colleague, Dr. Ernst Simmel, "In my opinion, psychoanalysis does not lend itself in any way whatever to the medium of the motion picture" (Freud, 1925b, p. 99).

In similar vein, he also turned down the chance to serve as an expert witness at the trial of the American murderers Nathan Leopold, Jr., and Richard Loeb, in spite of the offer of an enormous fee (Freud, 1924a, 1924b; Bonaparte, 1926; Seldes,

1953; cf. Kahr, 2005a, 2005b, 2007, 2014). Whether one attributes Freud's refusal to travel to Chicago, Illinois, to health reasons, having recently received his diagnosis of cancer (Romm, 1983), or to his long-standing anti-Americanism (e.g., Freud, 1915, 1921, 1925c; cf. Falzeder, 2012), or to his loathing of coarse publicity, one cannot say with certainty. But, without question, he missed an opportunity to bring psychoanalysis into a more public arena.

Although Freud – born in 1856 – did not contribute to what we might describe as the technological dissemination of psychoanalysis, he certainly did not object to its popularisation, if undertaken in a truly serious way. When, in 1935, the Polish-born Dr. Gustav Bychowski paid his last visit to Vienna, prior to his emigration to the United States of America, he spoke with Freud about this very matter. As Bychowski (1948, p. 9) later recalled, "I asked him what contribution he thought psychoanalysis might eventually make to the solution of the appalling crisis with which our civilization was threatened. "How can we," I said, "devote our time and energy to curing a few individuals at a time like this when our entire civilization, our very existence, is imperiled [sic]?" Freud replied that in his opinion we could not hope to save mankind, but could best help by advancing and popularizing our psychoanalytic knowledge, so that eventually it would become public property, a part of universal thought, so to speak. Then, in the distant future, the day might come when these horrifying reactions of the collective psyche would no longer be possible."

In spite of Freud's ambivalence towards public engagement, some of his early disciples immersed themselves in disseminatory activities with far more enthusiasm. As early as 13th April, 1910, Dr. Ludwig Jekels, an early Freud supporter, suggested that his colleagues in the Wiener Psychoanalytische Vereinigung should consider some strategies for "Propaganda" (Rank, 1910c, p. 431) ["publicity"]. Jekels proposed, in particular, that the psychoanalytical society should mount courses for physicians and pedagogues, as well as provide touring lectures to various Austrian cities and, also, organise talks for the "akademischen Jugend" (Rank, 1910c, p. 439) ["academic youths"]. A true enthusiast, Jekels underscored that any propaganda campaign should be "intensive" (Rank, 1910c, p. 439) and, also, "agitatorische" (Rank, 1910c, p. 439) ["agitating", even "rabble-rousing"].

In 1922, Dr. Sándor Ferenczi (1922) published a book entitled Populäre Vorträge über Psychoanalyse [Popular Lectures on Psycho-Analysis], designed specifically to reach a wider public. This text contained a welter of essays on many broad-ranging topics, including the links between psychoanalysis and such arenas as criminology, philosophy, and literature. In the "Vorwort" ["Foreword"] to his book, Ferenczi (1922, n.p.) described his tome as a collection of "psychoanalytische Themen für ärztliche und nichtärztliche Laien." ["psycho-analytical themes for medical and non-medical laymen."]. Hitherto, no psychoanalyst, to the best of my knowledge, had used the word "Populäre" in the title of a seminal publication.

Shortly thereafter, on 9th May, 1925, Dr. Heinrich Koerber, an early pioneer of psychoanalysis in Germany, delivered a short presentation to the Berliner

Psychoanalytischer Vereinigung [Berlin Psycho-Analytical Society] discussing the attacks against psychoanalysis in the press (Anonymous, 1925); and not long thereafter, on 27th March, 1926, the same organisation devoted a discussion to the topic of psychoanalysis and publicity, with opening speeches presented by Dr. Franz Alexander and Dr. Siegfried Bernfeld (Radó, 1926; cf. Bernfeld, 1930). Clearly, these younger practitioners harboured great concerns about the negative reactions to psychoanalysis and, hence, endeavoured to understand something about the source of the resistance.

Although we cannot offer a completely comprehensive history of what I shall refer to as "media psychoanalysis" (cf. Kahr, 2023a) – namely, the intersection between clinical psychoanalysis and newspapers, radio, cinema, and other organs of communication – I shall highlight just a few of the truly important moments of collaboration which have helped psychoanalysis both to survive and, also, to flourish.

On 23rd January, 1941, a new musical comedy opened at the Alvin Theatre on Broadway, in Central Manhattan, entitled *Lady in the Dark*, directed by the great American playwright Moss Hart, who also scripted the libretto, while the remarkable songwriters Ira Gershwin and Kurt Weill wrote, respectively, the lyrics and the music. Based largely on Moss Hart's own experiences undergoing psychoanalytical treatment with the venerated clinician Dr. Lawrence Kubie, *Lady in the Dark* provided an extremely serious and well-researched portrait of the psychoanalytical process (Kahr, 2000). Indeed, Kubie served as a consultant to the project, thus guaranteeing psychoanalytical authenticity. The collaboration between psychoanalyst and patient proved very rich, so much so that Hart dedicated the script to "L.S.K." (Hart, 1941, p. [v]) – the initials of Lawrence S. Kubie. And Dr. Kubie, in turn, wrote a full eight-page "Preface" under the pseudonym of the psychoanalyst in the piece "Dr. Brooks" (1941).

This Broadway show, which starred the internationally noted actress Gertrude Lawrence in the role of "Liza Elliott" – a woman who becomes cured successfully of her neurotic indecision – ignited a huge public interest in Freudianism (Bach, 2001; Brown, 2006; mcclung, 2007[1]), so much so that Paramount Pictures purchased the film rights to this Broadway musical and, in 1944, released a cinematic version of *Lady in the Dark* starring Ginger Rogers. Thus, through both a stage musical and a film, psychoanalysis acquired a much higher public profile than from any clinical publications or conference papers.

During the 1940s and beyond, several psychoanalysts collaborated closely with Hollywood even more directly. Indeed, when David O. Selznick commissioned Alfred Hitchcock to direct a big-budget thriller film, *Spellbound*, starring Ingrid Bergman and Gregory Peck – set in a private psychiatric clinic – he also engaged the services of his own personal psychoanalyst, Dr. May Romm, as psychiatric adviser to the film (Leff, 1987). Although a consummate filmmaker such as Hitchcock already knew a great deal about psychological depth, his collaboration with Romm helped to foreground the notion of the unconscious; and throughout the course of *Spellbound*, released in 1945, viewers will have had the opportunity to enjoy a dream sequence designed by none other than Salvador Dalí, and to learn of the horrific childhood trauma which propelled the character of "John Ballantyne" (portrayed by Gregory Peck) to develop a crippling dissociative amnesia. Romm repeated her role as consultant (Farber and Green, 1993), albeit this time in an uncredited capacity, to another mainstream Hollywood film, *The Dark Mirror*, released the following year, in 1946, in which Olivia de Havilland starred as a pair of twins – one sweet and one psychopathic – alongside Lew Ayres, who played the role of a psychologist and twin specialist who, using word association tests and Rorschach inkblots, actually managed to figure out which twin had committed murder.

In similar vein, another psychoanalyst, Dr. Robert Lindner, formerly a forensic psychologist, wrote a best-selling book entitled *Rebel Without a Cause ...: The Hypnoanalysis of a Criminal Psychopath*, published in 1944, which served as the basis for another Hollywood blockbuster, the eponymous *Rebel Without a Cause*, released in 1955, starring the popular, though short-lived, actor James Dean. A superb writer for the general public, Lindner (1955) reached wide audiences, notably, through his hugely popular book of case histories, also released in 1955, entitled *The Fifty-Minute Hour: A Collection of True Psychoanalytic Tales*. Lindner's work proved so successful that the celebrated American television programme *Playhouse 90* – a fixture in the late 1950s – dramatised one of his chapters, "The Jet-Propelled Couch", starring the actors Donald O'Connor and Peter Lorre. The television version of *The Jet-Propelled Couch* aired on 14th November, 1957; and in the wake of its transmission, Broadway songwriter Stephen Sondheim, best known then as the lyricist of the smash hit production *West Side Story*, attempted to adapt Lindner's work into a Broadway musical in 1958, albeit without success (Secrest, 1998).

Although the American psychoanalysts engaged with the media in a far more enthusiastic manner than their British counterparts, several London-based psychoanalysts did, from time to time, cooperate. The British Psycho-Analytical Society sponsored a Public Lecture Sub-Committee (later restyled as the Public Lecture Committee) during the 1930s, which hosted talks for a general audience on such topics as "Family Problems" (e.g., Glover, 1935). And one of its committee members, Dr. Adrian Stephen – the younger brother of Virginia Woolf – broadcast on radio from time to time on such topics as "Normal and Abnormal Personalities" (Berenson, 1934; cf. MacGibbon, 1997).

Mrs. Susan Isaacs (later Dr. Susan Isaacs) hosted a column, pseudonymously, as "Ursula Wise" in the publication *The Nursery World*, between 1929 and 1936, answering readers' letters about parenting and child-care (Isaacs, 1948; Gardner, 1969). Isaacs (1939) also wrote frequently for the monthly magazine *Home and School*, addressing such topics as "Security for Young Children".

In 1939 and 1940, Dr. Ernst Kris, a Viennese-born émigré to war-torn London even worked for the British Broadcasting Corporation Monitoring Service, utilising his fluent knowledge of the German language and his psychoanalytical skills to decipher Nazi radio propaganda broadcasts (Kris, et al., 1944).

Dr. John Rickman (1935), one of the most creative and productive of the first generation of psychoanalysts in London, appeared occasionally as a radio commentator on the British Broadcasting Corporation, discussing psychological matters. In 1932, he became the Convenor of the Public Lecture Sub-Committee (*Institute Board Minutes: 16.1.1925 to 30.4.1945*, 1925–1945); and with some pride, Rickman reported to his psychoanalytical colleagues on 27th February, 1933, that he had arranged for the circulation of some 1,000 copies of the flyers for the British Psycho-Analytical Society's public lecture series; nevertheless, in spite of this effort, the lectures barely recouped their expenses (*Institute Board Meetings: 16.1.1925 to 30.4.1945*, 1925–1945). An enthusiast for working with the media, if not especially proficient in doing so, Rickman certainly encouraged his own students to speak loudly. When Miss Pearl King (2001), while still a trainee at the Institute of Psycho-Analysis, had to deliver a paper, Rickman told her that she must visualise a barrier across the lecture room, and that she should project her voice over that barrier so people at the back could hear her properly.

The founder of the British Psycho-Analytical Society, Dr. Ernest Jones, also worked with the media, appearing several times on the radio and, also, on one famous occasion, providing a consultation to the distinguished actor Laurence Olivier. In preparation for his starring role as "Hamlet" in the 1937 production of William Shakespeare's play at London's Old Vic theatre, Olivier visited Jones, along with the actress Peggy Ashcroft and the director Tyrone Guthrie, to discuss the deeper psychology of the protagonist. Jones (1910, 1911), who had already written extensively about this *opus classicus*, pontificated about the psychodynamics of the Danish prince; and as Olivier (1982, p. 79) recalled, "I have never ceased to think about Hamlet at odd moments, and ever since that meeting I have believed that Hamlet was a prime sufferer from the Oedipus complex – quite unconsciously, of course, as the professor was anxious to stress."

When the Old Vic hosted a follow-on production of *Othello* in 1938, starring Laurence Olivier as "Iago" and Ralph Richardson as "Othello", both Olivier and Guthrie drew further inspiration from Jones, who spoke to them about the play: "Tony Guthrie and I were swept away by Professor Jones's contention that Iago was subconsciously in love with Othello and had to destroy him. Unfortunately there was not the slightest chance of Ralph entertaining this idea. I was however, determined upon my wicked intentions, in cahoots with Tony; we constantly watched for occasions when our diagnosis might be made apparent to the discriminating among an audience, though I must say I have never yet discovered any means of divulging something that is definitely *subconscious* to any audience, no matter how discerning they may be. In a reckless moment during rehearsals I threw my arms round Ralph and kissed him full on the lips. He coolly disengaged himself from my embrace, patted me gently on the back of the neck and, more in sorrow than in anger, murmured, 'There, there now; dear boy; *good* boy....'" (Olivier, 1982, p. 82).

In spite of these valiant early efforts to penetrate popular culture, the first generation of British psychoanalysts failed spectacularly. The British Broadcasting

Corporation dropped John Rickman (1935) from its list of contributors because they found his speaking voice to be quite "unsuitable"; and worse still, the B.B.C. placed Ernest Jones (1932, p. 694) "on a black list as a morally dangerous person" (cf. Jones, 1957; Maddox, 2006).

But of all the psychoanalysts – whether Austrian, German, American, or British – who experimented with public communication, none achieved quite as much of an impact as the English paediatrician, child psychiatrist, and psycho-analyst, Dr. Donald Woods Winnicott, who, as a radio broadcaster (Winnicott, 1945a, 1949a), as a writer of popular books and magazine articles and reviews (e.g., Winnicott, 1941, 1942, 1945c, 1950, 1954, 1957a, 1957b, 1963, 1964, 1965a, 1965b, 1967a, 1967b), and as one of the first psychoanalysts in history to appear on television (Taylor, 1956; Britton, 1968), made a massive contribution to the public dissemination of psychoanalysis. Although I cannot do justice to the enormity of Winnicott's media work in this context – having done so elsewhere (e.g., Kahr, 2015, 2018, 2023a) – we can, nevertheless, mention a few highlights.

Winnicott advocated the sharing of psychological knowledge with the widest possible audience. As he wrote, back in 1955, in an unpublished letter to Miss Nancy Russ, the Assistant Secretary of the Bollingen Foundation in New York City, New York, "I consider that there is a very strong need at the present time for a spread of the ideas that come from the various kinds of analytical work into the literature which is read by a public of thinking people who do not happen to be involved in therapeutics" (Winnicott, 1955).

While the B.B.C. did not relish the sound of John Rickman's vocal timbre, the producers at Broadcasting House became increasingly enamoured by the high-pitched but slow and mellifluous tones of Winnicott, and throughout the 1940s, 1950s, and 1960s, he enjoyed the status as the preferred commentator on a range of psychological subjects. Most famously, his wartime radio broadcasts brought great comfort to listeners, especially in view of his emphasis on the strengths of ordinary mothers. Indeed, during the bombings of the Second World War, a lis-tener, Mrs. Helen Trevelyan (1944), wrote to thank Winnicott, exclaiming, "At a very bleak moment I turned on the wireless + heard your voice – you can imagine how it sustained me!"

Miss Isa Benzie, one of the B.B.C.'s stalwart producers for the Talks Department, and one of the pioneering women in broadcasting, championed Winnicott and com-missioned his landmark radio programmes, subsequently published in pamphlet form as *The Ordinary Devoted Mother and Her Baby: Nine Broadcast Talks. (Autumn 1949)* (Winnicott, 1949a). As he reminisced years later,

> She was, of course, on the lookout for a catchphrase, but I did not know this. I told her that I had no interest whatever in trying to tell people what to do. To start with, I didn't know. But I would like to talk to mothers about the thing that they do well, and that they do well simply because each mother is devoted to the task in hand, namely the care of one infant, or perhaps twins. I said that ordin-arily this just happens, and it is the exception when a baby has to do without

being cared for at the start by a specialist. Isa Benzie picked up the clue in a matter of twenty yards, and she said: "Splendid! The Ordinary Devoted Mother." So that was that (Winnicott, 1966, pp. 3–4).

These broadcasts proved extraordinarily popular among British mothers. For instance, in 1952, a woman named Florence Bantin wrote a fan letter to Winnicott, thanking him for having provided such a helpful corrigendum to the regnant forms of child care which stipulated that one must never feed a baby at night-time; one must let the baby scream; one must never pick the baby up; and so forth. As Bantin explained, many believed, during that era, that, "Babies are very cunning, and will master you if you don't master them" (quoted in Bantin, 1952). Thus, Winnicott's more relaxed approach to the mother-baby relationship represented quite a relief.

In spite of the fact that millions of Britons welcomed Donald Winnicott into their homes, many of his conservative colleagues criticised him for ostensibly watering down the purity of psychoanalytical doctrine. As Dr. Brendan MacCarthy, sometime President of the British Psycho-Analytical Society and Director of the London Clinic of Psycho-Analysis, recalled, Winnicott would often become the subject of snide gossip and dismissal for daring to speak outside the halls of the organisation's headquarters on New Cavendish Street (Kahr, 2002; MacCarthy, 2002, 2005). But in spite of the lack of support from some of his contemporaries, Winnicott persevered undaunted, and he used his potent voice not only to educate grateful mothers about the vicissitudes of child care but, also, to attack publicly what he regarded as the vicious forms of psychiatric treatment then prevalent, namely leucotomy and electroconvulsive shock (Winnicott, 1943a, 1943b, 1943c, 1944a, 1944b, 1944c, 1945b, 1947a, 1947b, 1949b, 1949c, 1951a, 1951b, 1951c, 1954, 1956).

In this respect, Winnicott served, quite powerfully, as both a champion of psychology, and, also, as a politician of psychology, daring to promote psychodynamic concepts while criticising injustice as well.

As a matter of some small interest, Winnicott not only made extensive contributions to the public dissemination of psychoanalysis, but, also, he supported other writers and media personalities in their own work. In 1961, Winnicott (1961) sent an unsolicited fan letter to a young Welsh writer, Mr. Andrew Davies, congratulating him on a very engaging play, *The Carriers*, which Winnicott had heard on the radio. This letter meant a very great deal to Mr. Davies (1961), who replied immediately to thank Winnicott, and then kept this missive – the very first such fan letter that he had ever received – safe for decades thereafter (Davies, 2016). Winnicott might have smiled if he had lived long enough to know that this early encouragement of a struggling, fledgling writer made an impact and that Andrew Davies eventually became the most celebrated adapter of numerous works of literature for television, whose many impressive credits have since come to include having crafted the scripts for *House of Cards*, *Pride and Prejudice*, *Bridget Jones's Diary*, *Tipping the Velvet*, *Little Dorrit*, and *War and Peace*.

We cannot even begin to do justice to the many pioneering psychoanalytical workers who contributed to the publicisation of the profession over numerous years, and we must not forget such influential figures as the American psychoanalyst Dr. Karl Menninger, who wrote a regular column about children from 1929 until 1942 for the American magazine *Household* (Faulkner and Pruitt, 1997), and who then supplied personalised letters to readers' queries for the *Ladies' Home Journal* between 1930 and 1932 (Menninger, 1997). His family's private, eponymous psychoanalytical sanatorium, the Menninger Clinic in Topeka, Kansas, even employed a public relations expert – one Laura Knickerbocker – who wrote for *The New York Times* (Grotjahn, 1987). Such efforts helped the Menninger Clinic to become the principal centre for psychologically troubled Hollywood celebrities who then spread the word about psychoanalysis. Celebrity patients at the Menninger Clinic included the noted Hollywood star of the 1940s, Robert Walker (Farber and Green, 1993), and many others besides, such as the prominent American film personalities Dan Dailey, Jane Froman, Akim Tamiroff, and Gene Tierney (Friedman, 1990; cf. Tierney and Herskowitz, 1979). Karl Menninger's family clinic became such a go-to place that when Montgomery Clift, best remembered in this context for his portrayal of the title character in John Huston's film, *Freud: The Secret Passion*, released in 1962, began to struggle with alcoholism, his physician urged him to attend the Menninger Clinic for rehabilitation (Farber and Green, 1993).

In similar outward-reaching manner, Dr. Karen Horney delivered public lectures at the New School for Social Research in New York City, New York, on topics such as "At War with Oneself" (Willig, 1991). While in Great Britain, Dr. Ismond Rosen, a pioneering psychiatrist and psychoanalyst, lobbied hard with the media and eventually created a television series for the British Broadcasting Corporation about dreams, entitled *Fantasies of the Night*, for which he served as both writer and presenter (Kahr, 2017a).

These foundational collaborations between psychoanalysts and the public at large stand out as exceptional amid a great deal of protective conservatism among many of the post-Second World War generation of psychoanalysts who attempted to ensure that a once-reviled profession would maintain high standards of seriousness.

In many respects, Anna Freud, the inheritor of her father's mantle, typified the strong reluctance among psychoanalysts to collaborate with the media in any way. Indeed, Miss Freud perennially refused to cooperate with filmmakers. As a younger woman, Anna Freud did agree to be profiled in the Viennese newspaper *Die Stunde* [*The Hour*] which appeared in print on 3rd December, 1932 (Molnar, 1992); and in 1940, she granted an interview likewise to Ralph Ingersoll, the editor of the left-wing newspaper *PM*, on survival measures in the Freud household in London during the Blitz (Roazen, 2000). But as Miss Freud aged, she became increasingly antipathetic to the media.

Her unpublished correspondence in the Anna Freud Papers, part of the Sigmund Freud Collection in the Library of Congress in Washington, D.C., heaves with numerous serious requests for television interviews, all of which Miss Freud seems to have refused. For instance, in 1974, one Phillip R. Blake (1974), Assistant Professor in the Department of Psychiatry at the Neuro-Psychiatric Institute in the Center for the Health Sciences at the University of California at Los Angeles, approached Miss Freud about the possibility of making a serious documentary film about her contributions. He explained that he had already worked with such distinguished personalities as the paediatrician Professor Benjamin Spock and would soon be meeting with the eminent zoologist and Nobel Laureate Professor Konrad Lorenz. Anna Freud (1974) replied to Blake's letter immediately, explaining, "I am sorry to disappoint you by my answer that I am not willing to cooperate. I have been approached several times already for similar projects, all of an equally serious nature and I have turned them down over and over again", underscoring that, "Behind the refusal is probably the old dislike to appear on any kind of film" (Freud, 1974).

Several years later, in 1979, Anna Freud received a further request for a television interview of note. Her trusted American psychoanalytical colleague Professor Peter Neubauer interceded on behalf of the sober television interviewer Bill Moyers – a noted political commentator and former White House Press Secretary under President Lyndon Johnson. As Neubauer (1979) explained to Miss Freud, "Bill Moyers is the most outstanding, thoughtful television journalist with a non-commercial television station. His programs hav [*sic*] dignity and are on a high cultural and educational level". Professor Neubauer had vetted Mr. Moyers and, also, had discussed the prospect of such an interview with Miss Freud's lifelong friend Professor Marianne Kris, who had already telephoned her to discuss the project. Neubauer thought that the interview might be of particular use in terms of raising funds for Miss Freud's beloved Hampstead Child-Therapy Clinic. Unsurprisingly, Anna Freud (1979) declined, explaining, "I am sorry to say No to the idea of an interview for television, since you suggest it, and since it might have been of help for the fundraising. But even though I am willing to do a lot for the Clinic, my ability to be willing stops when it comes to publicity".

And just as her father had refused to collaborate with either Samuel Goldwyn or with Georg Wilhelm Pabst over films based on psychoanalytical ideas, so, too, did Anna Freud and, also, the entire Freud family, boycott John Huston's aforementioned biopic of Sigmund Freud, released in 1962, starring Montgomery Clift as the great Viennese physician. As Anna Freud's brother Ernst Freud (1964) wrote, in an unpublished letter to their American cousin, Edward L. Bernays, that he and his relatives refused to watch the movie, "As far as I know no member of the family felt inclined".

Although one must respect a family's prerogative to avoid watching a fictionalised version of their father's biography, such an attitude very much reflects the wider Freudian disengagement from public representations of psychoanalysis.

Anna Freud's suspicion of the media even impacted upon her very close and long-standing relationship with Mrs. Eva Rosenfeld, one of her oldest friends and colleagues and, also, a former analysand of her father's. It seems that, on one occasion, Rosenfeld delivered a very favourable address on the British Broadcasting Corporation, singing the praises of Sigmund Freud; but, in spite of the benign contents, Anna Freud became quite incensed. As Rosenfeld's son, Victor Ross (1992, p. 46), recalled, "Anna's wrath was quite disproportionate to the offense and suggests deeper apprehensions: if anecdotes today, why not letters tomorrow?" (cf. Roazen, 1995).

But Anna Freud and her father cannot be held completely responsible for the reluctance of certain psychoanalysts to collaborate with the project of public dissemination. Many others shared their suspicion of the media.

As early as 1911, Dr. Eduard Hitschmann and Herr Otto Rank (1911a, p. 201) cautioned their colleagues in the Wiener Psychoanalytische Vereinigung to exercise "zur strengsten Diskretion" – namely, "the utmost discretion" (Hitschmann and Rank, 1911b, p. 209) – when inviting guests to meetings, especially members of the press. Others, such as Dr. Judith Silberpfennig Kestenberg (1947, p. 192), objected to the potential for "'shallowness'". In view of such attitudes, it made sense to psychoanalysts of this era to collaborate with the press only very sparingly.

The early psychoanalysts had good reason to fear the media, not least with the rise of Nazism. Indeed, from the mid-1930s onwards, the members of the Wiener Psychoanalytische Vereinigung made a pact to censor any overtly public activities in order to avoid inflaming the wrath of the *Nazionalsozialisten* (Aichhorn, 1995). Nevertheless, even bad publicity proved essential for generating referrals in Freud's Vienna. Indeed, during the 1920s, the Austrian journalist Josef Bettauer published a magazine article about sexuality, recommending that those with concerns about their erotic lives should seek psychoanalytical treatment. In consequence, the Ambulatorium – the out-patient clinic run by the Wiener Psychoanalytische Vereinigung – received so many referrals that it could not accommodate them all (Sterba, 1982).

And just as Freud had to endure the experience of being misrepresented in the press (*vide supra* the story about his waiting-room full of thirty to forty patients), so, too, did many of his disciples. In 1922, Miss Barbara Low, an early British psychoanalyst, granted an interview to *Lloyd's Sunday News*, but she could certainly not have known that the article would eventually be published under the incriminating title, "Psycho-Analysis Dangers. Need for Protection Against Quacks Who Exploit Hysterical Women". In consequence, she evoked great displeasure from Dr. Ernest Jones (1922b), not least as his photograph had appeared in the newspaper alongside the article.

Other media psychoanalysts had to endure a great deal of envy from their colleagues. When, for instance, Dr. May Romm began to work for David O. Selznick and Alfred Hitchcock on the film *Spellbound*, Dr. Karl Menninger (1944a, 1944b,1944c) wrote letters of concern, worried that such a collaboration would lampoon psychoanalysis in some way (cf. Mankiewicz, 1944; Romm, 1944; Selznick, 1944). Although one might appreciate Menninger's concern for high standards, one cannot help but wonder whether this admittedly star-struck psychoanalyst experienced jealous feelings towards Romm for having landed such a rare piece of consultative work. Indeed, one can sense the excitement of this esteemed psychiatrist and psychoanalyst when, in 1937, he spoke of his pleasure in lunching at the glamorous Vendôme restaurant on Sunset Boulevard in Hollywood, California, where he had the opportunity to observe film stars "at close range" (Menninger, 1937, p. 235).

Practitioners of media psychoanalysis have needed to be brave; indeed, they have had to worry about a multitude of concerns, ranging from primitive envy, to incurring the wrath of Anna Freud, to the ravages of Nazism. Sometimes, one's promotion of psychoanalysis could even threaten one's livelihood. Circa the 1950s, Mrs. Lucy Freeman, a pioneering journalist at *The New York Times*, who championed psychoanalysis, not only by virtue of having written a best-selling memoir of her own experience on the couch, *Fight Against Fears* (Freeman, 1951), but, also, through a raft of newspaper articles on the subject (Kahr, 1999a, 1999b), had to navigate a most difficult situation. Apparently, one day, the managing editor of *The New York Times* told Mrs. Freeman that under no circumstances would she be able to write any further articles on psychoanalysis. Apparently, the editor's wife had undergone psychoanalysis, and, in consequence, she decided to divorce her husband; and so, in retaliation, this man tried to quash any public dissemination of psychoanalytical ideas (Freeman, 1986).

Having now provided an overview of the early efforts and reluctances of the pioneering psychoanalysts to forge a relationship with the press, let us now examine the current situation in greater detail. In view of the fact that psychoanalysis seems to have survived the early accusations of being a pornographic discipline developed by cocaine addicts, and in view of the fact that members of the British Royal Family have embraced the talking therapies with tremendous enthusiasm, does our profession really need to engage further with radio, television, film, newspapers, magazines, social media, and the Internet? Since we seem to have become part of the cultural furniture, perhaps mental health professionals no longer need to engage in acts of widespread public dissemination.

Of course, in spite of the huge successes which have devolved from the prescient work of transmission undertaken by Donald Winnicott and others, I would argue that now, more than ever, psychoanalysis requires the most impactful, profound, and sustained of campaigns for public engagement.

Unlike our tiny band of forefathers and foremothers who had to endure antisemitic revilements and accusations of sexual licentiousness, those of us who practise nowadays have to contend with a whole new set of difficulties, not least the fact that, due to the tremendous competition from psychopharmacology and from cognitive-behavioural interventions – each, in my estimation, an expression of an infantile desire for a magical feed at the breast – we must lobby now, more than ever, to ensure that the talking therapies, broadly defined, will enjoy a proper forum. Let us not forget that, in recent years, the oldest surviving psychotherapeutic organisation in Great Britain, namely, the British Psycho-Analytical Society (subsequently renamed as the British Psychoanalytical Society, without a hyphen) and its training body, the Institute of Psycho-Analysis (likewise dehyphenated as the Institute of Psychoanalysis), had to sell its Central London premises and move to a converted dairy in Maida Vale in West London. Likewise, three very long-standing and substantial organisations – the British Association of Psychotherapists, the Lincoln Clinic and Centre for Psychotherapy, and the London Centre for Psychotherapy – had to merge to become the British Psychotherapy Foundation, due, in large measure, to the fact that these bodies simply could not attract enough candidates to fill three separate psychoanalytical training programmes. And other organisations have begun to merge as well, including the Arbours Association and the Association for Group and Individual Psychotherapy, which amalgamated for a time as the Alliance of Psychotherapy Trainings.

Interestingly, in the immediate aftermath of Prince Harry's public comment about having undergone some type of counselling experience, the United Kingdom Council for Psychotherapy – Great Britain's largest registration body specifically for psychotherapists – issued a statement: "UKCP welcomes both the Duke of Cambridge and Prince Harry's efforts this Easter to reduce the stigma of mental illness – but says much more needs to be done to meet the mental health needs of the nation" (UKCP Welcomes Royal Mental Health Stance But Says More Needs Doing, 2017, n.p.). The organisation also quoted its Chair, Mr. Martin Pollecoff, who praised the royal efforts but decried the emphasis on the so-called "'quick fix'" (quoted in UKCP Welcomes Royal Mental Health Stance But Says More Needs Doing, 2017, n.p.), stressing that, "Unfortunately, these admirable words aren't being translated into action" (quoted in UKCP Welcomes Royal Mental Health Stance But Says More Needs Doing, 2017, n.p.).

At the present time, many senior psychoanalytical practitioners have few patients in treatment due to the proliferation of non-psychodynamically orientated mental health services. And thus, in spite of the great historical success of psychoanalysis, the discipline still struggles hugely to sustain itself and to invigorate itself for the twenty-first century.

Thankfully, the British mental health community and, of course, the general public more widely, have benefited enormously from the creative contributions of a small number of practising media psychologists who have devoted themselves to the forging of relationships with the popular press in its many forms. Few practitioners, however, have done more to foster awareness of psychological matters than Dr. Susie Orbach who, over multiple decades, has become in many respects "The People's Psychotherapist".

As a writer of books and newspaper articles, as a broadcaster on radio and television, as a consultant to theatrical and film companies, and, moreover, to cultural organisations, Orbach has made a unique lifetime contribution to the development of media psychology and media psychoanalysis. In consequence of her efforts, extremely large numbers of Britons have come to acquire a much better understanding of the psychotherapeutic process and have entered treatment as a result of Orbach's inspiration. Of course, these labours on behalf of the public dissemination of psychoanalysis represent only a fraction of Orbach's extraordinary *oeuvre*, which includes her work as a full-time clinician, supervisor, and teacher, and, also as a progenitor of projects ranging from The Women's Therapy Centre in London, to The Women's Therapy Centre Institute in New York City, to AnyBody, and so many more. She has, of course, also distinguished herself as a leading theoretician of gender, of bodies, of sexuality, and of the clinical process.

This extraordinary career has taken Orbach around the world and has provided her with the opportunity to speak to such august international organisations as the United Nations. Memorably, in 2012, she addressed the United Nations' Commission on the Status of Women about some of the horrors of bodily treatment – whether the extremities of female genital mutilation or the administration of Botox to small children – and through such public work she has managed to raise awareness not only about the nature of the psychotherapeutic process but, even more so, about the challenge of being a human who must inhabit a body and who might, therefore, require psychological support.

Susie Orbach's work in the media began, officially, in 1976, or thereabouts, not long after she and her lifelong colleague Luise Eichenbaum launched The Women's Therapy Centre in Islington, North London, in order to provide a safe and available space for females to access psychological services, many of whom could neither afford traditional psychotherapy nor feel safe in the presence of patrician practitioners. Together, these two women consented to an interview for the *Islington Gazette*, in an effort to make local residents more aware of the service that she and Eichenbaum had just initiated. In the wake of this, Orbach and Eichenbaum received an enormous number of invitations to talk to newspaper reporters, to speak on the radio, and so forth (Kahr, 2017b). And after nearly fifty years, the invitations have not stopped.

To offer only a small glimpse into the media world of Dr. Susie Orbach, it might be of interest to know that in the first quarter of 2017 alone, she appeared live on stage at the National Theatre, discussing the art of psychotherapy; she enjoyed the heaving success of the second series of her "hit" radio programme *In Therapy* for the British Broadcasting Corporation, which attracted approximately 3,000,000 listeners per each episode; and moreover, she consulted to stars of the West End production of Edward Albee's play *The Goat, or Who is Sylvia?* at the Theatre Royal Haymarket; and, furthermore, she delivered a keynote address before approximately 2,500 people at a conference hosted by the British Association for Counselling and Psychotherapy, speaking about "A Life in Therapy: Learning, Every Day"; and, not long thereafter, she offered a talk to the British Library. This list represents only a tiny portion of Orbach's tireless undertakings, all achieved only weeks after having celebrated her seventieth birthday!

Whether consulting to the World Bank or to the London Gay Men's Chorus, whether serving as a Trustee for the Freud Museum London or as a Consultant Psychotherapist to The Balint Consultancy, whether writing for *The Guardian* newspaper or whether appearing on *The Colbert Report*, Susie Orbach has found a way to bring a depth of psychological knowledge to a wider public in both a digestible and, also, an expansive manner. One would need the literary skills of a great novelist to capture the essence of Orbach's style – a deeply important ingredient in her abilities as a transmitter – but at the risk of attempting to capture this essence in mere words, I would suggest that she succeeds through her unusual combination of intelligence, erudition, warmth, and humour, as well as her ability to be provocative and to hold her ground; and, moreover, she triumphs by engaging with her interlocutors in a style which we might describe as both interesting and interested.

From an historical vantage, Orbach has found herself, in some respects, in a relatively privileged position, having entered the field during the 1970s, rather than the 1910s. Although psychotherapy could not be described as mainstream in the 1970s, she did not have to deal with accusations of being a Jewish pornographer, as Sigmund Freud and his earliest disciples will have done. But, Orbach did, nonetheless, have to fight some battles, as many still regarded psychological ideas with a certain suspicion at that time. Fortunately, Orbach has mobilised her private courage to persevere in the tradition of Winnicott and others who pioneered media psychology *avant la lettre*.

To review and examine her corpus of contributions to the public engagement of psychoanalysis would require a much longer text; therefore, in the space remaining, I wish to highlight two particular Orbachian achievements, which, I believe, deserve special recognition, both for their potency and for their cunning in terms of outreach.

The year 2016 proved to be rather a landmark one for Orbach. Not only did her classic work, *Fat is a Feminist Issue ...: The Anti-Diet Guide to Permanent Weight Loss* (Orbach, 1978), appear in a new, updated edition entitled *Fat is a Feminist Issue: Book One. The Anti-Diet Guide & Book Two. Conquering Compulsive Eating* (Orbach, 2016a), which includes an inspiring and fresh introductory essay (Orbach, 2016b), but, moreover, in this same year, she also launched the first series of her now legendary fifteen-minute radio programmes for the British Broadcasting Corporation, entitled *In Therapy*, subsequently immortalised in book form (Orbach, 2016c, 2018). Working in close partnership with the theatre director Ian Rickson, formerly artistic director of the Royal Court Theatre, Orbach facilitated imaginary psychotherapy sessions with skilled actors portraying patients, all briefed beforehand by Mr. Rickson. This genius format protected any "real" psychotherapy patients from the possibility of unwelcome public exposure; but at the same time, permitted Orbach to demonstrate her skill, her compassion, her style, and her vocalisations as a clinical practitioner before an audience of millions.

In Episode 2 of Series Two, broadcast in 2017, Orbach facilitated a session with an actor portraying a late-fifty-something-year-old advertising executive called "Charles" who, *inter alia*, confessed to Orbach that he had just resumed smoking after a hiatus of ten years, in the wake of a stressful merger between his firm and a brash new media company. Charles spoke of the resurgence of his smoking symptom with some shame and, also, perhaps, some fear, not least as he explained that his father-in-law had died from a slow and dreadful battle against lung cancer. Furthermore, Charles found himself to be a hypocrite, as he had only recently lambasted his own son for smoking.

When listening to this conversation unfold, one finds oneself struck by a number of qualities, perhaps, first and foremost, Orbach's use of silence. A rare experience on chatty radio, one can actually hear the long pauses in between Charles's statements: pauses which allow Orbach time to think and which also permit Charles to digest the contents about which he has just spoken. Although psychoanalytical practitioners have deployed silence as an active intervention for more than one hundred years, Orbach has always communicated in a way which does not leave the patient hanging but, rather, allows some breathing space for both participants in this sometimes-charged conversation.

After one of these key silences, Charles then explains to Dr. Orbach that his partner, "Caroline", has not managed to offer much support over either the stressful merger or, indeed, the resurgence of the smoking, as they have not had the opportunity speak directly, not least because Caroline had begun to spend increasing amounts of time away from the family home. As Charles explains, "we don't really talk". In response, Orbach underscores the importance of what Charles has told her, realising that her patient has had very little opportunity to discharge and process the many thoughts in his head and, also, the many words forming in his mouth.

After having admitted that he feels quite "sordid" for smoking, and that he does not experience himself as properly cherished either at home or at work, Orbach provides Charles with an experience of being psychologically cherished through her understanding. She wonders aloud and expresses a concern that smoking might provide a few moments of relief for Charles, but not much more. She then reflects, "the smoking's got a lot in it", and renders an interpretation, suggesting that puffing on cigarettes has stopped Charles from thinking about the meaning of either his medically endangering symptom or of any of the other challenges in his life. Orbach never diagnoses Charles as self-destructive *per se*; her language remains far too compassionate. Instead, she explains that, in her estimation, Charles has short-changed himself!

Although Orbach does not consider herself to be a classical nineteenth-century Viennese psychoanalyst – quite the contrary – I suspect that Sigmund Freud – a consummate smoker in his own right – would have enjoyed her seminal interpretation to Charles. Dr. Orbach by no means offers the ubiquitous British transference interpretation; instead, she renders a traditional interpretation of a defensive process, arguing that by putting something *into* his mouth – namely, the cigarette – he has prevented ugly and difficult words from coming *out* of his mouth.

Had Orbach presented this case in Vienna, circa 1920, certain colleagues might well have conceptualised Charles's symptom as an unconscious blockage of his oral zone. But Orbach, in spite of her interest in the body, has had no need to mention early orality; instead, she elected to focus on why Charles has utilised this part of his body – his organ of speech – as a vehicle for cigarettes rather than for speech. In this respect, she has facilitated the age-old psychoanalytical process of the "talking cure" (quoted in Breuer, 1895, p. 23), helping to analyse a point of resistance so that the patient can begin to speak.

In a gentle, almost conversational manner – unlike the more phallic pronounce-ments of her male counterparts – Orbach explains to Charles, "You know, you could use your mouth to speak". The patient chuckles, delightedly, in recognition of what his psychotherapist has just verbalised, and then he thanks Dr. Orbach and departs.

Whether Susie Orbach would agree with me or not, I do not know, but I would argue that she has succeeded, quite brilliantly, in offering a classical psychoana-lytical insight of symbolic depth in a very light-handed and accessible manner. In many respects, this stylism epitomises how she collaborates with the media, providing something very engaging and absorbable while also undertaking all the heavy lifting at the very same time.

In her work on *In Therapy* – only one manifestation of her broader contribution to world mental health – Susie Orbach has not only promoted psychological ideas but she has also rendered them extremely interesting. One cannot help but listen to the recordings of her radio programmes with rapt attention.

Not only has Orbach mastered the complex art of being both accessible and pro-found *à la fois*, she has also succeeded in solving a crucial difficulty that has foxed clinicians for decades. In fact, I believe that she has found a very high-integrity answer to a very disturbing ethical question, namely, that of confidentiality.

For decades, classical psychoanalysts have navigated the subject of confidenti-ality by breaking it. In a previous study (Kahr, 1995; cf. Kahr, 2024), I underscored that virtually every single one of the founders of psychoanalysis, from Sigmund Freud onwards, had engaged in gross betrayals of privacy through sheer gossip (cf. Kahr, 2023b, 2023c). For instance, in 1935, Freud (1935, p. 343) wrote at some length about his psychoanalytical session with the famous composer Gustav Mahler, blabbing to Dr. Theodor Reik that Mahler suffered from a "Mutterbindung", namely, a "mother complex". In similar fashion, Freud's disciple, Dr. Ernest Jones (1922a, p. 454), betrayed the confidentiality of his one-time analysand, the medical psychologist Dr. William Brown, when he wrote to Freud, "I know him well as a scoundrel with a thoroughly bad character". One could of course provide hundreds more examples.

Orbach herself knows a great deal about the human propensity to gossip, having become the subject of gossip herself, in view of her status as a publicly recognised personality. Indeed, back in 1994, she even wrote a column on this very subject, entitled "Why Tongues are A-Wagging" for *The Guardian Weekend* (Orbach, 1994).

In private conversation, and no doubt in public as well, Orbach has often reflected that, "Psychotherapy is not a spectator sport", and that what occurs in the consult-ing room must remain intensely private.

In view of this vital recognition, how then do we as psychotherapists talk about our work? How do we publicise our profession? How do we engage the general public … especially when the contents of what we experience in our offices must go with us to our graves?

Through two path-breaking books, Susie Orbach has, I would argue, solved the confidentiality problem in a most creative manner. In 1999, she published a landmark volume entitled *The Impossibility of Sex* (Orbach, 1999), in which she presented a series of rich, well-written, detailed, and compelling case histories of patients whom one can describe neither as "real" nor, strictly speaking, as "fictional". Forging a new methodology entirely, Orbach created imaginary characters based on her experiences in the consulting room, and then, having brought these personalities to life in her mind, she invited them to undergo psychotherapy with her and, soon thereafter, wrote up the substance of these creative conversations. Indeed, she presented herself as a character as well – a psychotherapist known as "Susie".

In other words, Orbach did not take a "real" patient and disguise the name by turning "John Smith" into "Mr. A.", or "Jane Doe" into "Mrs. B.". Rather, she conjured up many new personalities entirely, and then embodied the role of both doctor *and* patient, hence, creating what that patient might have said and, also, what *she* might have said. In doing so, Orbach succeeded, quite brilliantly, in my estimation, in providing a very full portrait of what actually transpires in the psychotherapeutic encounter, without jeopardising the privacy or the identity of any one particular person.

Orbach shared not only the verbal interpretations that she would make to these fictional-factional patients but, also, quite compellingly, she shared her silences. For instance, in the breathtakingly memorable chapter regarding "Adam", entitled "The Vampire Casanova", about a compulsive womaniser, Orbach (1999, p. 22) even introduced us to the notion of "silent interpretations", demonstrating for her general readership the ways in which the psychoanalyst formulates thoughts and ideas which remain confined to the analyst's own head. The practitioner does not rush to share these interpretations with the patient but, rather, digests them, and offers some sense of them to the patient in verbal form only if, and when, that might be deemed helpful.

In her radio programmes of 2016 and 2017, and in the book versions which appeared in print thereafter, Orbach (2016c, 2018) has expanded upon her creative methodology first developed in *The Impossibility of Sex* in a spectacularly successful manner. But on this occasion, with the collaboration of actors and a theatrical director, Orbach has now materialised the fictional-factional cases which she presented in *The Impossibility of Sex* and has brought them to life even more vividly with her radio programmes *In Therapy*. Through the magic of radio, everyone can now hear the patient speaking; everyone can now learn from Orbach's vocalisations and from her silences; and everyone can now enjoy the opportunity to listen to Orbach offering her own "off-camera" observations about the patient afterwards. Consequently, through the technological majesty of the B.B.C. on-line services, untold numbers of people around the world may happily access these remarkable radio episodes at a moment's notice (https://www.bbc.co.uk/programmes/b07v33xy/episodes/guide; cf. https://www.bbc.co.uk/sounds/brand/b07v33xy).

With tremendous ingenuity, Susie Orbach has not only disseminated psychoanalysis to a wide public audience, through her solo-authored books (e.g., Orbach,

1999), through her co-authored books (e.g., Orbach and Eichenbaum, 1987), and through her media work, but, in having shared her work so generously, she has offered a significant taste of some of the most sensitive and sophisticated psychoanalytical conceptualisations in town. Moreover, she has done so without violating the privacy or confidentiality of those men and women whose stories will become known to us only should they decide, one day, to write memoirs entitled *My Analysis with Susie*, or, *How Susie Saved My Life.*

The history of media psychology, as we have seen, has proved a challenging one. Sigmund Freud resented many reporters, and both he and his daughter Anna Freud – the two most influential Freudians of the twentieth century – did whatever they could to protect psychoanalysis and dynamic psychology from the press. But, undaunted by this Freudian anxiety, subsequent workers have made huge strides in the popularisation of psychoanalysis, hoping that they might thereby contribute to a demystification of the talking cure.

Although psychotherapy has finally arrived – witness its embrace by the royal families of both the United Kingdom and Hollywood – one must still beware our tendency to speak in alienating jargon, which the Berlin psychoanalysts Dr. Franz Alexander and Dr. Hugo Staub (1929, p. 17) referred to, in 1929, as "abstrakte Formeln" ["abstract formula"]. Fortunately, our Winnicotts in the last century, and our Orbachs in the present century, have helped to remove the abstraction from our work and have found a magnificent way in which to serve as lucid ambassadors of the psychological.

Not everyone can manage to become a psychotherapeutic representative. Indeed, few have had the bravery to engage with the media in the way in which Orbach and some of her predecessors, such as Dr. Donald Winnicott, have done. In fact, back in 1967, that venerated clinician and pioneer of British media psychoanalysis wrote to a young psychiatrist, Dr. Robin Hughes, "I think analysts are not very good as broadcasters" (Winnicott, 1967c; cf. Kahr, 2015, 2018, 2023a). This observation – quite an accurate one – remains as true now as it did fifty years ago. Happily though, not everyone must be an ambassador or a broadcaster. Fortunately, we already have some very good ones who can speak extremely well to the general public on our behalf.

Of course, we cannot attribute all of the success of the publicisation of psychoanalysis to the psychoanalysts themselves; that would be not only far too self-congratulatory but, also, far too historically inaccurate.

The public dissemination of psychological ideas has unfolded and developed as part of a much wider and greatly richer historical movement towards the democratisation of speech and as a sequela of the growing technologisation of our communication. At least one historian has argued that Queen Victoria deserves a great deal of the credit for having become the inaugural media-savvy monarch, having granted permission, for the very first time, for her royal image to appear on photographs and engravings, on street ballads, and on magic lantern shows, to extraordinary effect. Victoria's embrace of the media coincided with the huge growth in the mass print industry across the nineteenth century (Plunkett, 2003).

Indeed, had Queen Victoria lived today, she might well have hosted a Twitter feed of her own.

On 10th March, 1876, Alexander Graham Bell spoke to his assistant Thomas Watson for the very first time on a new-fangled invention called the telephone. On 6th December, 1877, Thomas Alva Edison recorded the ditty "Mary Had a Little Lamb" on a tinfoil phonograph, becoming the first person to preserve human speech in electronic form. These two pioneering moments in the history of transmitting sound and, also, recording sound formed the basis for what would eventually become the radio (Tritton, 1991).

In 1878, Henry Edmunds, an engineer and inventor from Yorkshire, visited Edison in Menlo Park, California, and came to build the first phonograph for Great Britain (Tritton, 1991), and, in due course, Queen Victoria asked to have a recording made. But as Edmunds could not meet Her Majesty in person, one Sydney Morse went in his stead in 1888, and brought a special machine to Balmoral, in Scotland, so that Queen Victoria could make a voice recording (Tritton, 1993). Thereafter, successive generations of British royalty have followed suit, and by 7th October, 1922, His Royal Highness The Prince Edward, the Prince of Wales, became the first British royal to deliver a public radio broadcast.

But in spite of the royal embrace of radio, and in spite of the fact the even Freud delivered a token address – only seconds in length – for the B.B.C., on 7th December, 1938, merely months before his death (Freud, 1938; cf. BBC Interview: Sigmund Freud (English – 1938: London, 1938), the bulk of our profession has not responded sufficiently well to the challenge of engaging with the outside world.

When, many years ago, I worked in the Child and Family Department at the Tavistock Clinic, members of the press would occasionally telephone, asking for an expert opinion about one or other specialist psychological subject. As virtually all of the staff members spent their days in session and could not, therefore, respond to telephone calls immediately, a secretary would take a message, jot it down on a memorandum, and stick it to the bulletin board in the common room on the second floor, with a little note attached urging any member of staff with free time to telephone the journalist in question. Inevitably, most psychotherapists at the clinic never even read these tiny notices; and those who did ring back a week or two later, found, to their dismay, that the story in question had already appeared in the newspaper without any contribution from a Tavistock Clinic member of staff.

For years, our profession has tolerated, and even facilitated, a certain blindness about our public image.

In the fifteenth century, the English reformer William Tyndale prepared an English edition of the Latin Bible, so that ordinary people could, at last, come to read this holy book. However, Tyndale did so in strict defiance of the decree of Archbishop Thomas Arundel who refused to grant permission to anyone to render the Bible into the vernacular. Even as enlightened a humanitarian as Sir Thomas More dismissed Tyndale as "the captain of our English heretics" (quoted in Rupp, 1957, pp. 16–17), and, not long thereafter, Tyndale would be strangled to death and then burned near Brussels. Supposedly, he spoke as his last words: "Lord, open the King of England's eyes" (quoted in Rupp, 1957, p. 24).

Through the good offices of Susie Orbach, whom we honour, and who has come to perfect what she herself has called the "crossover conversation" (quoted in Kahr, 2017b), our eyes have at last become opened. Mental health no longer remains a subject of shame and silence. In fact, our psychological wellbeing has now become part of the public agenda, spurred, in great measure, by Orbach's contributions. We remain grateful that we have a Susie Orbach among us, to educate us and, even more so, to inspire us.

Note

1   This particular author, Mr. Bruce D. mcclung, spells his surname without a capital letter; hence, in the interests of historical accuracy, I have rendered this reference correctly as "mcclung", rather than as "McClung".

References

Aichhorn, Thomas (1995). Personal Communication to Carol Ascher. n.d. October. Cited in Carol Ascher (2003). The Force of Ideas, p. 169, n. 46. *Luzifer-Amor*, *16*, Number *32*, 150–169.

Alexander, Franz (1960). *The Western Mind in Transition: An Eyewitness Story*. New York: Random House.

Alexander, Franz, and Staub, Hugo (1929). *Der Verbrecher und seine Richter: Ein psychoanalytischer Einblick in die Welt der Paragraphen*. Vienna: Internationaler Psychoanalytischer Verlag.

Anonymous (1925). Berlin Psycho-Analytical Society: Second Quarter, 1925, p. 523. *Bulletin of the International Psycho-Analytical Association*. *International Journal of Psycho-Analysis*, *6*, 521–529.

Anonymous (1965). Comedians at a Loss: Fight for Survival on Television. *The Times*. 7th August, p. 10.

Anonymous (2019). Prince William Opens Up About Mental Health Pressures. 18th May. BBC News. British Broadcasting Corporation. [https://www.bbc.co.uk/news/uk-48317 793; Accessed on 4th December, 2020].

Aschaffenburg, Gustav (1906). Die Beziehung des sexuellen Leben zur Entstehung von Nerven- und Geisteskrankheiten. *Münchener Medizinische Wochenschrift*. 11th September, pp. 1793–1798.

Bach, Steven (2001). *Dazzler: The Life and Times of Moss Hart*. New York: Alfred A. Knopf.

Bantin, Florence (1952). Letter to Donald W. Winnicott. 16th March. PP/DWW/B/A/2. Donald Woods Winnicott Collection. Archives and Manuscripts, Rare Materials Room, Wellcome Library, Wellcome Collection, The Wellcome Building, London.

BBC Interview: Sigmund Freud (English – 1938: London) (1938). YouTube. [https://www. youtube.com/watch?v=CVu2W33hw5c; Accessed on 15th November, 2020].

Berenson, Mary (1934). Letter to Judith Berenson. 28th May. In Barbara Strachey and Jayne Samuels (Eds.). (1983). *Mary Berenson: A Self-Portrait from Her Letters and Diaries*, p. 294. London: Victor Gollancz.

Bernfeld, Siegfried (1930). "Neuer Geist" contra "Nihilismus": Die Psychologie und ihr Publikum. *Die psychoanalytische Bewegung*, *2*, 105–122.

Blake, Phillip R. (1974). Letter to Anna Freud. 4th November. Box 6. Folder 4. Anna Freud Papers. Sigmund Freud Collection. Manuscript Reading Room, Room 101, Manuscript Division, James Madison Memorial Building, Library of Congress, Washington, D.C., U.S.A.

Bloom, Deborah (2017). Prince Harry Sought Counseling to Cope with Diana's Death. CNN. [Cable News Network]. International Edition. 17th April. [http://edition.cnn.com/2017/04/17/europe/uk-prince-harry-diana-death/; Accessed on 17th April, 2017].

Bonaparte, Marie (1926). Diary Entry. 8th January. *Journal d'analyse*. Cited in Célia Bertin (1982). *La Dernière Bonaparte*, p. 259. Paris: Librairie Académique Perrin.

Borch-Jacobsen, Mikkel, and Shamdasani, Sonu (2006). *Le Dossier Freud: Enquête sur l'histoire de la psychanalyse*. Paris: Les Empêcheurs de penser en rond / Le Seuil.

Breuer, Josef (1895). Beobachtung I. Frl. Anna O … In Josef Breuer and Sigmund Freud. *Studien über Hysterie*, pp. 15–37. Vienna: Franz Deuticke.

Britton, Karl (1968). Letter to Donald W. Winnicott. 27th June. Box 7. File 1. Donald W. Winnicott Papers. Archives of Psychiatry, The Oskar Diethelm Library, The DeWitt Wallace Institute of Psychiatry: History, Policy, and the Arts, Department of Psychiatry, Joan and Sanford I. Weill Medical College, Cornell University, The New York Presbyterian Hospital, New York, New York, U.S.A.

Brown, Jared (2006). *Moss Hart: A Prince of the Theatre. A Biography in Three Acts*. New York: Back Stage Books / Watson-Guptill Publications, VNU Business Media.

Bychowski, Gustav (1948). *Dictators and Disciples: From Caesar to Stalin. A Psychoanalytic Interpretation of History*. New York: International Universities Press.

Chodorkoff, Bernard, and Baxter, Seymour (1974). "Secrets of a Soul": An Early Psychoanalytic Film Venture. *American Imago*, *31*, 319–334.

Culpin, Millais (1940). Acute War Neuroses. *The Lancet*. 13th July, pp. 53–54.

Davies, Andrew (1961). Letter to Donald W. Winnicott. 13th July. Box 3. File 1. Donald W. Winnicott Papers. Archives of Psychiatry, The Oskar Diethelm Library, The DeWitt Wallace Institute of Psychiatry: History, Policy, and the Arts, Department of Psychiatry, Joan and Sanford I. Weill Medical College, Cornell University, The New York Presbyterian Hospital, New York, New York, U.S.A.

Davies, Andrew (2016). Personal Communication to the Author. 10th December.

Dicks, Henry V. (1970). *Fifty Years of the Tavistock Clinic*. London: Routledge and Kegan Paul.

"Dr. Brooks" [Lawrence S. Kubie] (1941). Preface. In Moss Hart. *Lady in the Dark*, pp. vii–xiv. New York: Random House.

Eissler, Kurt R. (1952). *Interview with Dr. Adolph Stern: November 13, 1952*. Unpublished Transcript. Box 122. Folder 10. Sigmund Freud Papers. Sigmund Freud Collection. Manuscript Reading Room, Room 101, Manuscript Division, James Madison Memorial Building, Library of Congress, Washington, D.C., U.S.A.

Eysenck, Hans J. (1985). *Decline and Fall of the Freudian Empire*. Harmondsworth, Middlesex: Viking / Penguin Books.

Falzeder, Ernst (2012). "A Fat Wad of Dirty Pieces of Paper": Freud on America, Freud in America, Freud and America. In John Burnham (Ed.). *After Freud Left: A Century of Psychoanalysis in America*, pp. 85–109. Chicago, Illinois: University of Chicago Press.

Farber, Stephen, and Green, Marc (1993). *Hollywood on the Couch: A Candid Look at the Overheated Love Affair Between Psychiatrists and Moviemakers.* New York: William Morrow and Company.

Faulkner, Howard J., and Pruitt, Virginia D. (1997). Introduction. In Karl Menninger. *Dear Dr. Menninger: Women's Voices from the Thirties.* Howard J. Faulkner and Virginia D. Pruitt (Eds.), pp. 1–14. Columbia, Missouri: University of Missouri Press.

Ferenczi, Sándor (1911a). Letter to Sigmund Freud. 16th February. In Sigmund Freud and Sándor Ferenczi (1993). *Briefwechsel: Band I / 1. 1908–1911.* Eva Brabant, Ernst Falzeder, Patrizia Giampieri-Deutsch, and André Haynal (Eds.), pp. 354–355. Vienna: Böhlau Verlag / Böhlau Verlag Gesellschaft.

Ferenczi, Sándor (1911b). Letter to Sigmund Freud. 16th February. In Sigmund Freud and Sándor Ferenczi (1993). *The Correspondence of Sigmund Freud and Sándor Ferenczi: Volume I, 1908–1914.* Eva Brabant, Ernst Falzeder, Patrizia Giampieri-Deutsch, and André Haynal (Eds.). Peter T. Hoffer (Transl.), pp. 255–256. Cambridge, Massachusetts: Belknap Press of Harvard University Press.

Ferenczi, Sándor (1922). *Populäre Vorträge über Psychoanalyse.* Vienna: Internationaler Psychoanalytischer Verlag.

Forsyth, David (1922). *The Technique of Psycho-Analysis.* London: Kegan Paul, Trench, Trubner and Company.

Frank, Gerold (1975). *Judy.* New York: Harper and Row, Publishers.

Freeman, Lucy (1951). *Fight Against Fears.* New York: Crown Publishers.

Freeman, Lucy (Ed.). (1970). *Celebrities on the Couch: Personal Adventures of Famous People in Psychoanalysis.* Los Angeles, California: Prince / Stern / Sloan Publishers / Ravenna Books.

Freeman, Lucy (1986). Personal Communication to the Author. 24th September.

Freud, Anna (1974). Letter to Phillip R. Blake. 11th November. Box 6. Folder 4. Anna Freud Papers. Sigmund Freud Collection. Manuscript Reading Room, Room 101, Manuscript Division, James Madison Memorial Building, Library of Congress, Washington, D.C., U.S.A.

Freud, Anna (1979). Letter to Peter B. Neubauer. 2nd July. Box 76. Folder 4. Anna Freud Papers. Sigmund Freud Collection. Manuscript Reading Room, Room 101, Manuscript Division, James Madison Memorial Building, Library of Congress, Washington, D.C., U.S.A.

Freud, Ernst L. (1964). Letter to Edward Bernays. 15th January. Box III:1. Edward L. Bernays Papers. Manuscript Reading Room, Room 101, Manuscript Division, James Madison Memorial Building, Library of Congress, Washington, D.C., U.S.A.

Freud, Martin (1957). *Glory Reflected: Sigmund Freud – Man and Father.* London: Angus and Robertson.

Freud, Sigmund (1875a). Letter to Eduard Silberstein. 9th September. In Sigmund Freud (1989). *Jugendbriefe an Eduard Silberstein: 1871–1881.* Walter Boehlich (Ed.), pp. 142–145. Frankfurt am Main: S. Fischer / S. Fischer Verlag.

Freud, Sigmund (1875b). Letter to Eduard Silberstein. 9th September. In Sigmund Freud (1990). *The Letters of Sigmund Freud to Eduard Silberstein: 1871–1881.* Walter Boehlich (Ed.). Arnold J. Pomerans (Transl.), pp. 125–128. Cambridge, Massachusetts: Belknap Press of Harvard University Press.

Freud, Sigmund (1900). *Die Traumdeutung.* Vienna: Franz Deuticke.

Freud, Sigmund (1910a). Letter to Sándor Ferenczi. 17th March. In Sigmund Freud and Sándor Ferenczi (1993). *Briefwechsel: Band I / 1. 1908–1911.* Eva Brabant, Ernst

Falzeder, Patrizia Giampieri-Deutsch, and André Haynal (Eds.), p. 231. Vienna: Böhlau Verlag / Böhlau Verlag Gesellschaft.

Freud, Sigmund (1910b). Letter to Sándor Ferenczi. 17th March. In Sigmund Freud and Sándor Ferenczi (1993). *The Correspondence of Sigmund Freud and Sándor Ferenczi: Volume I, 1908–1914.* Eva Brabant, Ernst Falzeder, Patrizia Giampieri-Deutsch, and André Haynal (Eds.). Peter T. Hoffer (Transl.), p. 152. Cambridge, Massachusetts: Belknap Press of Harvard University Press.

Freud, Sigmund (1915). Letter to Sándor Ferenczi. 23rd April. In Sigmund Freud and Sándor Ferenczi (1996). *Briefwechsel: Band II / 1. 1914–1916.* Ernst Falzeder, Eva Brabant, and Patrizia Giampieri-Deutsch (Eds.), pp. 119–120. Vienna: Böhlau Verlag / Böhlau Verlag Gesellschaft.

Freud, Sigmund (1921). Letter to Ernest Jones. 12th April. In Sigmund Freud and Ernest Jones (1993). *The Complete Correspondence of Sigmund Freud and Ernest Jones: 1908–1939.* R. Andrew Paskauskas (Ed.). Frauke Voss (Transl.), pp. 418–419. Cambridge, Massachusetts: Belknap Press of Harvard University Press.

Freud, Sigmund (1924a). Letter to George Seldes. 29th June. In George Seldes (1953). *Tell the Truth and Run*, p. 107. New York: Greenberg: Publisher.

Freud, Sigmund (1924b). Letter to George Seldes. 29th June. In Ernest Jones (1957). *The Life and Work of Sigmund Freud: Volume 3. The Last Phase. 1919–1939*, p. 103. New York: Basic Books.

Freud, Sigmund (1925a). Letter to Sándor Ferenczi. 14th August. In Sigmund Freud and Sándor Ferenczi (2003). *Briefwechsel: Band III / 2. 1925 bis 1933.* Ernst Falzeder, Eva Brabant, Patrizia Giampieri-Deutsch, and André Haynal (Eds.), pp. 48–50. Vienna: Böhlau Verlag / Böhlau Verlag Gesellschaft.

Freud, Sigmund (1925b). Letter to Ernst Simmel. 26th October, p. 99. In Frances Deri and David Brunswick (1964). Freud's Letters to Ernst Simmel. Frances Deri and David Brunswick (Transls.). *Journal of the American Psychoanalytic Association*, *12*, 93–109.

Freud, Sigmund (1925c). Letter to Ernest Jones. 21st December. In Sigmund Freud and Ernest Jones (1993). *Briefwechsel: Sigmund Freud. Ernest Jones. 1908–1939. Originalwortlaut der in Deutsch verfaßten Briefe Freuds.* Ingeborg Meyer-Palmedo (Ed.), pp. 40–41. Frankfurt am Main: S. Fischer / S. Fischer Verlag.

Freud, Sigmund (1935). Letter to Theodor Reik. 4th January. In Theodor Reik (1953). *The Haunting Melody: Psychoanalytic Experiences in Life and Music*, pp. 342–343. New York: Farrar, Straus and Young.

Freud, Sigmund (1938). Diary Entry. 7th December. In Sigmund Freud (1992). *The Diary of Sigmund Freud: 1929–1939. A Record of the Final Decade.* Michael Molnar (Ed. and Transl.), p. 38. New York: Charles Scribner's Sons, and Toronto: Maxwell Macmillan Canada, and New York: Maxwell Macmillan International, and New York: Charles Scribner's Sons / Macmillan Publishing Company, Maxwell Communication Group of Companies, and Don Mills, Ontario: Maxwell Macmillan Canada.

Friedman, Lawrence J. (1990). *Menninger: The Family and the Clinic.* New York: Alfred A. Knopf.

Gardner, Dorothy E.M. (1969). *Susan Isaacs.* London: Methuen Educational.

Glover, Edward (1935). Institute of Psycho-Analysis, London: Annual Report, 1933–34, pp. 254–256. In Edward Glover (Ed.). *Bulletin of the International Psycho-Analytical Association. International Journal of Psycho-Analysis*, *16*, 242–262.

Graf, Max (1942). Reminiscences of Professor Sigmund Freud. Gregory Zilboorg (Transl.). *Psychoanalytic Quarterly*, *11*, 465–476.

Grinker, Roy R., Sr. (1979). *Fifty Years in Psychiatry: A Living History*. Springfield, Illinois: Charles C Thomas, Publisher.

Grinker, Roy, Sr. (1985). A Memoir of My Psychoanalytic Education. Jay Martin (Ed.). *Psychoanalytic Education*, *4*, 3–12.

Grotjahn, Martin (1987). *My Favorite Patient: The Memoirs of a Psychoanalyst*. Frankfurt am Main: Verlag Peter Lang.

Hale, Nathan G., Jr. (1995). *The Rise and Crisis of Psychoanalysis in the United States: Freud and the Americans, 1917–1985*. New York: Oxford University Press.

Hart, Moss (1941). *Lady in the Dark*. New York: Random House.

Hitschmann, Eduard, and Rank, Otto (1911a). Vorschläge zur Regelung des Gästewesens: Erstattet vom Obmannstellvertreter und Schriftführer, p. 201. In Otto Rank (Ed.). Vortragsabend: Am 29. März 1911. In Herman Nunberg and Ernst Federn (Eds.). (1979). *Protokolle der Wiener Psychoanalytischen Vereinigung: Band III. 1910–1911*, pp. 200–208. Frankfurt am Main: S. Fischer / S. Fischer Verlag.

Hitschmann, Eduard, and Rank, Otto (1911b). *Suggestions for the Regulation of the Attendance of Guests*, p. 209. In Otto Rank (Ed.). Scientific Meeting on March 29, 1911. In Herman Nunberg and Ernst Federn (Eds.). *Minutes of the Vienna Psychoanalytic Society: Volume III: 1910–1911*. Margarethe Nunberg and Harold Collins (Transls.), pp. 208–216. New York: International Universities Press.

Institute Board Meetings: 16.1.1925 to 30.4.1945 (1925–1945). Archives of the British Psychoanalytical Society, British Psychoanalytical Society, Byron House, Maida Vale, London.

Isaacs, Susan (1939). Security for Young Children. *Home and School*, *4*, 43–45.

Isaacs, Susan (1948). *Troubles of Children and Parents*. London: Methuen and Company.

Jones, Ernest (1910). The Oedipus-Complex as an Explanation of Hamlet's Mystery: A Study in Motive. *American Journal of Psychology*, *21*, 72–113.

Jones, Ernest (1911). *Das Problem des Hamlet und der Ödipus Komplex*. Paul Tausig (Transl.). Vienna: Franz Deuticke.

Jones, Ernest (1922a). Letter to Sigmund Freud. 26th January. In Sigmund Freud and Ernest Jones (1993). *The Complete Correspondence of Sigmund Freud and Ernest Jones: 1908–1939*. R. Andrew Paskauskas (Ed.), pp. 454–457. Cambridge, Massachusetts: Belknap Press of Harvard University Press.

Jones, Ernest (1922b). Letter to Barbara Low. 12th February. CLA/F27/01A. Archives of the British Psychoanalytical Society, British Psychoanalytical Society, Byron House, Maida Vale, London. Cited in Brenda Maddox (2006). *Freud's Wizard: The Enigma of Ernest Jones*, p. 303. London: John Murray (Publishers) / Hodder Headline.

Jones, Ernest (1932). Letter to Sigmund Freud. 5th May. In Sigmund Freud and Ernest Jones (1993). *The Complete Correspondence of Sigmund Freud and Ernest Jones: 1908–1939*. R. Andrew Paskauskas (Ed.), pp. 694–695. Cambridge, Massachusetts: Belknap Press of Harvard University Press.

Jones, Ernest (1955). *The Life and Work of Sigmund Freud: Volume 2. Years of Maturity. 1901–1919*. New York: Basic Books.

Jones, Ernest (1957). *The Life and Work of Sigmund Freud: Volume 3. The Last Phase. 1919–1939*. New York: Basic Books.

Kahr, Brett (1995). Lecture on "Breaches of Confidentiality in the History of Psycho-Analysis". Conference on "Celebrating One Hundred Year of Psychoanalysis and Learning from Our Mistakes". European Society for Communicative Psychotherapy, Regent's College, Inner Circle, Regent's Park, London. 3rd June.

Kahr, Brett (1999a). The Adventures of a Psychotherapist: Lucy Freeman and Her Fight Against Fear. *Psychotherapy Review*, *1*, 199.

Kahr, Brett (1999b). The Adventures of a Psychotherapist: Lucy Freeman's Pioneering Contributions to the Study of Mental Health Journalism. *Psychotherapy Review*, *1*, 244–248.

Kahr, Brett (2000). Psychoanalysis on Stage: Moss Hart's *Lady in the Dark*. *Psychoanalytic Review*, *87*, 377–383.

Kahr, Brett (2002). Interview with Brendan MacCarthy. 24th July.

Kahr, Brett (2005a). Why Freud Turned Down $25,000: Mental Health Professionals in the Witness Box. *American Imago*, *62*, 365–371.

Kahr, Brett (2005b). Why Freud Turned Down $25,000.00: Mental Health Professionals in the Witness Box. All About Psychotherapy: The Online Resource for Psychotherapy. [http://www.allaboutpsychotherapy.com].

Kahr, Brett (2007). Why Freud Turned Down $25,000. In Jane Ryan (Ed.). *Tales of Psychotherapy*, pp. 5–9. London: Karnac Books.

Kahr, Brett (2009). Psychoanalysis and Sexpertise. In Christopher Clulow (Ed.). *Sex, Attachment, and Couple Psychotherapy: Psychoanalytic Perspectives*, pp. 1–23. London: Karnac Books.

Kahr, Brett (2011). Dr Paul Weston and the Bloodstained Couch. *International Journal of Psychoanalysis*, *92*, 1051–1058.

Kahr, Brett (2012). Le Divan taché de sang du Dr Paul Weston. Marcel Hudon (Transl.). In Louis Brunet, Jean-Michel Quinodoz, Pierre Dajez, Danielle Goldstein, François Gross, Florence Guignard, Céline Gür, Marcel Hudon, Luc Magnenat, Diana Messina Pizzuti, André Renaud, Michel Sanchez-Cardenas, and Patricia Waltz (Eds.). *L'Année psychanalytique internationale: 2012. Traduction en langue française d'un choix de textes publiés en 2011 dans* The International Journal of Psychoanalysis, pp. 199–210. Paris: Éditions In Press.

Kahr, Brett (2014). Television as Rorschach: The Unconscious Use of the Cathode Nipple. In Caroline Bainbridge, Ivan Ward, and Candida Yates (Eds.). *Television and Psychoanalysis: Psycho-Cultural Perspectives*, pp. 31–46. London: Karnac Books.

Kahr, Brett (2015). Lecture on "The Roots of Mental Health Broadcasting". Afternoon Workshop on "Donald Winnicott, the Public Psychoanalyst: Broadcasting Beyond the Consulting Room". International Conference on "Donald Winnicott and the History of the Present: A Celebration of the Collected Works of D.W. Winnicott". The Winnicott Trust, London, in association with the British Psychoanalytical Society, Byron House, Maida Vale, London, and the British Psychoanalytic Association, British Psychotherapy Foundation, London, and the Association of Independent Psychoanalysts, London, at the Board Room, Mary Ward House Conference and Exhibition Centre, Holborn, London. 21st November.

Kahr, Brett (2017a). Ismond Rosen: The Renaissance Man of Psychoanalysis. Unpublished Typescript.

Kahr, Brett (2017b). Telephone Interview with Susie Orbach. 8th February.

Kahr, Brett (2018). The Public Psychoanalyst: Donald Winnicott as Broadcaster. In Angela Joyce (Ed.). *Donald W. Winnicott and the History of the Present: Understanding the Man and His Work*, pp. 111–121. London: Karnac Books.

Kahr, Brett (2021). Freud and the Royal Families of Europe: From Kaiser Franz Josef to Princess Alexandra. Blog. Freud Museum London. [https://www.freud.org.uk/2021/07/27/freud-and-the-royal-families-of-europe-from-kaiser-franz-josef-to-princess-alexandra/; Accessed on 7th April, 2024].

Kahr, Brett (2022–2023). Freud and the Royal Families of Europe: From Kaiser Franz Josef to Princess Alexandra. *Athene: Magazine 2022/23*, pp. 14–17.

Kahr, Brett (2023a). *How to Be Intimate with 15,000,000 Strangers: Musings on Media Psychoanalysis*. London: Routledge / Taylor and Francis Group, and Abingdon, Oxfordshire: Routledge / Taylor and Francis Group.

Kahr, Brett (2023b). Filing Psychoanalytical Complaints: From Verbal Assaults to the Crushing of the Larynx. In Adah Sachs and Valerie Sinason (Eds.). *The Psychotherapist and the Professional Complaint: The Shadow Side of Therapy*, pp. 71–87, 220–222. London: Karnac / Karnac Books, Confer.

Kahr, Brett (2023c). Chapter 6. In Adah Sachs and Valerie Sinason (Eds.). *The Psychotherapist and the Professional Complaint: The Shadow Side of Therapy*, pp. 220–222. London: Karnac / Karnac Books, Confer.

Kahr, Brett (2024). *Foul Whisperings and Slanderous Tongues: Breaches of Confidentiality in the History of Psychoanalysis*. [In Preparation].

Kelley, Kitty (1984). Interview with Hildi Greenson. 27th April. Cited in Kitty Kelley (1986). *His Way: The Unauthorized Biography of Frank Sinatra*, p. 527. New York: Bantam Books.

Kestenberg, Judith Silberpfennig (1947). Letter to William C. Menninger. 15th November. Menninger Archives, Center for Historical Research, Kansas State Historical Society, Topeka, Kansas, U.S.A. Cited in Rebecca Jo Plant (2005), William Menninger and American Psychoanalysis, 1946–48. *History of Psychiatry*, *16*, 181–202.

King, Pearl (2001). Personal Communication to the Author. 4th November.

Kris, Ernst; Speier, Hans; Axelrad, Sidney; Herma, Hans; Loeb, Janice; Paechter, Heinz, and White, Howard B. (1944). *German Radio Propaganda: Report on Home Broadcasting During the War*. New York: Oxford University Press.

Lawrence, David Herbert (1921). *Psychoanalysis and the Unconscious*. New York: Thomas Seltzer.

Lawrence, David Herbert (1923). *Psychoanalysis and the Unconscious*. London: Martin Secker.

Leff, Leonard J. (1987). *Hitchcock and Selznick: The Rich and Strange Collaboration of Alfred Hitchcock and David O. Selznick in Hollywood*. New York: Weidenfeld and Nicolson / Wheatland Corporation.

Lindner, Robert M. (1944). *Rebel Without a Cause …: The Hypnoanalysis of a Criminal Psychopath*. New York: Grune and Stratton.

Lindner, Robert (1955). *The Fifty-Minute Hour: A Collection of True Psychoanalytic Tales*. New York: Rinehart and Company.

MacCarthy, Brendan (2002). Personal Communication to the Author. 17th July.

MacCarthy, Brendan (2005). Personal Communication to the Author. 16th March.

MacGibbon, Jean (1997). *There's the Lighthouse: A Biography of Adrian Stephen*. London: James and James (Publishers).

MacLellan, Kylie, and Chopra, Toby (2017). Britain's Prince Harry Sought Counseling More Than a Decade After Mother's Death. Reuters. United Kingdom Edition. [http:// uk.reuters.com/article/uk-britain-royals-harry-idUKKBN17J0KL; Accessed on 17th April, 2017].

Maddox, Brenda (2006). *Freud's Wizard: The Enigma of Ernest Jones*. London: John Murray (Publishers) / Hodder Headline.

Mankiewicz, Joseph (1944). Letter to Karl A. Menninger. 13th July. In Karl A. Menninger (1988). *The Selected Correspondence of Karl A. Menninger, 1919–1945*. Howard J. Faulkner and Virginia D. Pruitt (Eds.), pp. 401–403. New Haven, Connecticut: Yale University Press.

mcclung, bruce d. (2007). *Lady in the Dark: Biography of a Musical*. New York: Oxford University Press.

Menninger, Karl A. (1937). Letter to William C. Menninger, Charles F. Menninger, and John R. Stone. 27th February. In Karl A. Menninger (1988). *The Selected Correspondence of Karl A. Menninger, 1919–1945*. Howard J. Faulkner and Virginia D. Pruitt (Eds.), pp. 235–238. New Haven, Connecticut: Yale University Press.

Menninger, Karl A. (1944a). Letter to David O. Selznick. 7th August. In Karl A. Menninger (1988). *The Selected Correspondence of Karl A. Menninger, 1919–1945*. Howard J. Faulkner and Virginia D. Pruitt (Eds.), pp. 403–404. New Haven, Connecticut: Yale University Press.

Menninger, Karl A. (1944b). Letter to Joseph Mankiewicz. 8th August. In Karl A. Menninger (1988). *The Selected Correspondence of Karl A. Menninger, 1919–1945*. Howard J. Faulkner and Virginia D. Pruitt (Eds.), pp. 404–405. New Haven, Connecticut: Yale University Press.

Menninger, Karl A. (1944c). Letter to David Selznick. 2nd October. In Karl A. Menninger (1988). *The Selected Correspondence of Karl A. Menninger, 1919–1945*. Howard J. Faulkner and Virginia D. Pruitt (Eds.), p. 408. New Haven, Connecticut: Yale University Press.

Menninger, Karl (1997). *Dear Dr. Menninger: Women's Voices from the Thirties*. Howard J. Faulkner and Virginia D. Pruitt (Eds.). Columbia, Missouri: University of Missouri Press.

Mercier, Charles (1914a). Psycho-Analysis. *British Medical Journal*. 17th January, pp. 172–173.

Mercier, Charles (1914b). Psycho-Analysis. *British Medical Journal*. 31st January, p. 276.

Mercier, Charles (1916). Psycho-Analysis. *British Medical Journal*. 30th December, pp. 897–900.

Molnar, Michael (1992). 1932. In Sigmund Freud. *The Diary of Sigmund Freud: 1929–1939. A Record of the Final Decade*. Michael Molnar (Ed. and Transl.), pp. 117–137. New York: Charles Scribner's Sons, and Toronto: Maxwell Macmillan Canada, and New York: Maxwell Macmillan International, and New York: Charles Scribner's Sons / Macmillan Publishing Company, Maxwell Communication Group of Companies, and Don Mills, Ontario: Maxwell Macmillan Canada.

Morton, Andrew (1992). *Diana: Her True Story*. London: Michael O'Mara Books.

Neubauer, Peter B. (1979). Letter to Anna Freud. 15th June. Box 76. Folder 4. Anna Freud Papers. Sigmund Freud Collection. Manuscript Reading Room, Room 101, Manuscript Division, James Madison Memorial Building, Library of Congress, Washington, D.C., U.S.A.

Olivier, Laurence (1982). *Confessions of an Actor*. London: George Weidenfeld and Nicolson.

Orbach, Susie (1978). *Fat is a Feminist Issue ...: The Anti-Diet Guide to Permanent Weight Loss*. London: Paddington Press.

Orbach, Susie (1994). Why Tongues are A-Wagging. *The Guardian Weekend*. 19th February, p. 44.

Orbach, Susie (1999). *The Impossibility of Sex*. London: Allen Lane / Penguin Press, Penguin Books, Penguin Group.

Orbach, Susie (2016a). *Fat is a Feminist Issue: Book One. The Anti-Diet Guide & Book Two. Conquering Compulsive Eating*. London: Arrow Books / Penguin Random House, Penguin Random House UK.

Orbach, Susie (2016b). FIFI Today. In *Fat is a Feminist Issue: Book One. The Anti-Diet Guide & Book Two. Conquering Compulsive Eating*, pp. v–xxviii. London: Arrow Books / Penguin Random House, Penguin Random House UK.

Orbach, Susie (2016c). *In Therapy: How Conversations with Psychotherapists Really Work*. London: Profile Books.

Orbach, Susie (2018). *In Therapy: The Unfolding Story*. London: Profile Books / Wellcome Collection.

Orbach, Susie, and Eichenbaum, Luise (1987). *Bittersweet: Facing Up to Feelings of Love, Envy and Competition in Women's Friendships*. London: Century / Century Hutchinson.

Plunkett, John (2003). *Queen Victoria: First Media Monarch*. Oxford: Oxford University Press.

Prince Harry Joins Veterans' Mental Health Conference (2017). Institute of Psychiatry, Psychology and Neuroscience, King's College London. [https://www.kcl.ac.uk/ioppn/news/records/2017/March/Prince-Harry-joins-Veterans-Mental-Health-Conference.aspx; Accessed on 18th March, 2017].

Prince Harry on Diana Grief (2017). BBC News. British Broadcasting Corporation. [http://www.bbc.co.uk/news/uk-39619684; Accessed on 17th April, 2017].

Radó, Sándor (1926). Berlin Psycho-Analytical Society: First Quarter, 1926, pp. 531–532. *Bulletin of the International Psycho-Analytical Association. International Journal of Psycho-Analysis*, *7*, 531–537.

Rank, Otto (Ed.). (1910a). Vortragsabend: Am 6. April 1910. In Herman Nunberg and Ernst Federn (Eds.). (1976). *Protokolle der Wiener Psychoanalytischen Vereinigung: Band I. 1906–1908*, pp. 422–430. Frankfurt am Main: S. Fischer / S. Fischer Verlag.

Rank, Otto (Ed.). (1910b). Scientific Meeting on April 6, 1910. In Herman Nunberg and Ernst Federn (Eds.). (1967). *Minutes of the Vienna Psychoanalytic Society: Volume II: 1908–1910*. Margarethe Nunberg (Transl.), pp. 463–471. New York: International Universities Press.

Rank Otto (Ed.). (1910c). Vortragsabend: Am 13. April 1910. In Herman Nunberg and Ernst Federn (Eds.). (1976). *Protokolle der Wiener Psychoanalytischen Vereinigung: Band I. 1906–1908*, pp. 431–441. Frankfurt am Main: S. Fischer / S. Fischer Verlag.

Rapp, Dean (1988). The Reception of Freud by the British Press: General Interest and Literary Magazines, 1920–1925. *Journal of the History of the Behavioral Sciences*, *24*, 191–201.

Rapp, Dean (1990). The Early Discovery of Freud by the British General Educated Public, 1912–1919. *Social History of Medicine*, *3*, 217–243.

Rickman, John (1935). Letter to Roger Money-Kyrle. 26th June. PP/RMK/C.1. Roger Ernle Money-Kyrle (1898–1980), psychoanalyst Collection. Archives and Manuscripts, Rare

Materials Room, Wellcome Library, Wellcome Collection, The Wellcome Building, London.

Ries, Paul (1995). Popularise and / or Be Damned: Psychoanalysis and Film at the Crossroads in 1925. *International Journal of Psycho-Analysis, 76*, 759–791.

Roazen, Paul (1995). *How Freud Worked: First-Hand Accounts of Patients*. Northvale, New Jersey: Jason Aronson.

Roazen, Paul (2000). The Correspondence of Edward Glover and Lawrence S. Kubie. *Psychoanalysis and History, 2*, 162–188.

Romm, May (1944). Letter to Karl A. Menninger. 25th September. In Karl A. Menninger (1988). *The Selected Correspondence of Karl A. Menninger, 1919–1945*. Howard J. Faulkner and Virginia D. Pruitt (Eds.), pp. 407–408. New Haven, Connecticut: Yale University Press.

Romm, Sharon (1983). *The Unwelcome Intruder: Freud's Struggle with Cancer*. New York: Praeger Publishers / CBS Educational and Professional Publishing, Division of CBS / Praeger Special Studies / Praeger Scientific.

Ross, Victor (1992). Eva Marie Rosenfeld (1892–1977): A Woman of Valor. A Personal Memoir (with Illustrations). In Peter Heller (Ed). *Anna Freud's Letters to Eva Rosenfeld*. Mary Weigand (Transl.). pp. 23–48. Madison, Connecticut: International Universities Press.

Rupp, Gordon (1957). *Six Makers of English Religion: 1500–1700*. London: Hodder and Stoughton.

Sachs, Hanns (1944). *Freud: Master and Friend*. Cambridge, Massachusetts: Harvard University Press.

Secrest, Meryle (1998). *Stephen Sondheim: A Life*. New York: Alfred A. Knopf.

Seldes, George (1953). *Tell the Truth and Run*. New York: Greenberg: Publisher.

Selznick, David (1944). Letter to Karl A. Menninger. 22nd September. In Karl A. Menninger (1988). *The Selected Correspondence of Karl A. Menninger, 1919–1945*. Howard J. Faulkner and Virginia D. Pruitt (Eds.), pp. 405–407. New Haven, Connecticut: Yale University Press.

Spoto, Donald (1993). *Marilyn Monroe: The Biography*. New York: HarperCollins Publishers.

Stelzer, Dick (1977). *The Star Treatment*. Indianapolis, Indiana: Bobbs-Merrill Company.

Sterba, Richard F. (1982). *Reminiscences of a Viennese Psychoanalyst*. Detroit, Michigan: Wayne State University Press.

Stoddart, William H.B. (1940). Sigmund Freud. *Journal of Mental Science, 86*, 190–192.

Taylor, John Cranes (1956). Letter to Donald W. Winnicott. 30th October. PP/DWW/B/D/7. Donald Woods Winnicott Collection. Archives and Manuscripts, Rare Materials Room, Wellcome Library, Wellcome Collection, The Wellcome Building, London.

Thomson, David G. (1917a). Psycho-Analysis. *British Medical Journal*. 6th January, pp. 32–33.

Thomson, David G. (1917b). Psycho-Analysis. *British Medical Journal*. 27th January, p. 138.

Thornton, Elizabeth M. (1983). *Freud and Cocaine: The Freudian Fallacy*. London: Blond and Briggs.

Tierney, Gene, and Herskowitz, Mickey (1979). *Self-Portrait*. New York: Wyden Books / Simon and Schuster, Gulf and Western Corporation.

Torrey, E. Fuller (1992). *Freudian Fraud: The Malignant Effect of Freud's Theory on American Thought and Culture*. New York: HarperCollins Publishers.

Trevelyan, Helen (1944). Letter to Donald W. Winnicott. 16th December. PP/DWW/B/A/29. Donald Woods Winnicott Collection. Archives and Manuscripts, Rare Materials Room, Wellcome Library, Wellcome Collection, The Wellcome Building, London.

Tritton, Paul (1991). *The Lost Voice of Queen Victoria: The Search for the First Royal Recording*. London: Academy Books.

Tritton, Paul (1993). *The Godfather of Rolls-Royce: The Life and Times of Henry Edmunds, M.I.C.E., M.I.E.E., Science and Technology's Forgotten Pioneer*. London: Academy Books.

UKCP Welcomes Royal Mental Health Stance But Says More Needs Doing (2017). U.K.C.P. United Kingdom Council for Psychotherapy. [https://www.psychotherapy.org. uk/news/ukcp-welcomes-royal-stance-mental-health-says-needs-done/; Accessed on 21st April, 2017].

University Challenge (2016). Series 16. Episode 27. B.B.C. 2, British Broadcasting Corporation, London. London: I.T.V. Studios, for British Broadcasting Corporation. Producer: Irene Daniels. Director: David Kester. Date of Broadcast: 30th January, 2017.

Webster, Richard (1995). *Why Freud Was Wrong: Sin, Science and Psychoanalysis*. Hammersmith, London: HarperCollins Publishers.

Weiss, Edoardo (1970). My Recollections of Sigmund Freud. In Edoardo Weiss. *Sigmund Freud as a Consultant: Recollections of a Pioneer in Psychoanalysis*, pp. 1–22. New York: Intercontinental Medical Book Corporation.

Willig, Wanda (1991). My Reminiscences About Karen Horney as a Teacher and as a Person. *American Journal of Psychoanalysis*, *51*, 249–253.

Winnicott, Donald W. (1941). On Influencing and Being Influenced. *New Era in Home and School*, *22*, 118–120.

Winnicott, Donald W. (1942). Why Children Play. *New Era in Home and School*, *23*, 12–14.

Winnicott, Donald W. (1943a). Prefrontal Leucotomy. *The Lancet*. 10th April, p. 475.

Winnicott, Donald W. (1943b). Shock Treatment of Mental Disorder. *British Medical Journal*. 25th December, pp. 829–830.

Winnicott, Donald W. (1943c). Treatment of Mental Disease by Induction of Fits. In Donald W. Winnicott (1989). *Psycho-Analytic Explorations*. Clare Winnicott, Ray Shepherd, and Madeleine Davis (Eds.), pp. 516–521. London: H. Karnac (Books).

Winnicott, Donald W. (1944a). Shock Therapy. *British Medical Journal*. 12th February, pp. 234–235.

Winnicott, Donald W. (1944b). Introduction to a Symposium on the Psycho-Analytic Contribution to the Theory of Shock Therapy. In Donald W. Winnicott (1989). *Psycho-Analytic Explorations*. Clare Winnicott, Ray Shepherd, and Madeleine Davis (Eds.), pp. 525–528. London: H. Karnac (Books).

Winnicott, Donald W. (1944c). Kinds of Psychological Effect of Shock Therapy. In Donald W. Winnicott (1989). *Psycho-Analytic Explorations*. Clare Winnicott, Ray Shepherd, and Madeleine Davis (Eds.), pp. 529–533. London: H. Karnac (Books).

Winnicott, Donald W. (1945a). *Getting to Know Your Baby*. London: William Heinemann (Medical Books).

Winnicott, Donald W. (1945b). Physical Therapy in Mental Disorder. *British Medical Journal*. 22nd December, pp. 901–902.

Winnicott, Donald W. (1945c). Infant Feeding. *New Era in Home and School*, *26*, 9–10.

Winnicott, Donald W. (1947a). Physical Therapy of Mental Disorder. *British Medical Journal*. 17th May, pp. 688–689.

Winnicott, Donald W. (1947b). Battle Neurosis Treated with Leucotomy. *British Medical Journal*. 13th December, p. 974.

Winnicott, Donald W. (1949a). *The Ordinary Devoted Mother and Her Baby: Nine Broadcast Talks. (Autumn 1949)*. London: C.A. Brock and Company.

Winnicott, Donald W. (1949b). Hate in the Counter-Transference. *International Journal of Psycho-Analysis*, *30*, 69–74.

Winnicott, Donald W. (1949c). Leucotomy. *British Medical Students' Journal*, *3*, Number 2, 35–38.

Winnicott, Donald W. (1950). Neglected Children. *The Times*. 31st January, p. 5.

Winnicott, Donald W. (1951a). Leucotomy in Psychosomatic Disorders. *The Lancet*. 18th August, pp. 314–315.

Winnicott, Donald W. (1951b). Ethics of Prefrontal Leucotomy. *British Medical Journal*. 25th August, pp. 496–497.

Winnicott, Donald W. (1951c). Notes on the General Implications of Leucotomy. In Donald W. Winnicott (1989). *Psycho-Analytic Explorations*. Clare Winnicott, Ray Shepherd, and Madeleine Davis (Eds.), pp. 548–552. London: H. Karnac (Books).

Winnicott, Donald W. (1954). A Psychiatrist's Choice. *The Spectator*. 12th February, p. 175.

Winnicott, Donald W. (1955). Letter to Nancy Russ. 9th September. PP/DWW/B/A/34. Donald Woods Winnicott Collection. Archives and Manuscripts, Rare Materials Room, Wellcome Library, Wellcome Collection, The Wellcome Building, London.

Winnicott, Donald W. (1956). Prefrontal Leucotomy. *British Medical Journal*. 28th January, pp. 229–230.

Winnicott, Donald W. (1957a). *The Child and the Family: First Relationships*. Janet Hardenberg (Ed.). London: Tavistock Publications.

Winnicott, Donald W. (1957b). *The Child and the Outside World: Studies in Developing Relationships*. Janet Hardenberg (Ed.). London: Tavistock Publications.

Winnicott, Donald W. (1961). Letter to Andrew Davies. 11th July. Box 3. File 1. Donald W. Winnicott Papers. Archives of Psychiatry, The Oskar Diethelm Library, The DeWitt Wallace Institute of Psychiatry: History, Policy, and the Arts, Department of Psychiatry, Joan and Sanford I. Weill Medical College, Cornell University, The New York Presbyterian Hospital, New York, New York, U.S.A.

Winnicott, Donald W. (1963). Struggling Through the Doldrums. *New Society*. 25th April, pp. 8–11.

Winnicott, Donald W. (1964). *The Child, the Family, and the Outside World*. Harmondsworth, Middlesex: Penguin Books.

Winnicott, Donald W. (1965a). Acknowledge the Difference. *New Society*. 9th September, p. 29.

Winnicott, Donald W. (1965b). The Child Behind Society. *New Society*. 30th September, p. 35.

Winnicott, Donald W. (1966). The Ordinary Devoted Mother. In Donald W. Winnicott (1987). *Babies and Their Mothers*. Clare Winnicott, Ray Shepherd, and Madeleine Davis (Eds.), pp. 3–14. Reading, Massachusetts: Addison-Wesley Publishing Company.

Winnicott, Donald W. (1967a). Steps to Good Parenthood. *New Society*. 13th April, pp. 545–546.

Winnicott, Donald W. (1967b). The Persecution That Wasn't. *New Society*. 25th May, pp. 772–773.

Winnicott, Donald W. (1967c). Letter to Robin Hughes. 9th January. Box 6. File 1. Donald W. Winnicott Papers. Archives of Psychiatry, The Oskar Diethelm Library, The DeWitt Wallace Institute of Psychiatry: History, Policy, and the Arts, Department of Psychiatry,

Joan and Sanford I. Weill Medical College, Cornell University, The New York Presbyterian Hospital, New York, New York, U.S.A.

Wortis, Joseph (1954). *Fragments of an Analysis with Freud*. New York: Simon and Schuster.

York, Chris (2017). Prince Harry Sought Counselling After 'Total Chaos' Caused by Princess Diana's Death: He was 'very close to a complete breakdown on numerous occasions'. The Huffington Post. United Kingdom Edition. 17th April. [http://www.huffingtonpost.co.uk/entry/prince-harry-counselling_uk_58f44c42e4b0b9e9848cc982; Accessed on 17th April, 2017].

Part V

Orbach from a Personal Perspective

Chapter 8

A Reflection on Susie Orbach's Work

Risking the Radical Edge of Relationship-Seeking in Theory and Practice

Kate White

> "The desperation to belong is what makes us human … When we belong we can feel safe being separate."
>
> (Orbach, 2016, p. 107)

Introduction

What an honour to have been invited and what a joy it was to make this presentation at the conference in celebration of Susie Orbach's work. I had such an amazing journey preparing for it both personally and professionally.

Thank you, Susie, for your determination in the pursuit of the radical edge of relationship-seeking in theory and practice with all its complexity in an unequal world. You emphasise the riskiness of becoming attached in a socially divisive world, recognising our fears of loss and of feeling overwhelmed by too much closeness – the dialectic of attachment and its paradoxes.

You show so exquisitely the vulnerability in exposing our needs for belonging and the risks we take in expressing our desires, hoping we will be met and recognised, and fearing being ignored and rejected. This is especially complex when, as women raised in the patriarchal system trained to meet the needs of others, exposing our wants is so dangerous.

In this chapter I plan to start with more personal reminiscences and the impact you had on my life long before I ever met you. Then I want to trace just *some* of the pathways and theoretical influences that have informed your radical synthesis. Finally, I will illustrate how it all comes together in practice using two different papers of yours, the first on the theme of disappointment and the second on working with couples.

Personal Reminiscences

My first encounter with Susie Orbach's (1978) work was through reading *F.I.F.I.* (*Fat is a Feminist Issue*) way back when it came out in 1978. Arising from the very personal resonance it had with my own life, I then joined with a group of women like me, confused and distressed by a troubled relationship with our bodies and

DOI: 10.4324/9781003470090-14

eating, led by Clair Chapwell. It was through the innovative work in one of these self-help groups that emerged from The Women's Therapy Centre, established in London in 1976, that I finally found a deep and compassionate understanding of what was driving my own distress. I found recognition and soothing in my plight in the company of other women. There was an understanding of the emotional roots of our pain in early attachment relationships shaped by patriarchy, and in the impossible demands for perfection with the resulting sublimation of our own needs for nurture as we nurtured others including the men in our lives.

Alongside the emotional sharing there was the humour and delight in a feeling of liberation as we began to understand the individual and social and political context in which our longings for belonging had not been met. Our own mothers and grandmothers would often be starved of nurture, re-enacting their deprivation in subsequent generations. In the *Zeitgeist* of the times, we were listening to Joan Baez and Bob Dylan. These numbers, such as "Diamonds and Rust", echoed our experience of hope and betrayal. (You can listen here at https://www.youtube.com/watch?v=1ST9TZBb9v8).

The "F.I.F.I." cover boldly states:

- "Fat is not about lack of self-control or will power".
- "Fat is about protection, sex, nurturance, strength, boundaries, mothering, substance, assertion, and rage".
- "It is a response to the inequality of the sexes".

It was such a revelation and brought immense relief. Here Susie and her colleagues were contextualising this painful repetition, risking everything with the radical and empowering idea that relationship-seeking was central to women's lives and that troubled eating was a response to the inequalities that denied women's needs for love, nurturance, and equality.

This work was so imaginatively taken up by Clair Chapwell and the Spare Tyre Theatre Company (Noble, Powell, Chapwell, and Farrar, 1987), who wrote songs and performed shows on these themes. Ringing in my ears are the standards they played such as the memorable blues: "I woke up this morning (I'd put on two pounds)". Their songs were often accompanied by a unique cha-cha-cha percussion sound provided by two Ryvita biscuits being rubbed together, while the song "Mars Bar" contained the lyrics "Why is it every time my mother rings me on the phone I want a Mars Bar?" How we laughed 'til tears poured down our faces. (Listen here at http://www.clairchapwell.co.uk/music/).

Susie and colleagues at The Women's Therapy Centre developed a feminist understanding of women's psychology in the dominant social context of patriarchy and our response to it requiring from women:

- Deference – leading women to hide their desires from themselves.
- Subjugation – shaping women's lives in relation to men and to the needs of others.

- Emotional antennae that are attuned to others.

All of this emotional labour would leave women with a deep sense of neediness and deficit.

The following key issues were identified by Susie and her colleagues as central in their impact on women's psychology:

- Mother-daughter relationships in which the textures of all future relationships are learned.
- Impact of nuclear family structures and the absence of men from childcare.

Women conscious of the painful internalised inequalities looked to psychotherapy as one source for change. *Understanding Women: A Feminist Psychoanalytic Approach* by Luise Eichenbaum and Susie Orbach (1983b) was an amazing *tour de force*. It was described as "a complete introduction and guide to feminist psychotherapy, both theory and practice". It became central to our newly fledged psychotherapy training course at The Bowlby Centre as it embodied the principles of our radical attachment-informed approach.

Further Theoretical Influences

Susie summarised these succinctly in an internet post:

> *Relational Theory* is the practice of a psychotherapy which offers the possibility of seeing what arises from attachment patterns and can provide the possibility of risking new forms of relating.

> *Fairbairnian theory* illustrates the ways in which difficulties in early attachment relationships are managed internally. It illuminates the internal object relations which is to say when aspects of actual relationships disappoint and have to be withdrawn from and lived in fantasy (Orbach, 2012, n.p.).

As Orbach explained in a personal communication in 2014, these three differing theories are ways of approaching the human subject: developmentally, intrapsychically and intersubjectively. Indeed, they each address different aspects of our understandings.

The major influences on her work from psychoanalysis, feminist consciousness-raising principles, and gender identity theorists are extensively discussed in notes at the end of the first chapter of *Understanding Women: A Feminist Psychoanalytic Approach* (Eichenbaum and Orbach, 1983b). This was of course written prior to the contemporary influences of relational psychoanalysis on her work and to which she has subsequently contributed extensively.

Following both a recognition of and critique of Freud, these are a few of the authors she and Luise identified as influential to their theoretical thinking: Wilhelm

Reich, an inspiration to feminist psychotherapists interested in relating the social, political, and psychological worlds; Frantz Fanon, who spoke about the internalisation of race and class; and Karen Horney, who, in addressing issues that arise with women's lack of power – provided alternative theoretical explanations to Freud's. Harry Stack Sullivan, Clara Thompson, and Erich Fromm were important; however, "though they (Horney and Thompson in particular) understood the impact of cultural and social forces on child rearing they did not dissect the psychodynamics by which the outside world becomes transformed in its particular form in the individual psyche" (Eichenbaum and Orbach, 1983b, p. 30).

Within the "British Object Relations Group", Ronald Fairbairn has been a primary inspiration in Susie Orbach's theoretical and clinical developments as has Donald Winnicott, despite his use of the language of drive theory. Fairbairn's argument that the self develops in the context of relationships and is primarily relationship-seeking was a revolutionary departure from Freud's drive theory. Similarly, she drew inspiration from Winnicott's famous remark, "There is no such thing as an infant, meaning, of course that wherever one finds an infant one finds maternal care and without maternal care there would be no infant" (quoted in Khan, 1975, p. xxxvi). Each of these psychoanalysts has provided an extensive and nuanced understanding of the psychological development of individuals.

Fairbairn's influence also includes his notion of psychological maturation as being movement from infantile to mature dependence as distinct from the Freudian concept of developmental stages. Fairbairn's state of mature dependence implies a recognition of the separateness of individuals, even while they are involved in the most intimate and interdependent of relationships. Separateness thus in no way implies isolation, or even disconnection, but a place of interdependence. Rather in "mature dependence", separateness hinges on the recognition of the existence of the selfhood of the other, not subsumable by one's own selfhood. It involves the acknowledgment of the unique individuality of the other in a way that is in no way diminished by the existence of the relationship between the self and that other. Additional key Fairbairnian concepts include the internal saboteur, the antilibidinal ego, the libidinal ego, and the allure of the "bad object".

John Bowlby and attachment theory have proved crucial. As Susie herself has indicated in a personal communication, "For me *Attachment theory* is the scaffolding: it is about the shape of relationship offered to the developing infant / child and in turn it becomes the way the individual understands relationship and the kind of relationship she or he seeks."

Attachment theory provides an understanding of the universal need for others across the lifespan and how this develops in a cultural and social context. As Bowlby himself explained, "Intimate attachments to other human beings are the hub around which a person's life revolves, not only when he is an infant or a toddler or a school-child but throughout his adolescence and his years of maturity as well, and on into old age" (Bowlby, 1980, p. 442).

We are born with the inherent capacity for making emotional bonds and becoming attached to those who care for us in our childhood. By having enough of our early attachment needs recognised and met, we are enabled to explore the world with confidence, trusting that we have a safe haven to return to when the going gets tough. We thereby learn what to expect in the way of behaviour from others, and the likely consequences for how we feel, think, and act. Key Bowlby concepts include attunement, separation anxiety, loss and mourning, rupture and repair, and internal working models of relationships.

Bowlby was criticised and ostracised for his arguments which identified relationship-seeking as primary and for his focus in his attachment research on the impact of separation and real relationships. One can see in Susie's work how she has taken key concepts from attachment theory and its subsequent developments, for example, by Daniel Stern (1985) and Allan Schore (1994), and refreshed and extended these with her own unique take and clinical experience. I am only able to identify in the space of this brief chapter a few examples of her deft theoretical integration, drawing her ideas and extensive understanding, for example, from Marxism, and the latest neuroscience studies to contemporary relational psychoanalysis. It is her breadth and depth of understanding the struggles that we face which is dazzling. Alongside this is her immense personal and professional courage which from the beginning named the duplicity and deception of global capitalism, and with brilliant imagination and collaboration has brought into being a radical and compassionate approach to meeting human suffering. As Orbach (2016, p. 107) has written, "What consumerism and fundamentalism both highlight is the human desperation to belong. This is not pathological; the desperation to belong is what makes us human. When we belong we can feel safe being separate. If we can't, the expression we find for it when it goes awry can be deadly."

Relational Psychoanalysis and the Concept of Intersubjectivity

As Susie wrote in her contribution to The Relational School in 2014, "Relational Theory is the practice of a psychotherapy which offers the possibility of seeing what arises from attachment patterns and can provide the possibility of risking new forms of relating" (Orbach, 2014).

Intersubjectivity is a central concept for relational psychoanalysis with its long-standing critique of a one-person psychology and the notion of the "analyst who knows" delivering interpretations. It was interesting to find that Joan Riviere (1952, pp. 166–167), analyst to both Donald Winnicott and John Bowlby, wrote about the essence of the social context of human relationships as follows:

There is no such thing as a single human being, pure and simple, unmixed with other human beings [...]. That self [...] is a composite structure which has been and is being formed and built up since the day of our birth out of countless never-ending influences and exchanges between ourselves and others. These other persons are in fact therefore part of ourselves [...]. We are members of one another.

In Susie's project to develop a gender-conscious psychoanalysis, she and Luise Eichenbaum (Orbach and Eichenbaum, 1995, p. 94), in their paper "From Objects to Subjects", argue that there is a necessity "to critique the patriarchal perspective of object relations theory. We understood that the therapist was not only object but subject as well. And, moreover, for both women and men patients, the experience of the subjectivity of the female therapist was essential to the project of change. In hindsight, it seems obvious that that perception was most likely to come from feminists who had understood the struggle from object to subject with agency in daily life in very personal ways."

In the same paper they quote from Jessica Benjamin (1988, p. 20), who writes, "the idea of intersubjectivity reorients the conception of the psychic world from a subject's relations to its object toward a subject meeting another subject." The position of the therapist being a selfless, idealised other was now under scrutiny. After the bold foundation of The Women's Therapy Centre, gender-conscious psychoanalysis continued to evolve (Orbach and Eichenbaum, 1995).

In the paradigm shift represented by the emergence of relational psychoanalysis, influenced in turn by feminist writers, Stephen Mitchell (2001) saw the therapeutic relationship as one where there are two people who co-create the process and the meaning and the narrative. There is not a subject who knows (the analyst) and an object who struggles to understand (the analysand) but two subjectivities who bring their experience, values, attitudes, and feelings to a human and yet uniquely asymmetrical relationship. The emphasis is on countertransference and relational reenactments, recognition, mutuality, and the bidirectional impact of therapist and analysand on one another in which both are changed.

These are key concepts highlighted in Susie Orbach's work. I have chosen two examples. One is a lecture in memory of Sigmund Freud on the neglected theme of disappointment and the other is an article in which she describes her clinical work with a couple and discusses this therapeutic relationship in the context of the theoretical influences upon which she is drawing.

Beyond the Grand Emotions: the Challenges of Disappointment

It is now a year on from the Labour landslide victory of 1997. In her Freud Memorial Lecture, delivered in London on 14th May, 1998, Susie starts brilliantly by contextualising the moment and linking her audience into the feelings of hope and exhilaration which emerged from that election and now she is suggesting that around the corner we all are aware there is the voice of realism, which we can hardly bear to hear as we protect ourselves from impending disappointment. It is in her exploration of the emotion of disappointment that she brings together her unique synthesis of theory and practice. As she wrote: "Disappointment is the Cinderella emotion of the modern psychological lexicon. Less explosive than anger, less terrifying than hate, more hopeful than despair, more dynamic than depression; disappointment sits with hurt, regret, and shame outside the scope of the grand emotions offering us an insight into as well as a model for understanding a different class of emotions, the more subtle less catastrophised emotions [...]. Disappointment frequently shapes grander emotions but is so often unseen or misnamed that it cannot find a life of its own but has to live tucked into experiences that are described in other terms" (Orbach, 1998, p. 3).

Susie Orbach (1998, p. 3) argues that disappointment is strangely neglected in both our theories and clinical writing, even though it occupies a large part of our lived experience both as therapists and clients: "The hurt that comes from disappointment, the rage that is a response to disappointment, the bitter grief that masks habitual disappointment, the particular poignant let down that is disappointment, frequently goes unrecognised, rendering psychoanalysis less rich in its understanding than it is in its actual practice."

She conjectures that the neglected emotion that is disappointment is perhaps a product of the field itself facing disappointments of its own as the paradigm shifts towards the two-person, asymmetric relationship of collaboration and uncertainty that characterises contemporary relational psychoanalysis. Orbach (1998, p. 5) suggests that, "It is in the clinical domain that we can advance our understanding of the vicissitudes of disappointment." For it is in the clinical setting, in the quiet purposeful reflection and engagement that characterises the therapy relationship that the timbre of feelings states can be held, recognised and explored in all their subtlety, and she continues thus: "If the patient feels understood and can work through their disappointment about being misunderstood and their defences against being understood, then new psychic possibilities open up" (Orbach, 1998, p. 5).

According to Orbach, "This process, the search with another to connect with what has become detached or unthinkable is the means by which the self repairs and develops. It finds, through language and relationship, an acceptance of what has been thought to be unacceptable." She underscored that we "expand our vocabulary together so that subtlety, nuance, tone, shading and colour combine with precision and tact in our attempt to articulate what we understand of our own and our patient's experience" (Orbach, 1998, p. 5).

I find the description here is illustrative of Susie's eloquence as she courageously gives words to the delicate and hidden experiences of both therapist and client. As Orbach (1998, p. 6) has remarked, "To acknowledge disappointment in ourselves and in our patients, is to be infused with a hurt that bruises the heart and stains the image one has of oneself. Disappointment is not an easy emotion to contain. It implies and forces a confrontation with a self in which there is a great sense of being diminished."

What we might learn, Susie suggests, then becomes lost. Drawing upon Fairbairn, she asserts, "The refusal to accept this disappointment is, as Fairbairn would have put it, to show adhesion to those objects who have failed us" (Orbach, 1998, p. 7). This results in an endless and painful repetition: "If the disappointment cannot then be felt, the deflation is so devastating that anger, bitterness, belligerence, or contempt are mobilised in its place [...] reaching to reconfigure and expel, the disappointment is bypassed. Aspects of the self are left stranded and unable to develop, at the mercy of fantasy, vested in the hope of manipulating another – real or imagined" (Orbach, 1998, p. 7).

Susie argues persuasively that sitting with our unmet expectations is the means by which our disappointment can be shared and met and addressed: "Disappointment felt under these conditions reinforces the sense of being a subject with wants, curiosities, desires and hopes. When hopes are thwarted the feeling of being diminished is acute but it is temporary and short lived and serves as a reminder of both one's desire as well as one's humility" (Orbach, 1998, p. 7). She emphasises further the value of the psychotherapist "being able to feel disappointment with the patient creating a moment which involves connection" (Orbach, 1998, p. 7). In Stern's (1985) language this constitutes moments of meeting. As Orbach explains, "when disappointment can sit between them when the word can be spoken, when they both experience the particular hurt of hope gone wrong, of a loss that makes their muscles ache as the tension that has been held in them dissipates, then the feeling of being diminished dissolves too" (Orbach, 1998, p. 8).

Therapist and client each risk sustained connection and relatedness to stay alongside one another as they explore the agony of disappointment. Orbach (1998, p. 9) describes the process of restoration being made possible through "the presence of the other, who bears with the patient while what has been split off is gradually helped to find a psychic home". No longer living in a "slit under the stairs as tentative and concealed as the desire it covers" (Orbach, 1998, p. 9), disappointment, through its emergence, can become part of the rich repertoire of emotions available to us.

Extending Attachment Theory in Practice With Couples

The key concept Orbach (2007) introduces in her paper on "Separated Attachments and Sexual Aliveness: How Changing Attachment Patterns Can Enhance Intimacy" is how an extended understanding of attachment theory enables the couple and therapist to explore together the loss of sexual aliveness in their relationship in a creative and non-pathologising way. As her summary states: "This paper explores a common dilemma with couples: the disappearance of an active sexual relationship. Orbach shows how difficulties with merged or avoidant attachments which create implosion can be transformed in the couple relationship to enable a sufficiently separated attachment that allows for sustainable intimacy. The couple is encouraged to use the relationship as a joint psychological space, a third. This joint space takes on the psychic task of providing a secure enough platform to enable them to then individually attain a felt sense of separateness. In this way the tension between their commitment and their distinctiveness is managed and provides a base from which they can re-engage and sustain intimacy" (Orbach, 2007, p. 8).

She argues that lack of sex can be seen as a "regulator, a needed protection in the struggle of each in the relationship not to be merged" (Orbach, 2007, p. 15).

Complaints between partners may act as "spacers, creating enough distance [...] for them to get on" (Orbach, 2007, p. 16); but it came at a cost – each rather "stranded" (Orbach, 2007, p. 16) and thus isolated from their longings for closeness and recognition.

Susie identifies that dissonances in attachment patterns need to be recognised and explored. In fact, there is often a flux between merger with its insecure and avoidant attachments and their attempt to create a secure enough separated attachment where respect and excitement are both present (Orbach, 1999; Clulow, 2001; Mitchell, 2001). She argues that, "by asking the relationship to carry this sense of a secure base, there was more possibility for the risks, excitements and pleasures associated with intimacy to breathe rather than collapse." This is elaborated in the "Attachments trapezoid" diagram (Orbach, 2007, p. 9).

Her extension to the theory uses the individual person's attachment pattern of secure, dismissing, preoccupied, or disorganised, alongside a dimension of merger and separateness which can be seen in the diagram (Figure 8.1). As Orbach (2007, p. 10) writes: "A separated attachment would be equivalent to the couple having a secure base between them. The couple relationship creates a third category, the relationship, which in itself may function as an external and yet at the same time a lived attachment by which they are both underpinned."

Susie illustrates this in the example of her work with "Kusum" and "Jonathan", noting, "The difficulty Kusum and Jonathan encountered was how to climb out of that state of psychic merger, which at the beginning was experienced as so blissful and wondrous and completing, into a relationship in which they could use their attachment as a basis for supporting their individual senses of self (Eichenbaum and Orbach, 1983a; Orbach 1999). How could they be both connected and separate?" (Orbach, 2007, p. 14).

She goes on to explain, "We no longer assess the couple as only two individuals with their unique attachment history. It is the attachment which is co-created by the couple that is now of interest. The co-created attachment can provide either a secure or an insecure base for their relationship. The relationship itself becomes a

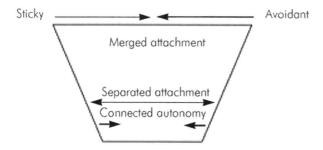

Figure 8.1 Attachments trapezoid
Orbach, 2007.

third kind of attachment, taking on the capacity to become a platform as well as a container from which the individuals relate" (Orbach, 2007, p. 15).

In conclusion, she writes: "By asking the relationship to carry this sense of a secure base, there was more possibility for the risks, excitements, and pleasures associated with intimacy to breathe rather than collapse" (Orbach, 2007, p. 16), noting that, "Sexual intimacy is dependent not so much on each individual sorting themselves out *per se* as it is on creating a platform of security from which the couple can nourish itself" (Orbach, 2007, p.16).

In this chapter I have concluded with these two papers of Susie's to illustrate for the reader examples of the originality, depth, and creativity of her work.

References

Benjamin, Jessica (1988). *Bonds of Love*. New York: Pantheon Books.

Benjamin, Jessica (2004). Beyond Doer and Done to: An Intersubjective View of Thirdness. *Psychoanalytic Quarterly, 73*, 5–46.

Bowlby, John (1980). *Attachment and Loss: Volume III. Loss. Sadness and Depression*. London: Hogarth Press and the Institute of Psycho-Analysis.

Clulow, Christopher (Ed.). (2001). *Adult Attachment and Couple Psychotherapy: The 'Secure Base' in Practice and Research*. London: Brunner-Routledge / Taylor and Francis Group.

Eichenbaum, Luise, and Orbach, Susie (1982). *Outside In ... Inside Out: Women's Psychology: A Feminist Psychoanalytic Approach*. Harmondsworth, Middlesex: Penguin Books.

Eichenbaum, Luise, and Orbach, Susie (1983a). *What Do Women Want?: Exploding the Myth of Dependency*. New York: Coward-McCann.

Eichenbaum, Luise, and Orbach, Susie (1983b). *Understanding Women: A Feminist Psychoanalytic Approach*. New York: Basic Books.

Khan, M. Masud R. (1975). Introduction. In Donald W. Winnicott. *Through Paediatrics to Psycho-Analysis*, pp. xi–l. London: Hogarth Press and the Institute of Psycho-Analysis.

Mitchell, Stephen (2001). *Can Love Last?* New York: W.W. Norton and Company.

Noble, Katina; Powell, Harriet; Chapwell, Clair, and Farrar, Judy (1987). *The Spare Tyre Songbook*. London: Virago.

Orbach, Susie (1978). *Fat is a Feminist Issue*. London: Paddington Press.

Orbach, Susie (1998). Unpublished Typescript. Beyond the Grand Emotions: The Challenges of Disappointment.

Orbach, Susie (1999). *The Impossibility of Sex*. London: Allen Lane / Penguin Press, Penguin Books, Penguin Group.

Orbach, Susie (2007). Separated Attachments and Sexual Aliveness: How Changing Attachment Patterns Can Enhance Intimacy. *Attachment: New Directions in Psychotherapy and Relational Psychoanalysis, 1*, 8–17.

Orbach, Susie (2012). The Relational School Internal Study Group on How Relational Psychoanalysis Marries Attachment Theory and the Fairbairnian Theory of Internal Objects. Unpublished Statement.

Orbach, Susie (2014). The Relational School Internal Study Group on How Relational Psychoanalysis Marries Attachment Theory and the Fairbairnian Theory of Internal Objects. Unpublished Statement.

Orbach, Susie (2016). *In Therapy: How Conversations with Psychotherapists Really Work*. London: Profile Books.

Orbach, Susie, and Eichenbaum, Luise (1995). From Objects to Subjects. *British Journal of Psychotherapy, 12*, 89–97.

Riviere, Joan (1952). The Unconscious Phantasy of an Inner World Reflected in Examples from English Literature. *International Journal of Psycho-Analysis, 33*, 160–172.

Schore, Allan (1994). *Affect Regulation and the Origin of the Self: The Neurobiology of Emotional Development*. New York: Psychology Press.

Stern, Daniel N. (1985). *The Interpersonal World of the Infant: A View from Psychoanalysis and Developmental Psychology*. New York: Basic Books.

Chapter 9

A Celebration of Susie Orbach

Valerie Sinason

All too often major pioneers whose findings have changed our lives face more envy than gratitude. A celebration is therefore a chance to redress the balance and to be grateful for the seminal way Susie Orbach and her work have affected our lives and the lives of our partners, families, friends, children, patients, and colleagues. Sometimes we are consciously and obviously aware of this gift from her and sometimes it is almost invisible. She has been a nourishing part of the fabric of the environment in which we have breathed for decades.

How do we even start to measure her international impact? As a practitioner, she has taken the term "applied psychoanalysis" to a completely different level, extending a therapeutic influence on the millions of people that she could not see in her consulting room. How moved Donald Winnicott would have been by her educational commitment, who, as Brett Kahr has often reminded us, cared deeply about educating the public through the media.

Her book, *In Therapy: How Conversations with Psychotherapists Really Work* (Orbach, 2016), has amassed over 16,500,000 internet links. And when we add on Susie's seminal books and articles, we have around 40,000,000 links. If only they were all mirror neurons – but some of them are! Additionally, we rarely publicly validate and celebrate something or someone who provides insight. To be popular without being a populist is indeed remarkable in this moment of time.

Celebration entered the English language in the early sixteenth century, derived from the Latin *celebratio*, meaning "big assembly". Initially, it meant the honouring of a day or season by appropriate festivities and soon came to mean a big assembly gathered to respect, commemorate, honour, and celebrate. In the 1570s, it meant performance of a religious assembly, the Eucharist; but from the 1670s it came to mean extolling in speeches. It is interesting that the religious meaning moved into a secular one in the 1670s, just at the pre-dawn of the Enlightenment. For secular people, a celebration can still carry a positive ritual meaning in that it is a day or book or event that affects our communality, our relational identity, and our society.

So, the writers of the chapters and those who attended the celebratory day which formed the basis for this book are a large gathering who have come together to

DOI: 10.4324/9781003470090-15

celebrate the life and work of Susie and her multiple contributions to such diverse areas of speciality as:

1) Working for national and international mental health.
2) Studying the personal and the political.
3) Co-founding the group Psychotherapists and Counsellors for Social Responsibility.
4) The media, including radio and television.
5) Writing for *The Guardian* newspaper.
6) Working in the theatre.
7) Consulting to advertising, especially the Dove campaign.
8) Consulting to Unilever.
9) Working with the World Bank and aiding poverty-stricken women.
10) Having held a professorship at the London School of Economics and Political Science in the University of London.
11) Theorising.
12) Facilitating her own clinical practice.
13) Lecturing on our sporting, lovemaking, procreating, and ageing bodies.
14) Having created The Women's Therapy Centre with Luise Eichenbaum and, subsequently, The Women's Therapy Centre Institute with both Luise Eichenbaum and Carol Bloom.
15) Having served as chair of The Relational School in the United Kingdom.
16) Convening AnyBody, an organisation that has campaigned for bodily diversity.
17) Co-founding Antidote, which promotes emotional literacy.

And this woman, with multiple pioneering strands – this person we are celebrating – is known mainly by only one name – a mononym – Susie.

Think Plato. Socrates. Voltaire. Cleopatra. Boadicea. Oprah.

This is something that happens only when there is enough public appeal. However, my small sample needs further filtering. There is arguably a difference in the public affection and esteem when a first name is used rather than a surname.

If we venture into the psychoanalytical community, we find only a handful of our revered ancestors have become known and recognised by one name only, denoting a public position of great significance: Freud, Klein, Bowlby, Bion, Winnicott, Segal, Jung. We never think of them as Sigmund, Melanie, John, Wilfred, Donald, Hanna, Carl.

We do hear, however, of Susie.

She is not known as the daughter of the Member of Parliament Maurice Orbach. Somehow her own individuality and her right-the-way-through sharp, warm honesty and brilliance have merited that single name of Susie. It is also particularly appropriate that the actual day on which these talks were first delivered, which now form the basis of this *Festschrift*, fell on "Earth Day". In fact, Earth Day was invented in 1970 – the same year as the first British National Women's Liberation Conference. And Susie was there, half a century ago.

Fifty-plus years! It might surprise some to consider that Susie shares some of the qualities of a soap opera. One of the pleasures of soap operas is that they become attachment sources – growing up with us weekly, dealing with or pinpointing the existential angst of our time. We tend to call someone a national treasure when that person has performed a similar function, aiding us iconically, symbolically, and literally. The role usually goes to someone in the arts and it is extremely rare that it goes to a psychoanalytical thinker and practitioner. But Susie has educated and inspired us for over four decades. I have been helped by her writing and thinking and advice over many areas and subjects, but, especially within the secure framework of her robust and lively ongoingness.

She applies an open, non-defensive inquiry of herself when in the public eye in the same way she interrogates other people or subjects. Some years ago, she commented in *The Observer* newspaper, "we had the fantasy that we were changing the world. We had the notion we had enormous impact" (quoted in Cadwalladr, 2008, n.p.). And of course, she did, in reality, but she always recognised the size of the problem.

Bryony Gordon (2016, n.p.) interviewed Susie Orbach for *The Daily Telegraph* newspaper, noting, "I tell her she did change things. 'Did I? I think I saw something and I had no idea how big it was. And then it got bigger, and bigger, and bigger.' Does she think it will ever get smaller again, so to speak? She lets out a deep sigh. 'Not really. I love the fact that lots of young women will dress in exuberant manners, whatever their size and shape. But it doesn't mean they feel OK about it. I think it's poisonous that we've done that.'"

At the same time, Susie can acknowledge what has changed. She was quoted as saying, "it was considered scandalous that we would let it be known that there was a therapy centre opening. The climate has really changed." (quoted in Gordon, 2016, n.p.).

With public attention on her private life, Susie has also managed impeccably. On being asked about her marriage to Jeanette Winterson, she replied non-defensively, "Well, I don't think all marriages are the same. You don't have the same kind of experience. I'm not raising children now. It's completely different." (quoted in Gordon, 2016, n.p.). Her relational attachment approach in therapy allows her to find a secure level of public being that aids security in her readers.

At the height of all the media madness as to Princess Diana coming to Susie for therapy (which, in truest analytical fashion she never commented upon), all that the media could find was an elderly relative (not a blood relative) who complained that Susie did not visit her enough!

Slowly and almost imperceptibly, she has also been responsible for two new literary genres that have been evolving, breaking through the separated worlds of literature and academic-clinical psychology and psychotherapy without proper fanfare or announcement.

Whilst Jung realised that there was always reality inside psychosis, there has long been a bipartite *cordon sanitaire* between the literary world and the psychoanalytical one over works of imagination and reality, both fiction and non-fiction.

From the psychoanalytical side of the barricade, literature was allowed to possess great human insights and, indeed, Freud considered that the artist delved deeper than the psychoanalyst. But the consensus was that literature needed the psychoanalyst to explain where the artist had gone and what treasures had been brought up from the deep.

But what happens when the artist is also the psychoanalyst or psychologist?

This new genre has been heralded by Susie Orbach's (1999) pioneering book *The Impossibility of Sex*. In that text, she made it explicit that she had created fictional characters, inspired by her experience, in order to elucidate a clinical meaning without infringing client confidentiality. In taking her work to literary festivals and in discussing the meaning of such writing through crucial interdisciplinary work, a new meaning could be ascribed to the increasingly composite case discussions that appear in clinical journals. Fear of breaching confidentiality has led to more and more clinicians providing such composites – a different approach from the invention of personalities.

Of course, not all published papers with composite case descriptions are good literary writing. It is particularly where the work follows the literary excellence of Freud's first case studies to which I am referring.

The leading American psychoanalyst and psychiatrist, Richard P. Kluft, provides a new entry into this field with novels, both published by Karnac Books, namely, *Good Shrink / Bad Shrink* (Kluft, 2014) and, subsequently, *An Obituary to Die For* (Kluft, 2016). Where else do you get a new novel with reviews by Professor Colin Ross, Professor Martin Dorahy, Professor Warwick Middleton, and Professor David Spiegel? Additionally, Kluft (2016, n.p.) dedicated the latter book to "The victims of brainwashing and torture it has been my privilege to assist [...] you have taught me more about human evil and human courage than I ever wanted to know." His afterword is entitled "When Truth and Fiction Collide ...". These books by Kluft occupy an important place in the tradition established by Susie herself.

Susie has developed a second genre of literature as well. Following her zeal to educate the public and colleagues without infringing confidentiality, Susie has crafted another type of writing – on the radio – in which an actor comes to see her for a consultation to tell a story about which she knows nothing in advance. The results of this experiment have intrigued millions of people, and these radio pieces, *In Therapy*, and the book versions of them (Orbach, 2016, 2018), have become profoundly popular. I witnessed a couple of live theatrical versions of this model in which Susie sat in the public eye faced with an actor, not knowing anything about the assessment she was about to undertake.

In 1980, I was present when Tillman Furness and Arnon Bentovim undertook media work while treating abused children at Great Ormond Street. There was one television programme in which Furness had to deal with an unknown scenario that the actors knew. But to my knowledge that was not repeated, whereas this new format has been repeated over and over. It is hard to convey the courage of a therapist lending himself or herself out publicly to an unknown assessment from an audience of theatre-goers.

An unusual reason for the success of this format is that the characters of the actors actually improve through the public therapy they receive. The "false" scripted selves they have brought to real therapy have to contain something of their understanding, and we witness real changes before our eyes.

A famous tragi-comic piece in *The International Journal of Psycho-Analysis* on how to destroy creativity in psychoanalytical communities, written by Otto Kernberg (1996), stated that senior analysts should never say or print publicly the interpretations they actually made to patients as it would destroy all mystique. Susie has openly allowed her art to be witnessed. In fact, Susie has been able to work with actors who lend themselves out bodily and mentally to become the characters they are portraying.

She has also tried to develop Winnicott's (1960) idea of the false self into an idea about the false body (Orbach, 2002). It is therefore not surprising that she has seen the gaps in theory, even in Winnicott, in her wonderful chapter "Towards a Gnosology of Body Development" (Orbach, 2012).

Susie also speaks about dissociative identity disorder (D.I.D.) as hyper-illumination and points out that the multiple selves in a D.I.D. system are not just psychic constructs but, rather, have different bodies, postures, and ways of being.

Remarkably, Susie has taught us that major theories of the self could be applied to the body using not only the idea of a dissociated body, but that bodies can be classified through the main attachment diagnostic categories. There could be a disorganised body, for instance, as well as an avoidant-dismissive body, and a preoccupied-ambivalent body and, even, a merged body.

Hence, while I had appreciated intellectually that one client with D.I.D. has a bulimic part to the personality and, also, an anorexic part and, moreover, thinks of herself as a ten-year-old male street urchin, I had not properly – until learning from Susie – taken in the fact that this ten-year-old boy in the body of a forty-year-old woman had a securely-attached male latency body. Somehow, the latency boy had received some emotional connection from the parents.

This also applied to what I had called the "secondary handicap" in children with adults with an intellectual disability. Who distorted their bodies in order to hide their shame of difference? Ten-year-old "Mary" – a girl with Down's Syndrome – came to me for an assessment, wearing a party dress. After she had spun around and said, "I am a special girl in a special dress and I go to a special school", my bodily countertransference was of a sense of falsity. I said that the word "special" sounded like a difficult word. Mary stopped pirouetting and replied angrily, "I hate this dress. Mummy made me put it on." She was becoming an insecurely-attached bodily wish of her mother in order to hide the shame each felt about Mary's disability. Therapy could help her cast off the body that was not hers, as previously she could not find a secure body.

Let me describe another patient. "John" lived happily with his mother. But, he explained, there was one thing wrong. Whenever he and his mother went to the pub, she would shout out loud, "I am here with my handicapped son John." He wanted his mother to stop saying that. As John described what she said, his hands went into a secondary handicap position – a caricature – and I could feel bodily how his mother's words had hurt him. I invited her to come to see me – an extremely obese woman who puffed her way into the room. I told her that John was really happy living with her and, also, with their relationship. She beamed lovingly at him. I also said that there was only one thing that she did that he would like to change. "Only one?" she smiled curiously. I replied, "We have not met before and I wonder what it would have been like if John had said to me, "Valerie, meet my fat Mum. Mum, meet my fat therapist." The mother looked confused for a moment and then we all burst out laughing. At this point, a tear came to her eye and she explained, "I say that in the pub so everyone will know", and then she added, "but they *would* know, wouldn't they?"

Twenty-five-year-old "Roseanne" was asked to show me round her beautiful new shared home in the community. She took me through the pristine building, pointing to the lovely new carpet, the shiny new freezer, and the lovely staircase. And then we came to her room. On her bedside table, she pointed gleefully to a broken ornament. "Broken", she said happily. Something about the excessively designed house and furniture felt false to her and she was now secure enough to show what was her current self-representation.

It is thanks to Susie Orbach that therapists can be free to be secure about how they speak about their bodies when communicating with patients.

It was the last session before Christmas for a group of women with intellectual disabilities. They presented my co-therapist and me with two small parcels covered with creased wrapping paper. My co-therapist, who was not English and was secretly planning to return to her country of origin to have her first baby, was given a second-hand book entitled *Poems for a Friend Who is Going Far Away*. On the creased cover was the image of a pregnant woman looking far out to sea. My book was entitled *A Woman's Health Book* with a picture of a slim woman playing tennis on the cover.

There was a pause in which the group members tried to make themselves look as handicapped as possible and with their heads downcast. As I spoke, they slowly lifted their heads higher and higher.

"Well," I said, "even though we have discussed not having presents you wanted to show us you care for us. You have given 'X' a book about a pregnant woman going far away because you know she is from another country and you wonder when she will go back to her country and have a baby. And on my book, there is a slim healthy woman on the cover. You want me to be healthy because you care about me, but you also wonder why the fattest woman in the group is one of the therapists."

They lifted their heads and burst out laughing – a happy, non-handicapped truthful laughter.

To end near the beginning, Susie's famous book, *Fat is a Feminist Issue* (Orbach, 1978), was first published more than forty years ago and remains a much-reprinted classic and a meteor, combining politics, society, research, and psychoanalysis.

Since that time, Susie has become a phenomenon, appearing on television and radio and treating patients and reaching out to untold millions. And she shows no signs of stopping. The mass public have expressed their gratitude to her for over five decades, and now, at last, we see the beginnings of the psychotherapy profession publicly expressing its gratitude as opposed to privately benefiting from her findings, while in the quiet consulting room.

There are many examples from the fields of trauma, disability, and dissociation that I could give of how helped I have been personally and professionally, thanks to insights and education from Susie. Here is to her continuing on-goingness and inspiration. Thank you, Susie.

References

Cadwalladr, Carole (2008). It's Been a Long Journey – And We're Not There Yet. *The Observer.* 7th December. *The Guardian.* [https://www.theguardian.com/lifeandstyle/2008/dec/07/women-equality-rights-feminism-sexism-women-s-liberation-conference; accessed on 31st August, 2021].

Gordon, Bryony (2016). Susie Orbach on Why Britons Are Increasingly Anxious – and Falling in Love with a Woman After 40. *The Telegraph.* 31st October. *The Telegraph.* [https://www.telegraph.co.uk/women/life/susie-orbach-on-why-brits-are-increasingly-anxious---and-falling/; accessed on 31st August, 2021].

Kernberg, Otto F. (1996). Thirty Methods to Destroy the Creativity of Psychoanalytic Candidates. *International Journal of Psycho-Analysis*, *77*, 1031–1040.

Kluft, Richard P. (2014). *Good Shrink / Bad Shrink.* London: Karnac Books.

Kluft, Richard P. (2016). *An Obituary to Die For.* London: Karnac Books.

Orbach, Susie (1978). *Fat is a Feminist Issue.* London: Paddington Press.

Orbach, Susie (1999). *The Impossibility of Sex.* London: Allen Lane / Penguin Press, Penguin Books, Penguin Group.

Orbach, Susie (2002). The False Self and the False Body. In Brett Kahr (Ed.). *The Legacy of Winnicott: Essays on Infant and Child Mental Health*, pp. 124–134. London: H. Karnac (Books), and New York: Other Press.

Orbach, Susie (2012). Towards a Gnosology of Body Development. In Valerie Sinason (Ed.). *Trauma, Dissociation and Multiplicity: Working on Identity and Selves*, pp. 96–109. Hove, East Sussex: Routledge / Taylor and Francis Group.

Orbach, Susie (2016). *In Therapy: How Conversations with Psychotherapists Really Work.* London: Profile Books.

Orbach, Susie (2018). *In Therapy: The Unfolding Story.* London: Profile Books / Wellcome Collection.

Winnicott, Donald W. (1960). Ego Distortion in Terms of True and False Self. In Donald W. Winnicott (1965). *The Maturational Processes and the Facilitating Environment: Studies in the Theory of Emotional Development*, pp. 140–152. London: Hogarth Press and the Institute of Psycho-Analysis.

Epilogue: In Dialogue with ...

Susie Orbach

My first thank you, for this stunning collection of articles, must go to Professor Brett Kahr, and to Jane Ryan and the staff at Confer, who made the day from which most of the pieces were first given. The day was beautifully chaired by Dr. Amita Sehgal, to whom, thank you ... and thank you also, to all the magnificent contributors.

The experience of listening to papers on my work and its impact was, and is, totally humbling. Reading the finished papers increases that feeling. It is insufficient to say it is also pleasing and heartening. To have been part of a dialogue with psychoanalysis and society for over half a century has been engrossing, challenging, and enhancing. It has given me the gift of developing rich collegial friendships. It has allowed ever more complex thinking while increasing my capacity to manage and delight in the many feelings that doing the work, writing about psyche, body, self, and society engender. The search for the right words for the session, for the page, for sharing with colleagues, for social activism, forces an expansiveness that I, for one, could never have envisioned as a young person. In responding to this collection, I am moved by what we as a group do day in and day out as we meet the troubles, the sorrows, the solaces, and the triumphs of the people with whom we work.

* * *

I want to turn first to Professor Brett Kahr's three specific contributions in this volume. As progenitor of the *Festschrift* and editor, I am mindful of the considerable work this has entailed, and I want to thank him again for what he has undertaken. Brett is a man of considerable intellectual capacity. He is today's historian of psychoanalysis and his deep interest in the field has led to his encyclopaedic knowledge from which we learn much. On his recent birthday, I told Brett that I always learn something new from a conversation with him. In bringing together this event he has given me the opportunity to say the same to all the contributors in this volume. Once again, thank you.

Professor Kahr's opening essay speaks to the heart of what I value in him. Our initial encounters in 1990 were around his lecture series on psychohistory. He is well able to situate The Women's Therapy Centre and my work in its historical and cultural context. He understands generational initiatives in their moment and

DOI: 10.4324/9781003470090-16

in their significance. He appreciates the longings and desires to change a field, who can belong to it, and who can benefit from it, and he links this with Freud's revolutionary project, both to comprehend and situate people in their explicit circumstances.

A student of psychoanalysis and of the arts, especially music, Brett soon got up to speed on contemporary politics to understand what was so compelling about the phenomena I was writing and thinking about. As we see in Radio Karnac, he is the kind of interviewer who makes conversation possible. We might think that all psychoanalysts are good at that, but we aren't. We may be well versed in facilitating a therapeutically-minded conversation in the consulting room but that does not translate to broadcast media or indeed to lecturing, at which Brett is unparalleled.

In his densely researched chapter, " 'Psychotherapy is not a spectator sport': The Dissemination of Psychoanalysis from Freud to Orbach", Brett deftly shows how psychoanalysis was, from early on, derided and ridiculed within medical circles. We can speculate that such derision and ridicule contributed to a kind of caution about what psychoanalysts should be saying and doing in public – even becoming circumspect about revealing their locations. Looked at from today's perspective, this can help us understand the many years of secrecy which led in part to the isolation of psychoanalysis outside of the academy and thus to its destructive splits within our profession. It is hard to have open dialogue when all around is threat. Paradoxically, and I want to stress this fact, such hiddenness is in contrast to the light psychoanalysis has to offer on the motivations, confusions, wishes, and fears of us humans.

Of course some psychoanalysts did publish for the wider public, notably Wilhelm Reich, whose early mission was to understand the relationship between class, society, sexual repression, authoritarianism, and fascism. I think it is no accident that Reich's pre-war writings (before he moved to the United States and went on a different trajectory) were taken up in the west by the baby boomers in the 1960s. There were several strands that came together to make psychoanalytic discourse vibrant at this time. There was the post-war reckoning by the German psychoanalysts Alexander Mitscherlich and Margarete Mitscherlich (1975) who looked at the inability of a society to mourn its own destructiveness and loss. There were the transplanted psychoanalytic thinkers of the Frankfurt School – Herbert Marcuse, Erich Fromm, and others. There was the secretive correspondence between analysts exiled to the United States known as the Fenichel papers (Jacoby, 1983) that aimed to keep psychoanalysis alive in the new continent. There were the contributions from Karen Horney and her colleagues bringing feminist concerns to psychoanalysis (e.g., Horney, 1967).

At the same time, the political movements of the 1960s in which civil rights and the struggle against the war in Vietnam crystallised the idea that who we are and what we do is political. *The personal is political*. The Women's Liberation Movement ran with this idea and it was this that led me, Luise Eichenbaum, Carol Bloom, and others to think about how psychoanalysis could be revived to address the difficult phenomenon that the psychological structures of the patriarchal family meant there was an unwitting involvement of women in their own subordination.

Contemporaneously, the Radical Therapy Movement opened up a reconsideration of society from a socially informed psychological perspective that brought into its discourse notions of gender, of war, of racism, and a critique of mental health services. Their motto was, "Therapy means social, political and personal change, not adjustment". All put together, it was these movements that made modern psychoanalysis not something to be hidden but something to be shared widely despite a continuing and often unexamined prejudice within training institutes that extreme discretion was the best. It was thus welcomed when, in 1976, The Women's Therapy Centre sent out a press release and did interviews to announce its service. It was seeking an engagement with women who might use it, and who might recognise the value that their experiences could be understood.

Twenty-three years later, the Tavistock Clinic allowed the B.B.C. to document some of its work, and the *British Journal of Psychotherapy* chose the first film for its clinical commentary (Orbach, 2000). This initiative can be seen as part of a further opening up of psychotherapy to the public which started with the entry of psychoanalytic ideas into public space in the 1960s in the United States and with The Women's Therapy Centre's 1976 decision to publicise its services widely.

To Brett's historical account of the attempting silencing of psychoanalysis outside of the clinic is the revived interest from the 1960s radical movements which penetrated the universities and radical institutes reshaping the field with the preoccupations of the post-war generation and bringing psychoanalytically-informed ideas to an ever wider public.

I am especially grateful to Brett for his appreciation of my efforts to find ways to hold on to confidentiality while finding a means of writing about the work that we do. In *The Impossibility of Sex* (Orbach, 1999), I wanted to show how theory is alive in the mind of the psychotherapist as she or he is involved in making a relationship which can fit with and, yet, gently challenge the ways of being of her patients. By making myself and the patients fictive, I gave myself the freedom to go where the fiction writer goes, which is to say, with her characters rather than with the facts. There were many surprises for me as I wrote *The Impossibility of Sex* and equally many, many surprises in my encounters with the actor characters who participated in *In Therapy*. In so far as actors and fiction writers work is to embody and convey aspects of the human condition, I have been thrilled to find this form to write about people who are imagined, and yet, as they enter the consulting room, are absolutely real to and for me. I was interested that Brett picked out "Charles" and sees my engagement with him in classical Freudian terms. I think he is right. Brett's commentary helps me to think again about what I was doing. Supervision and clinical discussions along with readings are vital for psychotherapists. To be read, even while I was in the process of invention, is a most marvellous gift.

Today psychotherapists populate TikTok and other social media sites. Book deals with publishers are made on the basis of followers that an "influencer" can garner. The hunger for knowledge about ourselves and others which opened the Freudian revolution has exploded.

* * *

It is always a pleasure to read Luise Eichenbaum. I am always in conversation with the ideas we developed together. And like other contributors to this volume, I am always learning from her. The pleasure in our working together gave us both, I believe, an intellectual companionship to which we could bring ideas and readings and new discoveries. I remember well her telling me about Harry Guntrip, whose clinical descriptions rang true for so many of the people we were seeing at The Women's Therapy Centre, and I know for her it was a delight when I would bring something to her.

The way we understood and understand the clinical situation – the dilemmas of the people who seek our help, the theory that guides us, the many aspects of the therapy relationship, the interplay between current notions of gender and what we once understood, the emergence of class and race within the psychoanalytic dialogue from those who would scorn it when we were first writing together – keeps our conversation lively and current.

Intersectionality was learnt early on from black and working class feminists in the 1970s, particularly for us at Richmond College at the City University of New York, where Carol Bloom was the co-director of the first Women's Studies Program in the United States and we were among its first graduates. The continual forgetting of what has been learned and then forgotten, and which we try to hold on to, is part of the political subversion of feminist, anti-racist, and progressive movements from the 1980s onwards, what Susan Faludi termed Backlash. Thus, progressive notions have to be rediscovered by each generation and written in a new vernacular.

Despite the myriad subsequent and different influences which have acted upon us because of what is current in British and North American psychoanalysis, we have continued to find a language for what we are observing and experiencing clinically. The foundations of our joint understandings are robust enough to allow us to keep our dialogue going. And gratifyingly, we now see much talk of the mother-daughter relationship, of the little girl inside, and of our concept of separated-attachments which are taken up by several writers on these pages. The mission we had to understand ourselves and the people we were meeting in the clinic – to see the continuities of experience, to see new iterations – is heartening but also heart-breaking because while women have been permitted to occupy more space in the world, the psychological costs of doing so continue to be psychically expensive.

We came to psychoanalysis out of the feminist project of remaking the world. We needed to understand how the outside structures became the inner structures of internalised misogyny. We hoped to shift them, but we can see in the explosion of fury around the control of women's bodies by the Supreme Court of the United

States, following in the wake of #MeToo, that the threat women's equality continues to pose is disturbing. The challenge to femininities and masculinities, now openly expressed in new movements and challenges to gender binaries, is heartening, and yet we know how tough the world still is. Luise will always be my theoretical buddy and sister in struggle.

* * *

Turning now to the consulting room, which is where, of course, Luise and I and all the contributors to this volume do so much of our learning, we see aspects of cultural forces occupying and forming the psyches of our patients' minds and bodies. I am immensely pleased to have Jane Haberlin writing here. She has elegantly brought us into both the world of infant development which has been so extensively developed in the last seventy-five years and which has helped us understand from Selma Fraiberg (1975) and Margaret Mahler, Fred Pine, and Anni Bergman (1975) through to Daniel Stern (1985) and Beatrice Beebe and Frank Lachmann (2014), that what we experience affectively in the clinic is rooted in the earliest of experiences between caregivers and infants. Donald Winnicott, of course, was pre-eminent in understanding this and writing about infancy and "mothering". These later observational studies have now enhanced our picture of the infant's journey in minute detail. They allow us to see conclusively the impact of early relationship on the formation of self and, in her paper, Jane addresses aspects of early misattunements that emerge in the therapy relationship with two of her analysands, "Mark" and "Alice".

In her work with Mark, Jane is edged into an uncomfortable confrontation with fraud and with descriptions of his compulsive pornographic activity, the discussions and sharing that Mark had with his friends. Her own discomfort does not lead her to a hackneyed moral stance or the expression of disapproval *per se*, but to explore the deeper meanings of Mark's behaviours. In finding ways to talk to him, she is brought into a version of his shame and shamelessness. She finds a way to share this with him with humour and delicacy and gives us an exquisite insight into how relational psychoanalysis works in the consulting room. This is the essence of an awkward encounter which is made palatable and useful. An enactment beautifully made of use. It is driven by her belief that "the most valuable thing we have to give them (the patients) is a report of how it is to be in a relationship with them; especially when we have an *in vivo* experience of what it is that can happen that leads the other to withhold / reject / disappoint them."

Jane brings us "Alice", a case which she feels was unsuccessful. Not hiding from this is something we learnt from Freud who showed how much there is for us to consider in such an account. What Jane brings to this honest appraisal of her work when it cannot reach the individual, is an authenticity which is a hallmark of who she is and of the very best of contemporary relational psychoanalysis. We cannot meet the patient if we are not real, if we do not know ourselves and if we are not prepared to know ourselves anew in our encounters with them. Every therapy relationship is a challenge. There is no coasting. Alice sadly is not interested, and perhaps Jane suggests the timing was wrong because Alice had recently been hospitalised following a breakdown. While Alice's dismissal of Jane shames Jane, it also pushes her to think about herself and her own set of judgements which are provoked by Alice's criticalness towards both Jane and herself. These are difficult challenges. Jane does not pretty this up or blame Alice. She takes responsibility herself.

In these two illustrations, Jane shows how we are enamoured and absorbed by the work. It is intellectually and emotionally challenging. It gives meaning and value to us as we focus on our primary endeavour to give meaning and value to the people with whom we work.

* * *

I turn now to Sarah Benamer and her fine paper. It is so wonderful to be so well understood by a colleague. In this chapter, she describes her work with "Mia", who had stopped eating and who had been, as a result, in a psychiatric facility that sought a resolution to the problem of her not eating by seeing her anorectic stance as the problem, rather than as an attempted solution to underlying problems and rather than addressing the routes of why she needed to keep things out and her body boundaries so highly protected. The hospital thus missed the fears and terrors that besieged her and from whom she attempted to get away at a corporeal and psychological level.

Sarah has gone deeper. She understood that Mia "could not tolerate the need for others that left her yearning for more". This is a dilemma of unmet needs as well as a dilemma of needs for attachment which have been twisted and perverted by the malign. Mia was unable to have integrity in either the corporeal or the psychic domains. Sarah understands well that every person's body contains her or his own story which is reflected by interactions with other bodies. What other bodies allow, disallow, project, and proffer in early childhood, shapes how and whether the individual will be able to achieve a reasonable level of body surety.

Sarah's body is not outside of the therapeutic but firmly part of it. Her body is as essential to Mia's development as is Sarah's mind. It is an embodied Sarah that Mia will use in Winnicott's terms – or engage with and rely on – in my terms and in Sarah's. The "relational turn" demands that the subjectivity of the therapist is in the room. The notion of a blank screen, long abandoned by so many schools of psychoanalysis because it forced certain cruelties on analysands and analysts themselves, is replaced by the beating heart and the reflective responses that are experienced internally by Sarah.

Synchronicity, which is rather more a Jungian concept than a post-Freudian one, intriguingly announces itself with Sarah's patient "Zoe", whose obsessive-compulsive disorder was originally manifested around a fear of needles and contamination at the time of the initial H.I.V. / A.I.D.S. advertisements on television. At the same time, Sarah has a medical condition, which might require the use of a "full syringe and medicine drawn up into it" in an emergency. She must keep it with her at all times, even in a bag in the consulting room.

At the onset of Zoe's obsessive-compulsive disorder, her family were advised not to countenance talk of her ruminations. There was a belief stemming from behaviourism that not "indulging" will allow the symptom to abate. It did not. Like my patient "Herta" (Orbach 2009), symptoms which are side-stepped in the interest of cure can end up feeling unaddressed and then either grow in the mind of the patient or transform into a different symptom. Sarah's medical condition constitutes a present threat and emergency. She knows that bodies are contingent and will be fretted about. She has an earned body security in the same way we earn psychic security through our trainings, through the therapy we receive and through paying attention and reflecting upon our responses to what comes up for us as subjects in the consulting space which we then work on privately. Sarah has much to convey to Zoe through the wisdom of her own existential fragility. She has understood that her body is contingent and in living in spaces in which she must both understand and surrender, and, also, survive, it enables her to be fully present for Zoe as the patient addresses her body terrors rather than shut them down. In reading Sarah, I am reminded of the silent collaborators we have with those who extend and enrich the work. Psychoanalytic theorising is always a work of collaboration, building as it does on what has gone on before and what is going on simultaneously.

* * *

Kate White and I first discussed attachment in the late 1980s, she, from a Bowlbian point of view, and me, from a descriptive perspective. Over the last thirty years I have come to be acquainted with Bowlby's attachment schema. I have wanted to use and extend those categories on the one hand and apply them to corpor-eality. Body troubles were creating the intergenerational transmission of troubled bodies. Concurrent with this work I was looking at Valerie Sinason's work with dissociative identity disorder patients whose differing self-states were represented in distinct body representations with respect to age, sex, and gender. I also looked at Beatrice Beebe's (2004) work with "Dolores" in which Dolores' embodiment is linked to affects and self-states. We see this most vividly on video in Beebe's work with infants and mothers where misattunement reshapes the infant's face in front of our eyes as it does in "Tronick's Still Face Experiment" video (https://www.youtube.com/watch?v=f1Jw0-LExyc; cf. Tronick, et al., 1978). Kate's knowledge about Bowlby has made her a generous teacher to generations of students making clinical and research use of it.

I think Kate's openness to Luise's and my concept of separated attachments and her ability to see how it might be useful for the individual, for the couple, and for the group is gratifying. A couple I have been working with for several years remembers a diagram I once drew for them. It was premature on my part. They were so reliant on each other for the disciplining of personal needs which they would foist in ingenious ways on one another. It was also out of character for me to make such a sketch, but the man was a mathematician, and I thought it might help him hold onto something. Just recently, the couple referred to that sketch and how they felt they were trusting the relationship to be the cradle from which they could find security, rather than thrusting insecurity on each other in cruel and hurtful ways.

During Brexit, I was led to extend the concept of separated attachments outside the clinic to the much wider conversation about how we might think about acting locally and yet globally. It also has relevance for the diversity agenda because the capacity to manage and be respectful towards difference is urgent. Psychotherapists know from the clinical settings about the necessity for holding and managing difference. This is something we are required to do, and we develop great skill in doing so. A question for us to ponder in the effort to develop emotional literacy in civil society is how to do this in other forums, within family and community groupings and so on. The screeching hate culture, which pervades many aspects of social and print media, substituting shouting and sloganeering for careful, and yet, passionate conversations, desperately needs a reset.

The concept of separated attachment came out of Luise's and my work with women, where the pull to merge was ubiquitous. In the struggle for women to recognise their own desires – whether or not they could be met – and to understand how feelings of envy, competition, and potential abandonment interfered with their longings, led us to develop this. Separated attachments are different to the depressive position. It is not only about the achievement of connecting with self and accepting the disappointment of relationships that we have reconfigured in our inner object world, but it is also about respecting the autonomy and differing desires of others. It is a relational reconfiguring of the depressive position and as such it has value outside the clinic as well. There is a pressing need to find ways to connect and yet hold autonomy in so many different interpersonal, cultural, and political settings, so I am happy to see her discussion of my paper of the importance in moving from merged to separated attachments in couple work.

It touches me to be reminded in Kate's discussion of my Freud Memorial Lecture in 1998 on my plea for disappointment to be accorded a place in the emotional canon. In that paper, I think I was responding to a collapse that I noticed in some psychoanalytic writing in which vocabulary was shrunken into a few buzz words leading to the textures of feelings from the consulting room being squashed into a lexicon more reminiscent of the Ten Commandments than the subtlety needed in order to be recognised and to find a home inside of the person or the couple. The grand emotions of love, hate, and envy predominated the British psychoanalytic conversation at that time and I wanted to inject the conversations with more subtlety and nuance.

The invitation to give that lecture said to me either something about my being accepted by the establishment or that the establishment wanted to ruffle its own feathers. It is indeed pleasing to have been asked to speak then and to find Kate's discussion of this paper many years on.

* * *

It feels appropriate now to come on to Andrew Samuels's paper. Andrew and I have been psychoanalytic siblings. We have been working in similar terrains of what our profession can bring to social policy and to our institutions. We have sought to reform aspects of our own field, including revamping curriculum – often unsuccessfully – and to resituate psychoanalysis within its historic and present moments.

The W.T.C.I. (The Women's Therapy Centre Institute) in New York is a success-ful example of this and is to be admired for offering socially-embedded analytic trainings.

I want to say something more about siblings and the extraordinary absence of the subject from our training curricula. In the past few decades, Juliet Mitchell (2003) and Prophecy Coles (2003) have urged us to consider their importance. The neces-sity to consider the significance of siblings is even more pertinent now as many of the people we see will have step- or half-siblings – sometimes acquired when they are already grown up, which in turn challenges their relationship with parents, add-ing new layers as the parent makes new attachments.

A crucial thing about siblings is how they differ. They have different parents even in a conventional nuclear family. One is a new parent only once. The anx-ieties and hopes brought to parenting differ. Again this is totally obvious but it is not often recognised. Raising a child, whether peripherally or intensely involved, changes the parenting person. My brother and I were not treated differently only because of gender or the presence and absence of war in our time but because of the standing of the parental relationship, the knowledge including the fears acquired during the first few years of their parenting. A parent is changed by par-enting. This can span the gamut from worn out to enlivened, following the first child's (or children's) arrival, a decrease in anxiety with the second, third, and fourth children, and so on, and anxiety can continue for a first child in the parental attitude. Then there are longings for a child of a particular sex or the need to cre-ate a saviour child and so on. Parents are developing subjects whose unconscious and purposeful treatment of each child is distinct. To say, as many do, particularly around gender, "I treated them equally", is to misunderstand how our experience and our longings shape us.

Let us return to Andrew and me as siblings. We met because of our politics. The post-war settlement that had birthed us, led us as late teenagers to disrupt the inequalities in the social contract so obvious from the civil rights movement in the U.S.A. and the student movements around the world over the American involvement in the Vietnam war. Radical challenges abounded from the emergence of the Black Panther Party in the United States and of the Notting Hill People's Association in London, Dagenham, and so on. Feminism was pursuing not just equality but a rethinking of gender. Nothing was stable. The streets, the univer-sities, and the factories were alive with protest.

We were learning history and the history of social movements alongside visit-ing our personal histories to understand better how we had come to be the way we were. Andrew and I seem to show up in the same sort of forums, with similar desires to create new organisational structures which could push forward a meeting between progressive politics and progressive psychoanalysis. He, the Jungian, and me, more of a mixture of a Fairbairnian and a contemporary Freudian. Later we were both to meet in Relational Psychoanalysis.

In more conventional political terrain, Andrew and I used to argue that we wanted psychotherapists to be seen as technical experts – in a similar fashion to statisticians and economists – to advise on social policy. For me, I thought such a contribution could alert policy makers to initiatives that might fall short because they failed to understand the psychopolitics of a situation. What do I mean by this? If we take the example of women's refuges and do not understand women's pull to "heal" their abusers, then we could understand why women might find the "victim" position as problematic and fund the governmental offer for the refuges, from which women sometimes leave precipitously, to be less attractive than it could be. The World Bank had already understood that they needed to include gender in decisions to do with the siting of bridges or wells or the psychological disruptions of schooling girls which could, for example, provoke violence if unaddressed. We wanted to extend this to human agency – what perhaps today would be called a buy-in or a stakeholder. Psychoanalytic ways of thinking endeavour to understand what makes participation meaningful and vibrant and what does not.

What I had not expected was that I would be on an expert committee or two. Not by dint of our argument but because of Liberal Democrat women's ministers in the Coalition government. I remember apologising to a senior civil servant for being bolshie and she reassured me that this is precisely what is required to move the needle. The more critical I was, the more the civil servants took things back to their ministers. We never did achieve our aim of having psychotherapists on all committees and we certainly did not understand how they worked, although during the coronavirus pandemic, Steve Reich's excellence as an articulate and thoughtful psychologist was extremely useful and important.

Andrew is a performer. He gets this from his theatrical background at Oxford and, like Brett, and Valerie, he brings prodigious performance skills to presentations which encourage audiences to really take note and listen, which is, after all, the point.

Andrew's extension of Winnicott's concept of "good-enough" to the realm of leadership is interesting. For me leadership must have expectations of itself by which I mean, take responsibility for providing optimum conditions in which the work team – whatever it is – can participate as fully as possible. I do not want to draw a distinction – for the moment – between leadership in a work setting or a political setting. I do think it is the responsibility of leadership to set a vision and in such a way that the particulars of that vision can be taken up by all participants and made to be their own. Leaders are counted on to develop a roadmap for others to walk with them. They need to be thoughtful and self-reflexive, expansive, and humble. In our time we have seen that with Jacinda Ardern and Nicola Sturgeon. At the same time OCCUPY, the brief political movement, developed a unique form of coming to consensus and empowering a collective leadership. In circular rows, in a low-tech environment outside St. Paul's Cathedral or Wall Street, a participant's voice, while making a point, would be amplified by the person in the row behind, and then the row behind and then the row behind acting as human megaphones. This practice was important. The repeating of words one might not agree with was a novel manner in which to consider those words without immediately rejecting them. One came to articulate a position that might be quite at odds with what one thought, and in the act of doing so one came to consider more seriously what was being said instead of unquestionably sticking with one's initial position. It was scary. It was invigorating and it was challenging. Like the psychoanalytic session, it allowed for complexity. For considering what one could otherwise automatically dismiss.

This leads me to Andrew's idea of reverse mentorship where leadership may be listened to and counselled by a *junior member* of a team. Listening to those on the ground is, of course, what politics is meant to do but does not. It is what psychotherapy is meant to do. Thus, bringing this into the workplace, where it is really important for junior members to be respected by their leadership so that their contributions are valued, is certainly an innovation. This inventive idea is a hallmark of Andrew. He likes to upset convention, not in a simply rebellious way – although he has done that too – but in the interests of participatory engagement.

The other thing I want to write about from the perspective of psychoanalysis's possible contribution to my World Bank and other encounters is a recognition of the unparalleled experience psychoanalysis has of research about people in the process of change (Orbach, 2006). This constitutes a novel form of research which should not be underestimated. We have learned about how change happens. What then do we have to give back to social policy makers about our findings? What do we understand about conforming and non-conforming, belonging and feeling an outsider, about how feeling one has agency allows one to participate usefully and so on.

* * *

The most consistent form of activism I have been involved in has been around the body. As a naïve thirty-year-old, I wrote a book and thought it might open up the ways in which women were able to relate more kindly to their bodies and to food. As the last century wore on and into the present, the situation for everyone from little children to adults here and globally has meant that the body has become ever more problematised. It has become the target of many industries as it steals the childhoods and adult lives – even our old age – as it ramps up body hatred and body insecurity. In 2001 we created AnyBody – an organisation to challenge the merchants of body hatred – and, eight years later, I met Roanna Mitchell, then studying at the Royal Central School of Speech and Drama, where I was chairing a discussion on the actor's body. Theatrical luminaries – Emma Thompson and Ian Rickson – contributed from the platform as did Wardrobe, and I was privileged to learn so much about the horrors visited on the profession then, which has only become exacerbated since. Producers and agents press upon the bodies of actors in ways that strike me as a kind of perverse form of uniform embodiment. The skill of an actor is matched by a capacity to size and resize their bodies to conform to the perceived desires of box office. The demand on actors exemplifies the pressure on all of us to appear both nonchalant in a body that at the same time is alluring and conformist to today's aesthetic.

Roanna's challenge to the neoliberal appropriation of the notion of self-care within the acting profession is particularly valuable, as is her highlighting of the industries and ideology of this throughout the body positive movement. Self-help (and its derivatives such as self-care) have been hijacked by those who would produce profit. The notion of self-help emerged as a challenge to conventional medicine and mental health services in the 1970s. *Our Bodies, Ourselves*, from the Boston Women's Health Collective (1973) was a revolutionary document. It demystified women's bodies, challenged the medical establishments, and heralded the possibilities open to women who dared to know their own sexual responses, their gynaecological stories, and so on. Self-help, like feminism, had deeply radical and subversive roots. It is part of the political process, and we need to understand that aspects of revolutionary actions – projects, demands, demonstrations, and so on – become absorbed by society. It is inevitable. Revolutionary politics inform us of what is wrong. Keeping the revolutionary edge is what subsequent generations of activists are able to do, as the revolutionary ideas get incorporated and weakened and manipulated into the workings of the structures that exist. The tragic truth is that women's bodies – and men's bodies and trans bodies – have become the targets of industries which promise to fix them while undermining their stability. Self-care with its so-called holistic sentiments has debased and diverted women's agency towards society's repair as it continues to find new ways to profit.

Roanna tells of the imaginative work of AnyBody and Endangered Bodies. The local global organisation, created at the turn of the century, campaigned against the spread of body hatred. One cannot do activism on one's own any more than one can do scholarship or thinking or develop theory. The work of AnyBody shows the combined and synergistic talents of its membership from the comedic and the theatrical to the visual, to the political, the legal, and the psychological.

Initially, we targeted the fashion industry with a protest at London Fashion Week in 2002. This led to us being involved in the Model Health Inquiry, which reported in 2007. It was agitations such as this that led the ministers Lynne Featherstone and Jo Swinson to set up Expert Groups and cooperate with members of AnyBody both before and after the International Summit of 2011 and with the Advertising Standards Agency.

* * *

If Andrew Samuels is one sibling, Valerie Sinason is another. Valerie is a poet, a child psychotherapist, and a trailblazing psychoanalyst, working in the areas of disability and dissociation. We shared both a column in *The Guardian* newspaper for many years as well as a political background. Her father, like mine, was a Jewish socialist. Her mother too. As post-war babies, we grew up with hope and a message about contributing to civil society. Valerie brings that dedication to all of her work. She is a campaigner, a theory-maker, and an explainer. She wants people to know what she has uncovered and learned. She broadcasts this widely and gathers around her those who are prepared to have their hearts broken by what they learn and hear. Her optimism is one aspect of her survival in the face of these horrors. Her resilience another. And her fear of treading where others will not is something to respect and to marvel.

Valerie and I have endeavoured to share understandings from our field – a field we have both sought to expand and challenge, while being deeply committed. It is our love for the complexities we find which reveal beauties and human agency within the cruellest of distress that I believe keeps us both going. Valerie is able to make quite wide claims given her experience of working in disability and dissociation. This contrasts with the delicacy of the presence and thoughtfulness she gives on the individual level to survivors of trauma and abuse. It is her capacity to see both the big picture – the social circumstances, the psychological structures, and the interpersonal and intrapsychic dilemmas of the people that she works with, which I value. It is in this sense that we are psychoanalytic siblings and, it can be said, both seen as troublesome members of our profession, as well in our ageing, sometimes even appreciated for being part of the awkward squad.

Valerie is, like Brett, indefatigable. Her interests are wide and her knowledge bases ever-expanding. Her achievements and the ongoingness of them are humbling. She, like everyone in this volume, keeps me company in my thinking and in my actions. It is the privilege of my life to work with so many thoughtful, inspiring, and beautiful people.

References

Beebe, Beatrice (2004). Faces in Relation: A Case Study. *Psychoanalytic Dialogues*, *14*, 1–51.

Beebe, Beatrice, and Lachmann, Frank M. (2014). *The Origins of Attachment: Infant Research and Adult Treatment*. New York: Routledge / Taylor and Francis Group.

Boston Women's Health Collective (1973). *Our Bodies, Ourselves*. New York: Simon and Schuster.

Coles, Prophecy (2003). *The Importance of Sibling Relationships in Psychoanalysis*. London: H. Karnac (Books).

Fraiberg, Selma (1975). Ghosts in the Nursery: A Psychoanalytic Approach to the Problems of Impaired Infant-Mother Relationships. *Journal of the American Academy of Child Psychiatry*, *14*, 387–421.

Horney, Karen (1967). *Feminine Psychology*. Harold Kelman (Ed.). New York: W.W. Norton and Company.

Jacoby, Russell (1983). *The Repression of Psychoanalysis: Otto Fenichel and the Political Freudians*. New York: Basic Books.

Mahler, Margaret S., Pine, Fred, and Bergman, Anni (1975). *The Psychological Birth of the Human Infant: Symbiosis and Individuation*. New York: Basic Books.

Mitchell, Juliet (2003). *Siblings: Sex and Violence*. London: Polity / Polity Press, Blackwell Publishing.

Mitscherlich, Alexander, and Mitscherlich, Margarete (1975). *The Inability to Mourn: Principles of Collective Behavior*. Beverley R. Placzek (Transl.). New York: Grove Press.

Orbach, Susie (1999). *The Impossibility of Sex*. London: Allen Lane / Penguin Press, Penguin Books, Penguin Group.

Orbach, Susie (2000). Comment by an Object Relational Psychotherapist. *British Journal of Psychotherapy*, *17*, 51–53.

Orbach, Susie (2006). The Clinic, the Nursery and the World Bank: Psychotherapy and Social Institutions. *British Journal of Psychotherapy*, *16*, 458–466.

Orbach, Susie (2009). *Bodies*. London: Profile Books.

Stern, Daniel N. (1985). *The Interpersonal World of the Infant: A View from Psychoanalysis and Developmental Psychology*. New York: Basic Books.

Tronick, Edward; Als, Heidelise; Adamson, Lauren; Wise, Susan, and Brazelton, T. Berry (1978). The Infant's Response to Entrapment Between Contradictory Messages in Face-to-Face Interaction. *Journal of the American Academy of Child Psychiatry*, *17*, 1–13.

Susie Orbach's Professional Biography

Brett Kahr

Educational, Clinical, and Institutional Work

Dr. Susie Orbach has worked in the mental health profession for over fifty years.

She trained initially at the City University of New York from which she received Highest Honors in 1972 for her B.A. degree, and then earned an M.S.W. degree from the School of Social Welfare at the Health Sciences Center at Stony Brook University, part of the State University of New York, in 1974. Subsequently, she would be awarded a Ph.D. degree from the Psychoanalysis Unit of University College, part of the University of London.

In 1976, she returned to London and began practising as a psychotherapist and later as a psychoanalyst, providing services to individuals, couples, and groups, and she continues to do so to this day. Since 1982, she has offered clinical supervision to colleagues working at such diverse institutions in the United Kingdom as the Arbours Association, the King's Fund, St. George's Hospital Medical School, the Tavistock Clinic, University College Hospital, and numerous other centres within the National Health Service. And, from 1986 until the present day, she has served as a consultant to many national and international organisations and women's groups, and she has worked, subsequently, as an adviser in both the voluntary and the corporate sectors.

Throughout her career, Orbach has delivered literally hundreds of lectures and seminars across the globe in such countries as Australia, Belgium, Brazil, Canada, Germany, Holland, Hong Kong, India, Ireland, Italy, New Zealand, Northern Ireland, Peru, Spain, Sweden, the United Kingdom, and the United States of America on a range of topics, including psychoanalysis, clinical practice, eating problems, gender issues, emotional literacy, psychoanalytical politics, social policy, and the politics of food to universities and medical schools and other clinical organisations such as the Anna Freud Centre, Bradford Social Services, the Erasmus University Medical School, Harvard University, the Institute of Psychoanalysis in London, the Institute of Psychiatry in London, Islington Social Services, the Jewish Family Services, the Middlesex Hospital Medical School, the Peru Psychoanalytic Society, the Royal Society of Medicine, the San Francisco Medical School, Smith College, St. George's Hospital School of Medicine in the

DOI: 10.4324/9781003470090-17

University of London, the Tavistock Institute of Human Relations, the Tavistock Marital Studies Institute, the Toronto Psychoanalytic Institute, University College London in the University of London, the University of Cambridge, the University of Chicago, the University of Nottingham, Vassar College, VicHealth, and the William Alanson White Institute of Psychiatry, Psychoanalysis and Psychology. She has also spoken at the Cabinet Office, the Canadian High Commission, the European Commission, Exploring Parenthood, the International Bank for Reconstruction and Development, the Labour Party, the Royal Festival Hall, Tate Modern, the United Nations, the Victoria and Albert Museum, the Vienna City Government, and the Weitzman Institute.

Dr. Orbach has maintained membership in many professional bodies such as the British Psychoanalytic Council, the British Society of Couple Psychotherapists and Counsellors, The Relational School, The Women's Therapy Centre Institute, and, also, the New Zealand Institute of Psychoanalytic Psychotherapy, as well as the Northern Ireland Institute for Human Relations. She is a state-registered psychoanalyst in New York and, also, a Consultant Psychotherapist at The Balint Consultancy in London.

Over many years, Orbach has contributed to large numbers of communities. In 1976, she became a Co-Founder of the Women's Therapy Centre in London with Luise Eichenbaum, providing psychotherapy and counselling to approximately 2,000 women annually, as well as in-service training programmes for psychological professionals. This institution raised the profile of the mental health needs of women in the United Kingdom and became the basis of much British government documentation. In 1981, she and Eichenbaum also founded and co-directed The Women's Therapy Centre Institute in New York City, New York, which included the offering of a three-year postgraduate training programme in psychoanalytical psychotherapy. Several years later, in 1995, Orbach became the Co-Founder of Antidote, an organisation committed to the development of emotional literacy in public and private life through schools, businesses, and N.G.O.s. Between 1999 and 2001, Susie Orbach served as a Consultant to the World Bank in Washington, D.C., advising on psychological issues in relation to the implementation of programmes for transitional societies and development programmes, and also provided advice on gender issues as well as aid to post-conflict societies. In 2002, she became co-originator and Consultant to Dove, advising on the delivery of an expanded visual imagery strategy for girls and for women, and producing written material for mothers and daughters. Moreover, Orbach worked from 2002 until 2018 as Convenor of AnyBody / Endangered Bodies, a worldwide campaign designed to save future generations of females from hating their bodies, while helping to promote diversity around body images.

Additionally, Dr. Orbach has contributed to many other organisations as a trustee, board member, or expert. These institutions include Antidote, AnyBody, Body Confidence (under the auspices of the Home Office), the Centre for Attachment-Based Psychoanalytic Psychotherapy, the Freud Museum, the International Association for Relational Psychoanalysis and Psychotherapy, Newsreel, the

Northern Initiative on Women's Eating, Psychotherapists and Counsellors for Social Responsibility, The Relational School, and the Spare Tyre Theatre Company.

Orbach has maintained many academic appointments over the years, having held the post of Lecturer in the Division of Social Studies at Richmond College, part of the City University of New York, and then, having become Visiting Professor in both the Gender Institute and the Department of Sociology at the London School of Economics and Political Science in the University of London. She also became an Honorary Fellow of Regent's College in London, and, more recently, in 2019, received the title of Academic Visitor at Hertford College in the University of Oxford.

In recognition of her multiple contributions to the fields of psychotherapy and psychology and literature, Dr. Orbach has received many honorary degrees and awards. Between 2001 and 2022, six universities gifted her with honorary doctoral degrees in the arts and in science: Stony Brook University, part of the State University of New York, as well as the University of Essex, the London Metropolitan University, the University of East London, the University of Westminster, and the University of Roehampton. Additionally, in 2010, the Association for Women in Psychology presented Orbach with the Distinguished Publication Award in recognition of her book *Bodies*. Several years later, in 2017, the British Psychoanalytic Council granted her its Lifetime Achievement Award, and, in the following year, 2018, the Freud Museum London created Orbach as an Honorary Fellow. In 2019, she became a Fellow of the Royal Society of Literature.

Dr. Orbach broadcasts frequently on psychological matters. Her radio series *In Therapy* attracted over two million listeners live. That programme has become a staple for many training programmes in mental health and, moreover, an introduction to the ways in which psychotherapists work.

Books By Susie Orbach

Fat is a Feminist Issue ...: The Anti-Diet Guide to Permanent Weight Loss (1978).
Fat is a Feminist Issue II (1982).
Outside In ... Inside Out: Women's Psychology: A Feminist Psychoanalytic Approach (1982), co-authored with Luise Eichenbaum.
Understanding Women: A Feminist Psychoanalytic Approach (1983), co-authored with Luise Eichenbaum.
What Do Women Want?: Exploding the Myth of Dependency (1983), co-authored with Luise Eichenbaum.
Hunger Strike: The Anorectic's Struggle as a Metaphor for Our Time (1986).
Between Women: Love, Envy, and Competition in Women's Friendships (1987), co-authored by Luise Eichenbaum.
Bittersweet: Facing Up to Feelings of Love, Envy and Competition in Women's Friendships (1987), co-authored by Luise Eichenbaum.
What's Really Going on Here?: Making Sense of Our Emotional Lives (1995).
Towards Emotional Literacy (1999).
The Impossibility of Sex (1999).

On Eating (2002).

Bodies (2009).

Fifty Shades of Feminism (2013), co-edited by Lisa Appignanesi and Rachel Holmes.

Understanding Women: A Feminist Psychoanalytic Approach (2013), revised edition, co-authored with Luise Eichenbaum.

Fat is a Feminist Issue: Book One. The Anti-Diet Guide & Book Two. Conquering Compulsive Eating (2016), revised edition.

In Therapy: How Conversations with Psychotherapists Really Work (2016).

In Therapy: The Unfolding Story (2018).

Bodies (2019), revised edition.

Fat is a Feminist Issue (2023), revised edition.

Acknowledgements

I extend my deepest admiration and warmest appreciation, first and foremost, to Susannah Frearson, the publisher at Routledge / Taylor and Francis Group, for her immense support of this project. As ever, it remains a true honour and a great treat to work with such a compassionate, intelligent, and facilitating person as Ms. Frearson, and I convey my sincere gratitude to this truly collaborative expert.

I also wish to express my huge regard to Susannah Frearson's many accomplished colleagues in the publishing firm, all of whom have provided so much encouragement over the years, including Jana Craddock, Ellie Duncan, Russell George, Constance Govindin, Dr. Elliott Morsia, Alexis O'Brien, Saloni Singhania, and Alec Selwyn. Furthermore, I offer my deepest respect to Nick Craggs, the Senior Production Editor at Routledge, for his extremely kind facilitation of this process, and to Pamela Bertram, the most meticulous and accomplished of copyeditors, for their vital contributions.

Furthermore, I wish to offer additional appreciation to Sian Putnam, the administrator to Dr. Susie Orbach, for having assisted with a number of important queries.

This *Festschrift* originated back in 2016 when I proposed that we might wish to commission a special event in honour of Dr. Orbach's impending seventieth birthday. Thankfully, Jane Ryan, the founder of the organisation Confer Limited, hosted a memorable conference, entitled "Psychotherapy is a Cultural Issue: The Influence of Susie Orbach's Work on Theory, Practice and Values", held on the sixth floor of the grand Foyles bookshop on Charing Cross Road in Central London, on 22nd April, 2017. As ever, Ms. Ryan organised this tributary gathering in the most splendid of manners.

I thank all of the contributors to both the conference and the *Festschrift* for having crafted such warm-hearted and much-deserved tributes to Susie Orbach.

I also wish to salute many other colleagues for their assistance with various manners, including Oliver Rathbone and Dr. Rod Tweedy, both of whom encouraged this project in the early stages.

We wish to express our thanks to Amy Godfrey-Smythe, Jo Harrison, Dr. Susie Orbach, and Emilia Telese for their kind permission to replicate the various compelling images which appear in Chapter 6 of this *Festschrift*. Likewise, we offer further tributes to Dr. Susie Orbach for her kind permission to reprint her diagram on "Merged attachment", which appears in Chapter 8.

Above all, I extend my tremendous acclaim to Dr. Susie Orbach, whose inspiring contributions to global mental health have proved such a gift to so many millions of people.

Index

Printed and bound by CPI Group (UK) Ltd, Croydon, CR0 4YY

29/10/2024

01780759-0003